BOUND FEET BLUES

BOUND FEET BLUES

A LIFE TOLD IN SHOES

By

YANG-MAY OOI

First published in Great Britain in 2015
by Urbane Publications Ltd
Suite 3, Brown Europe House, 33/34 Gleamingwood Drive,
Chatham, Kent ME5 8RZ

ISBN 978-1-910692-30-1
EPUB 978-1-910692-31-8
MOBI 978-1-910692-32-5

Cover design by Julie Martin
Design and Typeset by The Invisible Man

Printed in Great Britain by
CPI Group (UK) Ltd, Croydon, CR0 4YY

urbanepublications.com

The publisher supports the Forest Stewardship Council® (FSC®), the
leadinginternational forest-certification organisation. This book is made
from acid-free paper from an FSC®-certified provider. FSC is the only
forest-certification scheme supported by the leading environmental
organisations, including Greenpeace.

To the women, past and present,
who made this story possible - thank you.

A journey of a thousand miles begins with a single step
– *Lao Tzu*

Contents

Bound Feet Blues, The Book - Family Tree

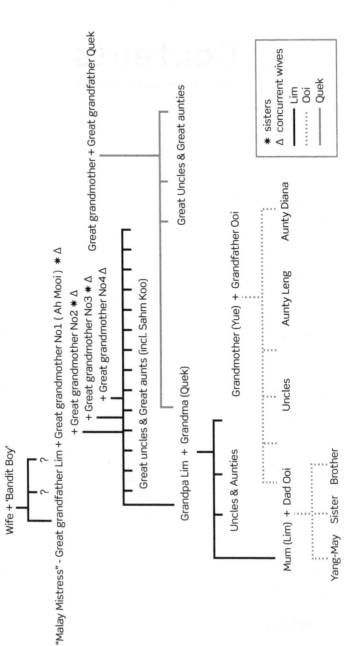

Acknowledgements

The performance script of Bound Feet Blues was developed in rehearsal with input from my director and voice coach, Jessica Higgs. I am indebted to her for her wise guidance, creative brilliance, patience and firm hand during our work together on the theatre piece.

I am grateful to many others in my life who have given me their guidance, stories, talent, time and also their love, friendship and support during the creation of both the theatre piece and this book. There are those, too, whose presence in my life made me who I am today and whom I will never forget – I owe my thanks also to them. Please join me in applauding:

Luke Dixon and Sean Bruno of The Centre for Solo Performance, and my co-participants in the Creating Solo Performance workshop

My producer Eldarin Yeong, videographer Claudia Rocha, photographer Xin Li, costumier Carol Alayne, lighting/ set designer Hanna Hua Tan, stage manager Crin Claxton

Ben Monks and Will Young and the team at the Tristan Bates Theatre

Helen Lewis and Sam Batt of Literally PR

Hi Ching, Annie Kwan and the past and present teams at the South East Asian Arts Festival

Ian Peacock, Piers Williamson, Fenella Edge and the directors and staff at The   Housing Finance Corporation

Wendy Wilks and her team at Maclay Murray Spens

Arts Council England

Zehan Albakri, Sunok Phillips, Betty Yao and everyone at the Pan Asian Women's Association

My handsome and innovative publisher Matthew Smith at Urbane Publications

Samiel Carolina Rodriguez Barros, Beverley Glick, Nicky Moran, Rona Steinberg, Lynn Tabbara and Sarah Lloyd-Hughes

Joanna Yates and Matt Hill of Spark London, and everyone at The Story Party

Katy Hunt, Anna Sayburn, Julie Bull, Jennie Walters, the late Charlotte Dawson, Ilin Chin, Veronica Lim, Marianne Aston, Alex Wood, Louise McDonald and Gerald the dog

"Josh", "Dana", "Karen", "Jane", "Lizzie", "Susan" and "Shane"

My family and especially my sister Yang Ming, my cousin Pey Colborne, Aunty Diana and my parents

Always and forever, the love of my life, Angie Macdonald.

Author's note

The original story of Bound Feet Blues was conceived as a solo performance piece for the stage, as you will see when you dive into this book. The script runs for an hour which means there was not enough space for all the stories I wanted to tell. This book therefore tells the stories behind the story in the show. Within the text you will find the actual script of the performance at the start of each chapter, except for the final chapter when it appears at the end.

The book and the show each stand alone as a distinct creative work in their own right. You can watch the show and never need to read the book. You can read the book without ever seeing the show. Or you can take in both of them for the ultimate life told in shoes.

While this book and the show are intended as a memoir, they are not a strict factual recording of events in my life. Neither are they fiction. Perhaps you might best think of them as a dramatized memoir or a creative work inspired by true events.

I wrote from memory so there are most likely inaccuracies. I have also taken liberties for simplicity and dramatic purpose. In some cases, different episodes are compressed into a single scene. In others, I have moved around the timeline and enhanced background detail. Every good story needs texture, but sometimes the exact details aren't as important as what was going on for me at that time as I tried to discover who I was as a woman.

Some scenes are imaginary, constructed in order to dramatize emotions or beliefs that are otherwise intangible. For example, in the show script I created the butch *pondan* woman and the scene in the school canteen. What happens in that scene represents the homophobia that I was aware of as I was growing up, manifested in the numerous comments, laughter, and stares directed at a range of queer folk over a long period of time. The canteen scene has dramatic impact on stage - a factually accurate discussion about my cultural awareness of homophobia would not.

Inevitably, in the story of one life, I need to talk about other lives, particularly those people who have had the most influence or impact on me. Names, personal details and locations have been changed in some cases for reasons of privacy. Sometimes, the qualities and traits of several people have been amalgamated into one character. My intention is to focus not on particular personalities, but on what my encounters with them means to me. It may be that that such folk have differing interpretations of what happened based on their own experience of the story. That is the nature of memory and stories.

I have aimed for factual accuracy in the historical and cultural sections – for example, about foot-binding and Chinese social history. My research has taken me to a number of rich and fascinating books as well as a wealth of information on the internet. These are set out in the Sources section of this book. I have aimed to show excerpts from original sources in quotations marks. Any factual errors or failures to indicate excerpts through quote marks are unintentional.

My invitation to you is not to read this memoir for factual or journalistic accuracy but to look within the stories for their emotional truth. My hope is that you might find in these personal stories a universality that takes them beyond just one individual life, and perhaps even into your own.

Yang-May Ooi
London, 2015

First Step

---

26 March 2014, Conway Hall, London.

I stepped out into the performance hall from behind the heavy wooden doors. I was still in shadow but the audience had sensed my entrance. There was an alertness now in the hall as they peered towards me in the gloom.

A blaze of light waited in the middle of the darkness a few steps away. Four powerful cross beams shafted down onto the stage from the theatre spotlights high above. The emptiness of the space seemed vast and exposed.

An emptiness waiting for me.

Even as my mind raced - taking in the empty stage, the dark shapes of bodies waiting in the audience, the specks of dust floating in the beams of light, the music fading out - my feet were already moving towards the moment of beginning.

The wooden floor boards felt cool beneath my bare feet. But there was a stickiness to my steps. I didn't know you could get cold sweat on your soles - but apparently, you can. Could the audience hear the *shlick-shlick-shlick* of my damp footsteps as I walked?

I could still turn back. While I was still in the shadows, before I stepped out under the glare of the lights, there was still time to call the whole thing off. No-one need see me freeze. No-one need see me make an utter fool of myself.

There were about fifty or more people out there in the auditorium. They had come on a cold Wednesday evening to

Conway Hall to watch three solo performers try out their material at the Going Solo scratch night. I had greeted audience members at the entrance, some of them my friends and family, others people I did not know. I had cheerfully hugged my pals, taking in their curiosity at this mad new project of mine. We had to put out more chairs and Luke and Sean, the producers of the show, said they normally had about fifteen people and were surprised by the large numbers. At that point, a mere half an hour ago, it had all felt like a bit of a lark. It was just some fun and the outcome did not matter.

But now the other two performers had completed their pieces and here I was walking slowly out of the darkness to stand alone in front of fifty or more people...fifty or more people who would watch me crash and burn.

Who did I think I was, to stand up in front of a paying audience and tell stories from my family and my life? What arrogance to think that anyone would be interested. What hubris to think I could take to the stage and give a dramatic storytelling performance. As a fifty year old woman, how ridiculous would I look acting as if I were a sexy, slinky twenty year old again? Did I really think that I could be convincing as my eight year old self, prancing around the stage in a childish gait?

Conway Hall scratch night

I pictured those dark figures in front of me filled with pity, squirming with embarrassment on my behalf, clapping out of politeness and then scurrying out as fast as they could without having to look me in the eyes.

Surely, they must hear my heart thudding in my chest. Was I wheezing for breath? That hee-haw of air scraping up and down my throat sounded like the trumpets at the walls of Jericho. Would I even be able to speak or stand up straight when I got to the pool of waiting light?

Everything seemed to slow down. It was only a few more steps now. The first soft edges of light waited like open palms to draw me into their power. In the back of my mind, I had a sense that these next few steps would change my life, and the terror of change held me suspended in the darkness.

How on earth had I got here?

* * *

In my mind, I saw an afternoon in 1986. I was twenty-three, an articled clerk - a trainee lawyer - at a law firm in Westminster. My desk was in the corner of the room I shared with the commercial law partner. My task was to call a complex government organisation and get an official document for the case we were working on.

Sitting there in my little grey suit, I managed to work my way through several layers of telephone bureaucracy. Finally, I got to the right department.

And suddenly, I was in trouble.

I could sense it in my chest and throat even as I began the sentence. The two words I needed to say thundered down at me like an unstoppable train wreck. There were no other words I could substitute. I had to say them. And I knew I couldn't.

"... so what I need is a …. s-s-s-s.." I couldn't breathe. But I had to keep speaking. I stopped and gasped for air. I was conscious of the partner sitting a few feet away, listening to me. My chest was tight. My tongue was rigid. I pushed on. "... s-s-ssolic-c-citors' c-c-certific-c-cate…"

The voice on the other end of the line was tentative. He said, "Y-y-yes, I c-c-can issue one for you. Wh-wha-which s-s-s-solic-c-citors' c-c-certific-c-cate d-d-do you need?"

You're kidding me! My mind shrieked fluently even as my lips and tongue went into a tighter spasm in sympathy with the man on the phone.

His train and mine had collided in an excruciating wreck. Amidst the carnage of twisted tongues and torn breath, we somehow made it through the next few minutes, neither of us - with true British politeness - daring to acknowledge the strangulated elephant in the room. I hung up exhausted but triumphant, knowing that the hard won solicitors' certificate was in the post to my firm.

For much of my young life, and especially in those few years in my twenties, I had a stammer. No-one knew because I could generally hide it well. Most of the time, I would be able to swap a word or phrase for the demonic one - especially if I could see it coming down the sentence track at me like a runaway train. So 'lawyer' would replace 'solicitor', 'evening' would take the place of 'night' - and fortunately, it was the era before the word 'digital' became ubiquitous.

However sometimes in large groups of people, especially if they were not my close friends, I would not be able to speak. We would hang out in the law college common room and everyone would be swapping jokes and stories. I would be bursting to share an anecdote or make a quip or tell a joke - but I would not be able to break in. Or I would start and suddenly I would be gasping for air, struggling with the words, and the joke would fall flat. And I would see their looks of pity and embarrassment.

So I made excuses when my law college classmates headed to the cafes or pubs after lectures. I would avoid social situations where I didn't know people very well. I shied away from group occasions where I had to fight for attention. And also times when

I might be the focus of attention - because all those expectant faces waiting for me to share my gems of wisdom or amusement would also set off the stutter train.

* * *

My days of stammering had long passed but sometimes, if I allowed myself to be vulnerable, the stuttering tension would return. Crossing the stage of Conway Hall was one of those moments and I felt on the edge of a vortex.

As I took another step towards the waiting spotlight, I tried to remember what Jessica, my voice coach, had taught me:

Feel the floor underneath you. Connect to your whole body. Connect with your feet. Breathe from your feet.

The breath that had been rigid in my chest exhaled. I let my lungs inhale by themselves. Like breathing in the sweet smell of a rose, Jessica's calm voice came back to me. And the air flooded in, swelling my diaphragm, melting the frozen muscles in my torso.

I had done public speaking before - even giving a TEDx talk a few months earlier. But they had all been miked. There was a safety in that - either standing behind a solid microphone stand, the bulb of metal and mesh in front of me like a magic talisman; or having a lapel mike that, although invisible, would amplify my voice to give it authority and power over the room.

I had been to Jessica for voice lessons only three weeks before. I'd had six sessions with her. Was that going to be enough to give my voice the *oomph* it needed to fill this cavernous hall without a microphone?

I was emerging from the gloom into the periphery of light. The glare of the bright beams from overhead flared into my eyes. I could just make out my sister in the front row and in the sweeping curve of chairs there were other faces, ones I did not recognize. They were all waiting expectantly.

Why had I felt the need to take to the stage to tell these stories? Why hadn't I simply written them down in a book and be done with it? After all, I was a novelist. A writer. An author. Words on the page were what I knew. What I was good at. They were safe, contained, predictable. And if they failed to impress my readers, I would not be there to see the disgruntled look on their faces, or their contempt or dismissiveness or sneering. I would not have to be humiliated in front of all these people.

I was not a performer. Yet here I was, within two steps of disaster.

* * *

When I first decided I was going to be a writer at age thirteen, I wanted to write about the stories in my family. There was so much to tell, so many intriguing tales. My great-great grandfather in China who had been abducted as a boy by a bandit gang, his home village razed to the ground, his family slaughtered. And the story of my great-grandmother with bound feet who had been married off to a man whose family made her work in the fields. And a mysterious mistress with shamanic powers who had taught my great-grandfather about love and jungle spirits prowling the night. Sisters who became concubines of the same man. My grandmother treading the water wheels to irrigate the fields after school, and on Sundays playing the piano to accompany missionary hymns in her father's chapel. My mother telling us stories of pea-soupers in 1960s London and meeting my father at a dance, their eyes meeting across a crowded room.

We have a recording of my *Kong Kong*, my Grandpa - my mother's father - telling us the story of our family history. I taped it on a cassette recorder one rainy evening in 1976. It was the school holidays and I had come back from my first term at school in England. We were spending some time with my grandparents in Taiping, the small town in Malaysia where my mother had grown up. The whole family gathered round after dinner on the

Grandpa carrying me

verandah. On the recording, you can hear the rain and the singing cicadas in the background, my aunt's laugh, a phone ringing at one point. My voice is high and childish as I ask him to tell us the story of our family. And he begins with the boy abducted by bandits. *Kong Kong* died the next year of a heart attack. This tape is the only recording we have of him and is one of the most precious things we have in the family, copied many times over and distributed among the vast extended group of relatives.

At thirteen, I started writing the family history in a school exercise book, sitting at my desk at boarding school in Brighton. It began, as Grandpa's story had, with the bandit boy, and ripped along like a Boy's Own adventure with thundering hooves and houses set on fire as the bandits stormed their way through the village. But the pages soon ground to a halt as I realised that I did not have enough historical information or knowledge to flesh out the story into a full blown book.

At thirty one, when I set out to become a proper writer, I tried again with a semi-autobiographical novel portentously titled *Ancestral Voices*. Again, it began with the bandit boy. And again, this version also ground to a halt - it was earnest, turgid, and unreadable. It's still there languishing unfinished in that proverbial drawer of abandoned manuscripts.

I turned my hand instead to a legal thriller that became The *Flame Tree*, my first published novel. It was published by Hodder & Stoughton as part of a two book deal. After the success of these two legal dramas, my publisher wanted more thrillers - but I found myself drawn again to my heritage. I had another go at the family memoir, this time split into two books, *Iced Tea and Laksa* and *Bound Feet Blues*. I was so confident that this attempt was going to be 'The One' that I even announced it to the world in the press. I was going to begin the first book with an homage to Proust, letting the taste of curry laksa and sweet milky iced tea transport me back to my childhood, and from there recount the stories that bound me so fast to my family. The second book would follow my own life, growing up and trying to find my own way as a young woman in the thrall of these stories.

And again, it all ground to a halt.

In the fifteen years or so since that last attempt, I would return to the stories every now and then, tinkering, trying out different approaches, seeing if I could find a new way in that would give me traction. There was too much material, too many stories, a vast unchartered rain forest of colour and texture and dappled light. I could not find my way, could not capture the shimmering past that flickered just out of reach. I knew I had to simplify, focus only on a tiny patch of abundance. But how?

What about poetry? Poetry was short, I thought. It would force me to pare things down, find the treasure and focus just on that. So I started a long form narrative poem - but the lines of lyrical text soon degenerated into prose. And I was back where I started.

Then suddenly, I was forty-eight.

How had that happened? Where had my writing career gone? It had been over fifteen years since my second novel, *Mindgame*, was published. I had been going to write all these books. And apart from a business book, nothing more creative had materialised. The family stories remained unwritten. Untold.

I was working in the garden with my partner, Angie. It was a Sunday in June. It was pouring with rain - we were in England after all. It was my birthday. My forty-eighth birthday.

I stood in the middle of the lawn, piling twigs and prunings into a brown garden bag. The rain was coming down harder now. My cap was no match for the pounding drops and my head was getting cold and drenched. My rain jacket shone with damp in the grey light and a trickle of cold water was sliding down the back of my neck.

Grandma - my mother's mother - came into my mind. She loved her garden and especially the orchids that she and Grandpa used to grow. A whole section of the garden would be devoted to these delicate plants, set out in rows like tall, ramrod straight soldiers on parade. As a child, I would follow her as she walked through the rows, appreciating their beauty, knowing each type by name. She and Grandpa created new specimens, carefully cross pollinating the plants to bring into the world orchids that had never existed before. They would send them off to the Royal Horticultural Society in England to be verified and registered - each new specimen named for each of their children and grandchildren. If you search the Orchid Register, you will find an orchid with my name.

Standing there in the English rain, I missed my Grandma.

She used to have a little rag doll she kept in a glass cabinet with all the beautiful ornaments she had collected on her travels around the world with Grandpa. It looked out of place there, a hand-sewn faded doll about 8 inches long, half-sitting, half-slumped against the back of the cabinet with two little tiny chickens at her feet.

She would say to me, "This doll will be yours one day. It was made for me by my grandmother, my mother's mother. She was the eldest daughter and I was her eldest grand-daughter. You are the eldest grand-daughter of the eldest grand-daughter so this doll will be yours."

The doll is a little five year old girl, with black threaded hair in pigtails and finely sewn Chinese eyes and features. She is in a faded green pinafore over a pink blouse with little shoes in black cloth. She is my grandmother at the time when her grandmother had made that doll for her. It sits now in an air-tight plastic container on a bookshelf in my living room. Whenever I see it, I think of a little old Chinese grandmother in rural China, sewing this doll by lamp light late at night after the day's work is done, thinking only of her grand-daughter and how much joy this gift would bring.

I am the eldest daughter of the eldest daughter of the eldest daughter going back at least five generations. That was Grandma's gift to me - that connection with a heritage that was greater than just my own small life. She gave it to me through her stories - she told stories to us not just about her own life as a pastor's daughter in China but also about her own family history and that of Grandpa's family. She talked about her life with Grandpa, how they met, brought up a family together, built a community, played their part in the creation of Malaysia, a new country after independence from the British.

In my memory, those moments of storytelling would take place as if outside of time, suspended in a sense of specialness. We would sit with her in the breezy hall, the overhead fan whirring in the hot tropical afternoon, and she would tell us about where and whom we came from.

In the grey drenching rain in London, I smiled as I remembered those magical afternoons on the other side of the world.

It struck me that Grandma had passed on that love of storytelling to my mother, her eldest daughter. As children me, my brother and sister would pile onto my parents' bed after dinner, scrubbed and clean in our pyjamas. Cuddled up between my parents in a tangle of arms and legs and pillows and bolsters, we would listen to Mum tell her stories - about how she and my father met, about her childhood and his, about being a new wife in a new family, about each of us and how special and clever we each were.

I had always thought that one day I would also have an eldest daughter and an eldest grand-daughter, just like Grandma. That I too would be a wife and mother like my Mum. That I would carry on their legacy - and the legacy of the family, ensuring its longevity for generations to come. I would have children and grandchildren of my own. And I too would sit with them all and pass on stories of my own life and stories about the people they came from.

I looked over at Angie, working on the vegetable patch in the pouring rain.

I was forty-eight and I could have been a mother and grandmother if I had made different choices in my life. But there was only Angie and me and a relationship that would have been impossible in another time and another place.

I felt a tinge of that old shame and disappointment. I had lived my own life - and in so doing, I had not lived up to the destiny that had been laid down for me by my heritage.

* * *

I stepped out of the shadows into the light.

I kept my gaze lowered, focusing on the semi-circle of blazing wooden floor in front of me. Beyond that, in the gloom, I caught glimpses of legs and shoes in my peripheral vision - the front row of the audience so close to the stage. So long as I did not look up into their eyes - like the proverbial ostrich with its frightened head in the sand - I could stay here forever, I thought, in a limbo of not beginning; and they would not see me for as long as I did not see them.

In the eighteen months since that rainy birthday, I had felt an odd restless creative urgency. I started writing again. I tried to find alternate ways of developing narrative – perhaps I could use my blog or experiment with some of those story-focused online sites. It was as if something inside was clamouring to get out. I was dimly aware that this urge had something to do with wanting to share my stories in whatever form they might come into being. But why with such fervour and why now, I could not yet see clearly. I had a go at live storytelling – most memorably at Spark London, a storytelling group inspired by the cult club in New York, The Moth. From there, I signed up to a public speaking course that eventually led me to tell a version of my coming out story at a TEDx Women event.

These moments in front of an audience were a little scary but ultimately fun and exhilarating. The pieces were ten to twenty minutes long and it didn't involve much more than making sure I had written out a good story, and then remembering what I wanted to say and adding some dramatic pauses. They were Public Speaking Plus, if you like. It was the words and story that mattered, not me. Even with the prestigious TEDx talk, where I told a very personal, intimate story without guile or pretension, I was simply talking – there was no element of dramatizing the events or people in the story, no attempt at performance, no stripping away of the speaker/ storyteller persona to reveal my deepest emotional self.

Then in January, I started on a workshop for Creating Solo Performance run by Luke Dixon and Sean Bruno at The Centre for Solo Performance. Over the next twelve weeks, I turned up every Saturday morning at one of the class rooms in the Conway Hall complex. In that time, writing in the evenings after work and presenting my weekly pages at the workshop, I developed a story I called *Bound Feet Blues*, cannibalising the title from that old memoir I had wanted to write. When I first signed up, the workshop was going to be just a way for me to improve on those ten to twenty minute stories I had been telling - learning a few tips on better delivery of lines and on shaping a tighter script. And it would be fun to have a go at the 'graduation' scratch night for these workshops in March at Conway Hall - called Going Solo - to see how the stories hung together.

But something changed during those workshops. The piece grew from ten minutes to twenty, to thirty; until finally I had forty-five minutes of material and it was still incomplete. Standing up in front of Luke and Sean and the five or six other participants, I began to experiment with dramatizing the different moments in the little stories that made up *Bound Feet Blues*.

In one of the workshops, I tried out a sexy, slinky walk to depict my twenty year old self walking to the ball 'in a delicate swaying manner'. Then without planning it, I let the words of the script take control. As if my body moved of its own will, I found myself mapping the shape of a stiletto shoe on my body, marking out its shiny black triangle at my pudenda, the arching foot on my arching body – and throwing my head back in a sigh of ecstasy.

Conway Hall scratch night

My slot ended and I came to rest in embarrassment. Where had all that come from?

I stood there awkwardly at the front of the class room. My fellow workshoppers were staring in astonishment. There was silence.

Luke had been watching without expression. I was suddenly aware that he was an internationally recognised theatre director with decades of experience and several books on stagecraft to his name. I cringed inwardly thinking about what I had just done and how ridiculous my posturing must have looked.

He said quietly, "Go for it more. Arch as far back as you can go. Make it even sexier."

So here I was in the spotlight, about to go for it – and not just go for it, but go for it *more*.

* * *

The scratch night that had just been for a bit of fun had somehow become something bigger. It would normally have taken place in a classroom in the Conway Hall complex, but due to a last minute room scheduling clash Luke told us one Saturday morning that we would have the chance to play in the main hall. That was when, in a panic about the weakness of my unmiked voice, I asked him to refer me to a voice coach. I had turned up on Jessica's doorstep hoping she might perform some magic in just a handful of sessions.

In another element of a perfect storm, a couple of the other workshoppers then dropped out of the show at the last moment. And Luke suggested that I may as well present what I had since there was now time to fill. So instead of doing just twenty minutes of my material, I was going to lay before the audience forty-five minutes of script with no break and me playing all the different characters.

Standing here in the crossbeams, at the heart of the grand central auditorium of Conway Hall, I felt overwhelmed by the

Conway Hall scratch night

theatre setting with the big spotlights, the professional sound system, the darkened auditorium, the anticipation in the crowded audience, the vast scope of the material I was about to perform and the sense of drama and occasion... This lark had turned into a serious performance.

The audience shifted. They were waiting.

Just start. That was all I had to do. But I couldn't. I wanted to stay here in this place of not beginning. Here I risked nothing. Nothing would change. No-one would have to see me make a fool of myself. No-one would see me crash and burn in this nightmare of hubris and arrogance.

But all this was only the surface of my anxiety. The real fear suddenly revealed its cold naked terror.

I had stripped myself bare in each of the stories that made up this piece. There was so much vulnerability and tenderness and

15

fragility bound into the material; *my* vulnerability and tenderness and fragility. I had, until now, hidden all of it so well from the world. People knew me as a confident, successful professional in the world of social housing finance, with a sideline as a talented author of legal thrillers and a business book. And now I was about to expose my heart in this piece – to offer up to the world the stories that meant the most to me.

I didn't have to do this. I had chosen to have a go – I could just as easily unchoose it. I didn't have to expose myself to ridicule and laughter and rejection. I could still just turn around and walk away and my life would simply go on as before.

I thought about Grandma and that rainy afternoon in my garden. And I suddenly knew why I could not turn back.

In Chinese tradition, the ancestors remained part of the family and looked out for their descendants from the ghostly realm. As the Christian God might help His children in times of need, Chinese ancestors would look out for their own down the generations. And only the eldest son could properly worship the family's ancestors and be the conduit between the living and the dead.

In my family, while the sons might have carried on the family line and passed on the ancestral name, it was the daughters who carried the soft beating heart of the family and let the ancestors come alive again through our stories. It was the daughters who gave voice and life not just to the dead but also to each one of us, listeners and tellers both. The stories that Grandma and Mum told me had taught me how to live, how to be a good person, how to make my way in the world, how to be a woman. My naked vulnerable self was part of that soft beating heart as theirs had been and there was no shame in it. I may never have children or grandchildren but the mother and grandmother I might have been needed to be heard. Needed to tell these stories. Here. This moment. Now. In this circle of light, about to begin. This was the coming together of all those times throughout my life I had said to

Mum, to Grandma, to my aunties, to all the women in my family: Tell me a story.

I looked up at the audience. And I began to speak.

Conway Hall scratch night

Tik-tok shoes

BOUND FEET BLUES – THE STORY

China Doll

It's a beautiful summer evening in Oxford in 1983. I'm twenty and I'm walking arm-in-arm with Josh. He's tanned and tall and looks gorgeous in his dinner jacket. We're going to a ball and there's a gang of us strolling up the High Street - the young men in black tie and us girls in our beautiful ball dresses.

I'm wearing a blood red *cheongsam* – that's Chinese for long dress. It's that traditional dress with a high collar and buttons down the side. It was made for me by our family tailor in Malaysia to fit my every curve all the way down to the ground. There are slits coming up the side, stopping just short of obscenely high on my upper thighs.

I'm wearing silk stockings and lacy suspenders. As I walk, the dress moves and there - can you see it? - a hint of that delicate strap, high up on my thigh.

I'm wearing a pair of Kurt Geiger stilettos - black patent leather with 3 inch heels. There's a shiny black triangle at their tip, where my toes are. There's a thin leather strap running up the middle of the foot like a thong to meet another strap that goes around my ankle like a bondage collar. The shape of the shoe makes my foot arch back like a woman in ecstasy.

And I swish along. The stilettoes make me walk in a delicate, swaying manner and I'm taking tiny baby steps. I feel a class above the other girls in their flouncy ball dresses, walking arm in arm with their young men.

Because the men – they are all looking at me.

Helpless

And every step is an agony. All my weight is on the balls of my feet and my toes are jammed into the tips of the shoes - crushed up against each other, overlapping, crooked. The arches of my feet feel contorted. And every time the sharp piercing heel slams down on to the pavement, my ankles wobble, threaten to snap over.

Josh has swagger in his walk; he loves having his China doll on his arm. He's picking up the pace, with a long masculine stride. I'm tottering after him with my tiny baby steps.

I say, please, Josh, slow down. And he does, but absently, not really understanding why I need him to slow down. And soon, he is picking up the pace again. And I struggle along beside him.

I look up at the High Street stretching out ahead of me. There's such a long, long way to go. How many tiny painful steps is it going to take me to walk that long, long way to the ball? I envy Josh his strong sturdy shoes, his long manly stride, that sense that he owns the world.

Whereas my world is so tiny, shrunken to the next painful little step.

THE STORIES BEHIND THE STORY

Above all else, Oxford was an idea in my mind. You cannot come up to Oxford, with all its history and mythologies, without an idea already constructed of what your time there will be. This was the city of dreaming spires, one of the top universities in the world, a place where I had been destined to come to since I was a little girl. It was a place where I would become everything that my family expected me to be – successful, ambitious, worthy of their hopes and dreams.

There had only ever been two choices for me: Oxford or Cambridge. Anything else would have been a failure. And I had chosen Oxford over Cambridge - despite my father having read Law at the latter - because my favourite uncle had been here studying Medicine. I had grown up with their good-natured rivalry – Cambridge was better than Oxford and vice versa. But both of them told stories that might have described one single golden place – stories of cycling to lectures given by world famous professors, crossing quads covered in snow, late night intellectual debates with brilliant students, dashing young men and beautiful young women punting and picnicking and dancing all night at May balls.

This single golden idea was going to become my Oxford, too.

There are photographs of me in that first Michaelmas Term in 1981. I am eighteen but I am still a child in these pictures. There is a tentativeness in my look, the sweetness of a teenager in my smile. My hair is part-tomboy, part girlish in a wispier, slightly longer version of a gamine cut. I'm wearing jeans and white coat over a rust and black butterfly jumper. I'm trying to stand in a feminine way as a grown up woman should in my little white low-heeled slip-ons.

I had this idea of what Oxford would be but I did not yet hold in my mind an idea of who *I* might be.

I was reading English at St Hilda's, at that time still an all-female college. Most of the other English Lit freshers seemed so tall and confident. They had such an abundance of beautiful hair cascading down their shoulders, like those glorious women in Pre-Raphaelite paintings. They talked about Sylvia Plath and obscure Virago Press novels as if everyone should be passionate about such authors and I felt embarrassed that I read Daphne du Maurier for fun. They had boyfriends who dropped round at all times of day and night and they were involved in the poetry and drama and film-making clubs. I wanted to be a writer, to be one of the *literati* – like Dorothy Parker with her Algonquin set or Virginia Woolf and the Bloomsbury crowd. These other women claimed their artistic selves with such conviction, while I hovered and hesitated. The creative writing that I had been so proud of at school seemed naïve alongside their ambitious literary conversations. These women had an impenetrable glamour about them that I could only look in on from the outer edges of their universe.

It seemed to me as if I was forever on the outer edges. These Pre-Raphaelite women might as well have been the cool girls back at boarding school – the ones who looked eighteen when they were sixteen, with their well-developed breasts and womanly figures. They knew what to do with make-up, wore heels as if they had been born in them, flaunted themselves in the latest fashions at weekends, danced to the latest music, smoked, drank and snuck out of the school grounds to meet their boyfriends or flirt with boys in pubs.

I had been one of the brainiacs at school. I was known as the writer, the clever literary one. I wrote for and edited the school magazine. I wrote and directed the house play. I won writing prizes. But my nerdy glasses made me a 'four-eyes'. I had terrible acne and lank Chinese hair in a limp page boy cut. I dressed like a tomboy and kept spraining my ankles in my brown Clark's wedges. My friends were the 'Nice Girls' - the ones who obeyed the rules, preferred The Carpenters and ABBA to Thin Lizzie and Bryan Ferry and dressed in 'good girl' clothes.

But here's the thing. Much as I loved my friends and loved the warm, fun times I had with them. Much as I loved being known as the clever writer...I would much rather have been the glamorous writer. I longed to be in with the in-crowd. To be cool, pretty and admired by boys – and by association, admired by other girls. To have a boyfriend and exude grown-up confidence. To be somehow more than my flat chest and skinny hips and awkward gait could muster.

And here I was again. I had updated my hairstyle, wore more stylish glasses and my dress sense had edged upwards on the fashion spectrum. But Oxford was a vast place and it was so easy to get lost in the crowds of students, all struggling with how to become someone in a place where we were all no-one. In my early weeks there, my friends were a God-Squadder who kept trying to get me to go to Christian fellowship tea parties, and other freshers who were as miserable as I was. There was a girl on a scholarship who was in a complicated relationship with an older man whom she was missing badly. Several others who kept moaning that they couldn't meet any men while sitting around in each other's rooms downing bottles of red wine.

This was not the Oxford Experience I had imagined. Infused within the golden idea in my mind was the Oxford of *Brideshead* and of literature and film, heaving with generations of great writers and thinkers and Bright Young Things. It was meant to be a place of vigour and vitality, love and friendship, intensity and hope. Everywhere people were beginning to form cliques – stylish fashionistas, languid bohemians, energetic sporty types, retro classicals channelling Bogie and Bacall. I had lost my nerve after the first week of trying to make friends with the cool kids and coming face to face with their disinterest – or worse, their disdain. So I had strayed towards the freshers who seemed grateful for a friend. And now, if I stayed too long here in the outer edges I might not escape the gravitational pull of their uncertainty and sadness – and they would become my clique.

I should be with the Pre-Raphaelites, or at least with a dazzling in-crowd of my own, discoursing on deep intellectual stuff. I should be hanging out with brilliant young men and glorious young women. But I didn't know how. How do you find friends who can make you laugh and see how terrific life can be? How do you break away from the cold, outer edges and swing into the orbit of sunlight and fresh air? How do you catch the attention of the Bright Young Things?

More to the point: how do you *become* a Bright Young Thing?

* * *

Oxford was a place where we could try out the idea of who we wanted to be. And crucially, how well that idea of ourselves matched the idea of the place made the difference between succeeding in the world that awaited us or collapsing into ourselves.

In my second year, in that first term after I had got together with Josh, I was sharing a house on Iffley Road with nine other girls. One night, Caroline, a shy Politics student, stood in the kitchen unable to decide whether to boil the potatoes or not have any at all. She kept hesitating between the two choices, berating herself for her indecision and stupidity, apologising to us again and again, her sentences incomplete and unravelling. At first, the few of us in the living area engaged with her, tried to help her make a decision but it only seemed to make things worse. As she grew increasingly agitated, one of us – Pippa – went up to her and gently took the empty pot from her hand. And then led her to her room and put her to bed.

"What should we do?" We all looked at each other when Pippa came back into the living room.

The next morning, I went to see the Pastoral Tutor in college and that evening, Caroline's parents arrived to take her home.

At that time, I didn't really understand what had happened to Caroline – and I didn't want to. Her frozen uncertainty frightened me – reached out icy tentacles that touched the stuttering anxiety that I was hiding so well. Oxford, in its cold implacable vastness, had opened up a crevasse and she had lost her idea of herself in it. I felt the chill wind in the silent place she had left and I was determined that such a thing would never happen to me.

Earlier – during the spring term of my first year – I had finally managed to pull away from the outer edges. I found myself drawn to a group of girls who sparked with wit and vitality – and whose idea of Oxford chimed with mine. At their heart was Pippa, also reading English in my year – not one of the Pre-Raphaelites but with a sensible page boy cut to go with her down to earth charisma. She was a tall, warm presence in the group, with a knack for being funny and kind while never letting any of us take ourselves too seriously. I hovered for a moment in their orbit and was soon drawn into their laughter and curiosity about the Oxford that was opening up to us like an expansive vista.

As the weather improved, I found myself with a gang of friends to do all those things that made up the golden idea of Oxford. Central to the group was Jane - Pippa's best friend. She was reading French and German, a pretty blonde with a delightful laugh and an incisive intellect - and she was going out with Anthony's best friend Sam. Best friends going out with best friends – it was like in those movie romances and it added to the charm of this bright circle. We went punting, boyfriends and friends who were boys, standing tall in bow ties and crisp shirts, handling the long poles with muscular arms. We girls sat before them in long floaty skirts, trailing our hands languidly in the water, the picnics we had prepared waiting in hampers by our sides. The young men sometimes raced the shallow crafts as we pretty passengers cheered them on, sometimes competed to see who could punt the furthest one handed, handkerchiefs tied round their wrists to catch the dripping water.

We picnicked on strawberries and cream, lounging on tartan blankets. Once, Anthony, Pippa's boyfriend, challenged the other young men to press ups and beat them all with one arm behind his back. Pippa rolled her eyes but we girls nonetheless giggled with impressed delight. Another time, Josh – then just a boy who was a friend – and the other men had a knife throwing competition to see who could hurl the picnic knife to land the furthest away into the grass. I wanted to join in, to feel the blade between my finger and thumb and to see that satisfying *thwump* as it stabbed into the soil – but I hung back. This was the men's game, their moment in the sun. I sensed that if I tried to take the knife, the game would be over. So I stayed with the other girls, chatting on the picnic blanket.

Pippa, Jane and I came to share that house on Iffley Road in our second year, between us gathering seven other girls from St Hilda's and St Hugh's to fill the ten rooms. After Caroline went home, we found another girl to take her room, a post-graduate who had a calm grown-up air we were all in awe of. We filled the house with everything I had dreamed that Oxford would be: parties and late night conversations about philosophy, literature, life. We laughed, teased, talked girl talk, played pranks on each other. Pippa had a habit of kicking her shoes off and leaving them in the common living room – we nabbed one of the pair of dark green heels and posted it to Anthony through the university mail network, the "pigeon post".

Josh and I had spent our first year as 'just friends'. He had been one of the first people I met during Fresher's Week. We had both gone along to the Backpacker's Society. I wasn't a backpacker but had travelled a bit in my gap year. Back then, international travel was still relatively expensive unless you were savvy enough to get a cheap flight through a 'bucket shop'. So I reckoned that anyone who loved travel would have a serious interest in different cultures and an appreciation of the world beyond English life. As usual, I was the only East Asian in the group of predominantly white faces.

Over the next few weeks, I dropped round to his room at Lincoln and he would come round to mine. We would drink coffee and talk about life – what we knew of it so far from school and a few weeks at university, at any rate - travel and different cultures. He had backpacked around Europe in his gap year and been as far as Turkey. He wanted to go further East – Indonesia and Thailand maybe. I told him about Malaysia and its multi-cultural history.

I liked the way he looked at me, with his warm brown eyes, friendly and appreciative yet a little shy. I had never had a boy look at me like that before. I had never had a boy look at me – period.

It was thrilling.

And more so because…well, it was a boy like him. I liked looking at him, too. I liked his curls, his dark lashes, his strong brow. I had read about chiselled features in romance novels and here they were just an outstretched hand away. I liked his muscular arms, the soft down on his forearms, his manly hands. I liked that he was tall and had broad shoulders and eye-catching abs.

Josh didn't have a girlfriend – and had not had anyone serious while he had been at boarding school, just a few dates with girls he knew back home in Worcester. We started to hang out together. I met his friends – mainly boys he had known at school and others reading Politics in his college. I drew him in to my circle and we became a couple in all but name, giving a nice symmetry to outings with Pippa and Anthony, Jane and Sam.

I had never had a boyfriend. There had not been much opportunity at an all-girls boarding school. But at home in Malaysia during the holidays throughout my teens, my mother had tried to open my chances. She introduced me to 'Nice Boys' via get-togethers with the children of family friends who were around my age. But I felt awkward with my glasses and unstylish hair. I could see the politeness and lack of interest in the boys' faces, and no doubt they could see my excruciating self-consciousness, all of us labouring under the duty that our parents had imposed upon us. I was potentially a good catch on paper in the eyes of their mothers – the daughter of a highly respected lawyer, educated in England, with a mother who was socially adept, poised and glamorous. As teenagers, we were a long way from marriage but who knew where such an early friendship – or family alliance - might lead? But there's nothing like the enthusiasm of well-intentioned mothers to throw ice water on any teenage friendship. So I remained boyfriendless throughout my years at school.

And now, here in Oxford, in the summer of my first year, finally the person I might be was beginning to take shape. I was becoming the kind of person who had witty, sparkling friends. Who could create an in-crowd of my own. Who was bright enough to hold my own in place full of the brightest and the best.

I was becoming the kind of girl who could have a boyfriend – and not just any old boyfriend, but one who was good-looking and tall and gorgeous.

* * *

In the summer holiday at the end of my first year, I went home to Malaysia a Bright Young Thing, with the promise of a golden second year to come in a shared house full of my sparkling gang of friends – and the promise of Josh to myself for a few weeks before term started again.

Josh was spending a month backpacking in Indonesia and stopped off in Kuala Lumpur to spend time with me. He impressed my father, discussing politics and history with the right level of intellect and deference. He charmed my mother with his good looks and good manners. He took an interest in my younger sister and brother and they responded to his easy going humour. We went on a road trip with some cousins up the West Coast of Malaysia, staying in a hilltop lodge in the rainforest, playing on the beach in Penang. Wherever we went, people noticed him, his tall lean form towering over everyone. My extended family all came out to see my new boyfriend, taking us out to dinner, dropping by laden with Chinese cakes for tea. "He's not my boyfriend," I kept saying to no avail.

Then one night, in the last few days of his visit, we sat on the verandah steps, just him and me. We were back at my parents' house. Everyone else had gone to bed. The moon was out, casting the garden in liquid silver. Palm trees fanned their dark shapes against the deep sky. The cicadas hummed and every now and then the *tok-tok* bird beat out its distinctive knocking call. The night jasmine filled the air with sweet scent.

He put his arm around my shoulders and drew me into his embrace. We kissed for the first time there on those cool stone steps.

* * *

As a child in Malaysia, I used to play and run around in the tropical heat in nothing more than shorts or my underpants. We would splash in the inflatable paddling pool in the garden in just our panties, my brother and sister and me, spraying each other with the hosepipe. One rainy afternoon, when I was eleven, I watched the swallows swooping all over the lawn catching insects, and I raced outside, throwing off my T-shirt and shorts. In my knickers, with the wild rain pelting on my bare body, I chased the birds to and fro wanting to catch one in my hands as they skimmed so close to the ground. The grass was cold and squelchy underfoot, the sky was dark with monsoon clouds. I loved the smell of the rain and sodden earth.

And I felt the jolting of my embryonic breasts with each step. I put my hands up to their tiny hard shapes in my chest. I knew I should stop. I knew I should hide them. But I wanted this – I couldn't put it into words in that moment, but it was this rain, this laughter, this chasing birds believing I could catch them, this childishness, all this – to last just a little longer.

When I came back into the house that afternoon, dripping wet and shivering in my drenched knickers, I knew that that was the last time that I would be able to run free and naked as a child.

Over the next few years, I hunched over my breasts, hid them from view. I didn't like their womanliness as they grew from tiny kumquats into shapely peaches. I hated having my period every month, the hormones ripping my insides to shreds and forcing me to take to bed with a pillow rammed hard into my abdomen. I hated the acne and oil smearing across my face and chest and back. I raged at the world like a werewolf caught beneath a permanent full moon, furious and horrified at the changes in my body.

I was afraid of being a woman.

And now here was Josh, taking in my body with his eyes, kissing my breasts with eager lips, touching all of me with his strong hands, longing for me with his powerful body.

The idea of myself as a woman suddenly stood before me. A desirable woman. I had never thought I could be desirable.

I let my hair grow longer, gentle tendrils nestling against my neck, a light fringe softening my brow. It couldn't be too long or its weight would bring back that limp look from my miserable teenage years. It couldn't be too short or I would look like a twelve year old boy. It had to be just right and trips to the hairdresser were fraught with anxiety. The stylist kept saying that Chinese hair was 'strong' – which I think meant it was difficult to control. But when he did get on top of the cut, it looked exactly as I wanted it – layered, soft, feminine.

I started to take an interest in jewellery. Yellow gold and silver brought out the caramel in my skin. I wore bangles and bracelets, liquid necklaces curling softly on my collarbone. I got my ears pierced and dangled them with bold pendant shapes.

Hanging out with Pippa and the gang in the Iffley Road house, I would wear jeans and trainers. But if I was meeting Josh or there were boys involved in our gatherings, I would change into skirts and feminine tops. I had floaty skirts in white, grey and turquoise that hugged my hips but swirled free around my thighs and knees. White showed off my caramel so I had numerous tops in white and pale colours with open collars and a bold translucence. I very rarely wore a bra and through the pale tops everything beneath was just a breath away.

I would swap the trainers for one of my little pairs of shoes. A grey set of 'fairy boots' were my favourite. They had a red trim which caught the eye when I turned down the cuff but they could also be worn with the cuff turned up. They looked clunky with skirts so I saved them to wear with skin tight jeans or leggings. There were several white pairs of more girly shoes, low heeled pumps and slip-ons with different coloured trim. Blue and red and black pairs with sharper toes and higher heels. And two pairs of stilettos – one black and one in pale brown that would almost seem to vanish against my skin.

Under my skirts I always wore suspenders and silk stockings. I loved the sheen they gave to my legs. No-one but Josh and I knew about the straps and buckles hidden from view, the small area of skin above the tops of the stockings, the freedom of air floating around my panties.

I did all this for Josh. For the way he looked at me. And the way he touched me and caressed me and made love to me. But I also did this for the way that other men looked at me. It was as if my body held a power that I had never been aware of until that moment.

* * *

I contemplated this idea of me – this me who was feminine and desirable - as if seeing a statue of the Venus for the first time. I walked around her, inspected her from top to toe. Like a Pygmalion with his new creation, I played with her, tried her out in different settings, dressed her up and dressed her in hardly anything at all.

One evening, Jane and I found ourselves at home in our student house with nothing to do. Sam was with his rugby team playing a series of away matches. Josh had gone away to St Andrew's to see some old school friends at uni there. Our other housemates were all out with their other friends.

"I can't believe we're home alone on a Saturday night," Jane laughed morosely.

"Us! Of all people."

I looked at her across the empty living room. We were the two in the house who had feminine glamour to our personas. But of the two of us, her bubbly, feline charm was wholeheartedly a part of who she was. I was envious of that guileless ease she had in her womanliness. She made being feminine look so natural.

Her blue eyes flashed. "I know! How ridiculous is that?"

"There must be a party somewhere." I got off the bean-bag decisively.

We ended up gate-crashing a staircase party at Jesus College. There was no-one we knew there amidst the heaving student rooms that wound up the medieval staircase. We tossed our coats on a bed in one of the rooms and pushed our way through the hot, fuggy hoards until we came to a cluster that might turn out to be an interesting crowd. There seemed to be an intensity here in this wood-panelled room near the top of the stairs. A din of voices roared above the loud music.

We hovered for a moment on the threshold. Jane was in one of her pretty frocks, her blonde hair flicking against her shoulders. Beside her, I was taller than usual in my tan stilettos - and startling sleek in a glittering black camisole and a pair of skin-tight gold lamé leggings. I had heavy make-up, my scarlet lipstick matching my immaculate nails. A number of young men scooped us up with their eager eyes and swooped in like a net around us.

Well, that hadn't taken long.

We let ourselves be drawn into the room and handed drinks in paper cups. I caused consternation asking for a soft drink and as a number of them scurried about trying to find me a Coke, the group split off with Jane taking some of them in her wake to another corner of the room. And I was left with a jostling cluster of my own.

"Hello, who are you?"
"I've never seen you before."
"Which college are you at?"
"I'm Edmund."

"Matt…"

"Wait, let me guess, you're Japanese, right? *Konichiwa*… I'm James"

I found myself half sitting, half leaning on a window seat. From here, I could see the whole room. I caught the glances of some of the women – sour, disapproving. They said, this is *our* college, how dare you come into *our* college and try to take *our* men.

I smiled at the huddle of testosterone around me, preening, glancing coyly up at them. The women's jealousy fuelled something in me.

My voice was an octave higher than my normal speaking voice when I said in a flirtatious tone, "I'm Winnie."

A fresh faced boy caught my eye. I said, "Are you Chinese?"

He beamed, pleased to be singled out. "Half. My mum is Chinese. My dad is from Wales. I'm Todd. Pleased to meet you, Winnie."

He reached out in the gesture of a handshake. I took his hand as a queen might, palm down.

And he was "in".

The others knew it and the tight group around me loosened.

His friend, Edmund, stayed close, body blocking the others. He was Asian, with gold rimmed glasses, in a tweed jacket and tie in contrast to Todd's open necked shirt. "Winnie, Winnie - do you like his Bruce Lee haircut?"

"That's why I noticed him – the Big Boss." I looked askance at Todd and back at Edmund. "He's the action man and you're the intellectual?"

And they were off. Neither wanted to be simply brawn or brain. Their voices clamoured, overlapping, joshing each other, flirtatious with me. The other men straggled off, finally admitting defeat, and I was left with my two vying courtiers.

I laughed and teased, moving my gaze from one to the other in a way that showed off my neck and shoulders. I gasped at the right moments at their cleverness, touching my hand softly to my heart, my fingers lightly on my collar bone. I listened with open lips, eyes expressive, overflowing with awe and wonder.

Writing it down now, all those mannerisms sound so cold and calculated. But in that moment, I had no forethought or deliberateness. I simply let my body respond. This was…well, this was how Winnie was.

As the evening progressed, I found out that Winnie was from the poly and was studying English Lit. She loved Jane Austen ("so romantic") and First World War poetry ("so sad"). For her, these boys were so clever, so handsome, so funny, so charming, so manly. Everything they said was wonderful and exciting and witty and profound. She touched their arms, pitted them against each other, and affirmed their friendship.

I don't know why that evening I decided to be Winnie. She just arrived in the moment I said her name. Perhaps it had been out of loyalty to Josh. I had no intention of starting anything with any other boy. That night was all about the fun of a party and the exhilaration of laughter in a crowd. Of not being two girls alone on a Saturday night while life swirled on around us. So Winnie kept Yang-May safe.

And also, knowing that I was with Josh meant that I didn't need Todd or Edmund or any other boy. I didn't care about the outcome of the evening. I didn't care whether I got anyone's full name so we could exchange 'pigeon post' notes in days to come. I didn't care whether or not I got an invitation to see any of the boys again. They wanted me more than I wanted them. And that power set me free to play.

I was fed up of being the brainiac – the clever girl who, in conversation, challenged the men, argued with them, met them at their own level. I had turned up at parties before in these gold lamé leggings and tan stilettos and I had seen the boys' delight turn to distance when I started to talk to them as me. My manner would still be that of a brainy girl, all angles and a headlong rush of ideas and excitability without thought for the men as men. And

I would feel the shame of rejection as they withdrew.

But not Winnie. In Winnie, what they saw was what they got. She was all the girls I had ever envied - for their confident sexuality, their playfulness with men, their willingness to put the boys first. She held within her all of their most potent feminine qualities that I had seen from afar – and more. Winne was as dumb as she needed to be to let Edmund's intellect shine and as fragile as Todd wanted her to be for him to broaden into his manliness. She was me thumbing my nose at those other girls and their glares, the Pre-Raphaelites with their abundant hair, the cool girls who had one time or another laughed at my gauche plainness, pitied my awkward dress sense or ignored me with disdain.

She was the me I never knew I could be.

I liked her easy sensuality and her enjoyment of her body and its impact on others – both men and women. I liked her mischievousness and her feline toying with the boys under her spell. I liked how she could get them to do things just for her – fetch her another drink, compete for her approval, try so hard to make her laugh.

And yet I also despised her. I despised how she was so willing to listen and *ooh* and *aah* and to hardly speak except in appreciation or praise, how she played down her own intelligence, used her body as bait. I despised how she became invisible other than as a sparkly mirror in which they could see the best of themselves.

I was jealous of Todd and Edmund and men like them who found it so easy to see the best of themselves in the eyes of girls like Winnie. They took the heroic image of themselves that she gave to them and fed on it, growing bigger and bolder as they took their place in the world. But what if she also gave them her intelligence, her opinions, her thoughts, her views – those that were her own and not an echo of theirs – her boldness and ambition, her drive to take her own place in the world? Would they walk away as other men had walked away from the me who was just me without Winnie? Or would they be willing to be the mirrors that reflected back to her the best of herself, the hero that she too could be?

Jane and I cycled back through Oxford in the early hours of the morning, riding side by side through the empty streets. We laughed and giggled, swapping stories of the boys we had met, repeating jokes we had heard, comparing our experiences of the night. It was awkward cycling in my high heels, especially when we stopped and I had to put one foot down to steady the bike. I wished I had had a pair of trainers to change into – but no-one ever did that, all of us doing whatever we did in girly shoes. I was glad that I had managed to sit for most of the evening and that Todd and Edmund had been talky intellectual types rather than dancey lads. I rarely wore these stilettos. They made me anxious, especially on the old uneven stone floors of Oxford colleges; that I would misstep and go tumbling over, a hideous cracking sound in my ankle, shooting, unbearable pain making me spew expletives. But I had carried them off tonight with terrific aplomb.

I would never see Todd and Edmund again and that was fine with me. I didn't want to think about how they might have responded to me if I had turned up at that party as just me. Without the stilettos, without the heavy make-up, without the dumb act. If I had engaged with them as an equal, discussed Wittgenstein and Chomsky with the same ardour they had, talked passionately about the Great Victorian Novels that I loved, ventured to tell them about my ambition to write my own novels someday.

Winnie never came back. I couldn't express it at the time but much as I loved the power she gave me over the men at that party, I had a sense that she was casting our true power to the wind.

Yet, even as I let her slip off into the night, I knew that she had left something precious with me. Her sensuality, her enjoyment of her body, her confident sexuality, her mischievousness and feline playfulness – they were all mine now.

* * *

On a dark moonless night, a man is coming home from a business trip to a faraway town. He is walking the last few miles home, along a lonely road through the rice *padi* fields and banana groves. The thick forest encroaches in between the cultivated areas and all around the sounds of the tropical night hum and whirr and call. He hears a low moaning from time to time, so close he can reach out and touch it.

But there is nothing there. No-one there.

And then in a dark patch of shadow close to a cluster of banana trees, she is hurrying towards him, a pale feminine shape. She moves delicately like gossamer in the breeze, hardly seeming to strain against the ground. As she nears, he sees a woman of unearthly beauty in an embroidered tunic and soft, flowing sarong that trails down to the ground.

"Help me," she says, her imploring dark eyes touching his heart. "I am lost and weary."

And even as her mellifluous voice trails away, she swoons and he catches her in his arms.

He carries her home, wisps of scented hair catching in his mouth as her long tresses drape across his face. Her head nuzzles against his shoulder in her fitful faint, her breasts rising and falling as she moans and draws breathe. Her long sarong flows like streamers in the wind along the path behind him even though it is a still night.

At home, he lays her on his bed and brings a bowl of water, a flannel, some tonic for her to drink. He wipes her clammy brow. He cannot help but think how beautiful she is and how he longs to kiss her.

When he turns away to reach for the tonic, he does not see her reptilian eyes flit open and watch him. He does not see her lips curl, the fangs like those of a snake glinting in the half light.

He turns back and holds her head as she sips gently from the cup in his hand. He smells her sweet scent of frangipani and aches to lie with her.

He turns away again and stands up. He needs a brandy. He passes the end of the bed to go out to the drinks cabinet.

He recalls a funeral. The scent of frangipani heavy in the air. White wreathes against the coffin, overflowing with the flowers of death.

Glancing down at the woman on his bed, he sees the endless flowing sarong swirling like a beautiful cloud at her feet.

Only – she has no feet.

A chill runs its dead fingers down the nape of his neck.

He has brought home a *pontianak*.

While she sleeps he leaves the room. He hurries past the drinks cabinet. He needs a spike; that is the only way. There isn't a moment to spare. If she wakes… if she discovers that he knows… she will tear out his entrails with her claws, gouge out his heart, and gorge on his blood. Devour him.

He finds a screwdriver – yes that will do – and slips it into his pocket. Heading back to the room, he stops by the cabinet. Perhaps he will have that drink. He downs a shot and pours himself another. And he walks back into the bedroom, one hand holding the glass, the other hidden and clutching the steely shaft.

The *pontianak* lies on the bed, tossing and turning. This was how she would have died, lying alone in her own bed, writhing in pain as she delivered the stillborn heir to a man who no longer even thought of her. She had been once sweet and guileless like a child, had hoped for so much in her love for him. She had given him so much that had been most precious to her – her heart, her body, her innocence. And now while he rested in the bosom of his wife and family, she howled in agony and gave up that one last precious thing: her life. And all for nothing - a dead child and a man whose heart had been dead.

So she prowls the night to wreak her vengeance on all men, to seduce them with her feminine charms and then devour them as the seed of a faithless man's lust had once devoured her from the inside.

As he sits down by her side, she wakes and the dark liquid of her eyes holds him captive. She moves against the soft mattress like a snake, showing off her caramel neck, parting her moist red lips, arching her back, her breasts straining against the tight tunic. He can see her hips moving beneath the sarong, the crease where her pudenda waits. He feels the intoxication swirl around his head. He is hard and desperate for her.

But he must hold on to the cold, deadly shaft in his hand.

She draws herself up and entangles him in her arms and hair and long, lingering kisses. The smell of death fills his lungs but there is an allure in it, a longing to merge with her scent, her soft flesh, her destructive power. He feels himself falling into the vortex of her seduction.

But in the moment her fangs flash, her cobra eyes spark, her face decays into a triumphant, disgusted, malicious, joyous mask, and she rears her head back to plunge her jaws into his flesh, his hand pulls out the screwdriver and jams it into the back of her neck.

They are suspended there in a tableau of horrific ecstasy, his body curved over hers as the weapon penetrates her, breaking flesh and bone, entangled in her hair, her head thrown back in shock, her mouth open in a soundless shriek, her breasts hard against his chest.

He lets her fall onto the bed, the shaft of the screwdriver disappearing from view beneath her thick black hair. She is lifeless and still.

She opens her eyes.

But they are soft and docile. A sweet smile makes her lips even more desirable. The fangs are gone, her face is perfect and glows with good health.

"I am yours," she says with charming devotion. "My husband."

He watches as she sits up demurely, her legs curled under her on the bed. She gathers her long hair and coils it up into a bun, hiding the stub of the shaft within it. She slides off the bed and kneeling at his feet, she brings her hands together in a gesture of subservience and bows in a deep obeisance before him.

For as long as the spike remains in the back of her neck, she is the perfect wife - obedient, submissive, docile but also erotic, skilful, uninhibited. All for him. Only for him.

We grew up with many versions of the *pontianak* story. This is my version.

* * *

The *pontianak* is the most famous ghost in Malaysian and Indonesian folk lore. There are films and dramas and comics about these seductive vampires. Gathered round with my cousins as a child in Malaysia, we would sit round and scare each other on dark nights when anything might be lurking in the dark beyond the house. The details might differ - we might imagine a Malay man or a Chinese man or a white colonial planter, or he might use a nail or a spike or a sharp stick. But the core details were always the same – the meeting on the road, her seductive allure, the deadly transformation waiting to occur, the sharp shaft into the back of the neck bringing her under his control.

Something about her had always fascinated me as a young girl.

It was partly her fury. That fury at the man who had abandoned her. At the child who had killed her. At her loneliness that had led her to that fatal liaison. It was a fury that defied the laws of nature and brought her back to life – a transformative, powerful, uncontainable fury.

And it was also her sexual power that fascinated me. Freed from the confines of being a wife and mother, she is the eternal *femme fatale*, seductress and devourer of men, careless with them as the one man had been with her. In life, a man had held her in his thrall and taken her innocence without a thought. In living death, it was she who held the power to destroy them all.

I had been the girl this ghostly demon had once been, longing to be liked and loved despite my lanky hair and thick glasses and awkward manner. I hated that loneliness. I hated that neediness that felt like a shaft in the heart.

I wanted to not need. To be the one that others longed for. To hold the power.

The detail of her missing feet seemed to make the legend of *pontianak* more alluring. That is how you know that the beautiful woman you meet on a dark lonely night is not of this world: she has no feet – and yet, time and again, the foolish man sees nothing sinister in her delicate, ethereal movement, only the floating glide that he expects of all beautiful women.

That's why we wear our little shoes, isn't it? Women's shoes are thinner, more delicate, daintier, and more ethereal than those of men. They are not meant for walking but for being adored in. Even those women's brogues you see these post-modern days have a flimsiness and lightness to them compared to a pair of men's brogues. We are meant to glide, to float, to swish. To be not of this world – but transcendent, heavenly, divine.

Picture a beautiful woman in a gorgeous evening gown. Her feet may not be visible, but you are probably imagining a pair of high heels, with hardly any strap or casing but somehow almost invisible.

Now picture her with a pair of heavy, clunky Doc Martens or wellies. She looks ridiculous, right? Or like a rebel or someone who doesn't care about conventional rules of dress. But she is no longer aloof, elegant, dignified, goddess-like.

In shoe shops, they always display size 4 in the ladies section – that is the smallest Western size for adult women that doesn't look like a child's shoe. It speaks to the image of the ideal woman in our collective psyche, one who is feminine and dainty. As an object of desire, a size 4 shoe in your hand has an allure – but pick up a size 7 and its length and width hints at masculinity and sturdiness and stirs our cultural anxiety.

And the higher the heel, the smaller the shoe seems, the smaller the surface area in touch with the ground and the smaller our feet appear. And as the heel rises higher and sleeker, so our feet disappear and we become floating, gliding beings, goddess-like beyond the hold of this dirty, fraught world. And the stiletto, the highest and sleekest of the shoes, named for violence and desire, gives us our greatest sexual power.

So we can all become *pontianaks*.

* * *

Yet the fate of this powerful ghostly creature troubled me. From a ferocious being beyond the laws of nature, she becomes a wife in all but name. She belongs to the man, for so long as his shaft stays embedded in the back of her neck. With her docile eyes and placid beauty, she will do whatever pleases him. Her drive, her will, her fury no longer matters – she exists only for him.

Is this what we will all become as we slot into the roles expected of us, even if we are wild and uncontrollable demons from another realm? Is this what was happening to me - as I let go of my innermost desires, gave up on being a writer and creative artist and tomboy, and instead embedded the shaft of fitting in and being loved in my own back?

The thought flitted just out of reach. I knew it was there but I did not seek it out. In my twenty year old mind, I expected one day that I would get married. That's what we all wanted, wasn't it? That's what we all expected of our lives. What my family expected for me. Those thoughts were bright and graspable right there in front of me. But this other thought…Sometimes, like a bat fluttering in the darkness of my mind, I would see it but I would turn away towards the light.

But it was there.

I did not want to be a wife.

I didn't understand why. I felt ashamed that I even had such a thought. Surely, getting married was every girl's dream? There were so many layers of meaning embedded in that word but they were blurred and ghostly in my mind. At that time, I could only see the most brightly coloured of its manifestations and it pushed its way to the forefront like an accusation. Becoming a wife gave us the ultimate power, didn't it? Wife trumps mistress, right? And spinster. He, our husband – and the world of acceptability that he represented - would belong to us even as we might belong to him. That gave us the power to take our rightful place in the world, even as he might have the power to tame the demon in us. And that was worth it. Wasn't it?

And yet…

* * *

For Josh's twenty-first birthday, we headed to his parents' house in Worcester for the weekend. There was a big lunch party at home, the food spread out across the dining table, buffet-style. The house was overflowing with his friends from school and the neighbourhood, cousins and uncles and family friends. I was the only friend he brought home from Oxford. And I was the only person who was not English.

It felt like a big thing, this weekend – coming home as his girlfriend to meet his parents and stay in their house on this special occasion. At the time that he had come to visit me in Malaysia, he had been 'just a friend'. My parents had welcomed him as a friend and no more. But now that he was my Boyfriend, my parents were different with him – still friendly and warm because they liked him but I could see them thinking: could he be our son-in-law one day? What would *his* parents think of me, meeting me for the first time as his Girlfriend? Would they also start picturing me one day in the role of his wife and their daughter-in-law? And if they did, would they like what they saw?

Josh looked as handsome as ever in his blazer and tie. I wore my floaty turquoise skirt and a soft white top with my demure black pumps. I wanted his family to like me – or rather approve of me. No trace of Winnie or her legacy or the physical intimacy that Josh and I shared could be seen. I was polite, interested in everything. I was friendly and chatty, but not too much, still a little shy and reserved.

It was intimidating, all these people so curious about me. What they did not say was almost audible. *So - this is Josh's Girlfriend. She's quite exotic, isn't she? But why her? Why not one of us?* There were those who wanted to find out all about me, others who stole glances at me from a distance. His parents were kind and welcoming. His sisters, older than Josh, were warm and funny, affectionately conspiratorial with me – "How do you put up with him?" The young men were friendly but also appraising – and I sensed that I passed. Some of his girl friends eyed me glacially.

And then his Uncle Richard said out loud what was on everybody's mind. He was giving the toast. The older people – or grownups, as we thought of them – sat on the sofas and armchairs, and lined the room on upright dining chairs. I was among the other young folk on the floor, my flowing skirt spread around me. Josh was standing up by Uncle Richard, beaming awkwardly. The older man, a family friend 'uncle', spoke jovially about how Josh had grown into an adventurous young man, doing well at Oxford, with a thirst for new places and new ideas. He talked about his travels and his most recent trip to Bali.

"So he comes back home to us this weekend a man of the world, bringing back new perspectives from his studies in Oxford, a growing understand of the different cultures from his travels. We expected all that from him. But no-one expected him to bring back a dusky maiden…"

A roar of laughter broke out. I glanced up. Was he talking about me?

I looked at Josh. His excruciating embarrassment said it all. I felt the flush of red rise in my face as Josh pleaded "sorry" silently. For a moment, I didn't know what to do.

And then I held my head up and laughed with them. After all, it was *me* he had chosen - *me*, the dusky maiden - above all the other girls.

I liked the idea of myself as a dusky maiden. It made me exotic. Interesting. Intriguing. Alluring. Up till now the only references to my ethnicity I had heard had been the usual ones. Chinky-Chong. Hong Chong. Ah Chong. Slitty Eyes.

At my boarding school, there were only two Chinese girls for the first few years I was there – me and a sixth former. Girls called me those names, with no malice – and sometimes with affection. When I went to stay with school friends during half-term in provincial towns around the UK, kids in the street would shout names at me as we walked by. At Oxford, when I waited with my friends for a table at Chinese restaurants - if I was in low-key casuals - other customers would signal to me to take their order or expect me to seat them at a table. Once when a gang of us went to a country pub, I was first through the door into the smell of beer and wood fire and the noise of laughter and chatter - and the whole place fell silent as everyone inside turned to stare at me, the one non-white face amongst them all.

So for a long time, I didn't like to think of myself as Chinese. Within a couple of terms at school, I submerged my Malaysian accent under a cut glass public school one. I had no Chinese ornaments in my room at school, no Asian food in my locker other than pot noodles. A third Chinese girl who came to the school got special dispensation from chapel every morning for being Buddhist – with my Methodist background I couldn't get out of this daily morning ritual much as I would have loved 20 minutes after breakfast to myself. But a part of me also took pride in doing everything the English girls did and being just like everyone else. I watched and learned and reproduced all the manners and mannerisms of the English. And soon I forgot that when people looked at me, they didn't see a white English girl.

At Oxford, my voice mellowed into the languid superior vowels of the dreaming spires. I found it impossible to switch to my Malaysian voice in front of my English friends even though privately with my family I might chat happily in sing-song Malaysian slang. I dressed in Western clothes and wore only Western jewellery – no padded Chinese *meen lap* winter jacket, no jade. I ate only Western food and when I went to Chinese restaurants with my friends, I made a point of proclaiming that I couldn't read the Chinese version of the menu.

But the way Josh looked at me began to change things. Our few weeks together in Malaysia gave us a warm, jasmine-infused common memory that was ours to luxuriate in. His interest in South East Asia opened up the Eastern part of my life again and we talked about Asian customs and culture and history. He told me about the things he noticed in Indonesia and I threw in comparisons from Malaysia – the smell of *kretek,* the distinct clove cigarettes of that region, the difference between *sarongs* for men and those for women, how he had adopted the Eastern custom of taking of his shoes when he came to see me in Iffley Road.

It wasn't only his interest that nourished my Eastern self. Pippa and Jane and my other friends were curious about where I came from. Lizzie, a friend of Jane's who was also reading Modern Languages, would come by and we would all hang out in the upstairs living room, drinking tea. They asked me about my family, wanted to know what Malaysia was like – trying to imagine a place that was hot all year round, where everyone ate rice all the time and had curry for breakfast. I found a small Chinese grocery store in Summertown in North Oxford and bought Chinese tea and Chinese tea cups. Sometimes, instead of downing large mugs of PG Tips, we would sip the fragrant, milkless tea from the delicate little cups. It made me laugh that to them drinking tea like this at home and not in a Chinese restaurant felt exciting and exotic.

I asked them about where they were from and learnt about their childhoods in Derbyshire and South London and Scotland. Pippa explained about having dinner at lunch time and tea at dinner time and they all had common memories of English seaside holidays in the rain. They waxed lyrical about chip butties and walks to a countryside pub while Christmas dinner cooked in the oven.

I came to love the question, "Where are you from?" I don't see it as racist or condescending. It can be celebration of curiosity and when I ask it right back at the other person, we each see into each other's human hearts. Because before too long, we are talking about our families, our homes, our cultures and what we love and value most in our lives.

It can take a while for me to answer that question "Where are you from?"

Are you ready? Here goes… I come from Malaysia originally but I'm British now. My family are Chinese. Malaysia is made up of a mix of Malays (the majority and who are related to Indonesians), Chinese and Indians. The Indians would have been originally from India or Sri Lanka, and the Chinese from China. My family, many generations ago, arrived in Malaya (as it then was) from different parts of China. My parents still live in Malaysia although my brother and sister and I now all live over here.

So if you were to ask me, "Where are your family *originally* from?" I would have to say "China".

And that second question is one I love even more. Because when I ask it back to the person I am chatting with, we find ourselves delving into the history of Britain. The answer can involve part Danish, part Russian Jew, part East Indies, part Welsh - or in rare and unique moments, generations upon generations within a single British locality. I hear stories about seamstresses, miners, teachers, grocers. A great-great-grandfather committed to Bedlam, a great-uncle who died in the trenches in the Great War, an auntie who was a Land Girl during World War II. There are stories of love, making do, hardship, secrets never spoken of.

And sometimes, there are those who don't know their family history, who never sat down together to hear family stories and never asked their parents or grandparents. I've seen a curiosity stir in them that they never thought to have. It starts with a pang of envy - that I know so much of where I am from and they know so little of their own history. And then a determination to go and find out.

In that shared house on Iffley Road, I began to cook Malaysian meals. In those days, it was hard to find East Asian ingredients outside of London's Chinatown and speciality Asian grocers tucked away in odd corners of market towns. I brought back a *wok* from KL - all Malaysians refer to the capital city, Kuala

Lumpur as KL – along with packets of spices and specially mixed curry powder and dried bits and pieces: shrimp, mushrooms, cloves, aniseed. There was *keropok*, hard prawn-based disks like gambling chips which, when deep fried in the *wok* and fished out with chopsticks, grew and crackled into giant fluffy white crisps. Sometimes, I made *poppadoms* that same way, too and my friends would cluster round to see the Asian magic happen.

My signature meal was Malaysia's national dish *nasi lemak*. These meals were special occasions. We cleared the dining table to the side of the living room and laid out *rattan* mats on the carpet. Sometimes, guests had to come with *sarongs* to change into and go barefoot. Once we went all out for the full tropical experience, turning the heating up and decorating the room with papiêr maché palm trees. Pippa came in a full sari she had bought on a trip to India, others came in Hawaiian shirts and beach outfits. Josh and I wore our *sarongs*. Another time, we had lunch in the overgrown garden and pretended we were in the jungle and Josh wore a solar *topi* that I found for him in a costume shop.

I would flavour the rice with coconut or fragrant *pandan* leaves which I had brought back from Malaysia, preciously wrapped in plastic and stored in the fridge. I stir-fried prawns with garlic and onions and added *sambal belacan*, an explosive chilli paste made with shrimp. Then came the hard-boiled egg and a sprinkling of *ikan bilis*, tiny crunchy fried whitebait-like fish. Without banana leaves, we made do with ordinary dinner plates – but I made everyone eat with their right hand, sitting on the floor, Malay-style.

I loved sharing my culture with my friends. I loved seeing them discover these tastes that were so familiar to me and yet so new to them. In their turn, they held traditional English dinner parties – with starter, main and dessert, followed by cheese and port. We all dressed up like grownups. The young men wore blazers and ties, us girls in smart dinner frocks. They laid the table smartly with rows of proper cutlery, candles and different glasses for all the different wines – sometimes mismatched and scrounged from other student houses. Anthony had worked as a waiter in a hotel in the holidays and he took pride in serving each course as if were in a top notch restaurant, a tea towel draped over his arm. We girls stayed at the table at the end of the meal – after all, this was the 80s – and we all passed the port and smoked cigars and talked about life, the universe and everything.

Looking at Josh and my friends in the candlelight or cross-legged across the *rattan* mats, it seemed to me in those moments that I had everything that I had ever dreamt of amidst those spires of hope and possibility.

One thing, however, still remained unfulfilled.

I had not yet been to a ball.

Balls have a mythical quality to them. In our collective unconscious, they are magical and other-worldly. Beyond merely being big parties, they are transformative spaces or prizes to be won like a heavenly kingdom on earth or arenas for an ultimate challenge. In my mind, going to a ball would be the iconic symbol that I had conquered Oxford – beyond Caroline and her frozen sense of not being good enough, beyond the earnest intimidated girl I had been on my first day here, beyond honeypot Winnie and her dimwit act - going to a university ball would place me at the heart of everything that mattered to me and to my family: intellectual success, social acceptance, a rite of passage into a golden future as a grown up woman with its unspoken promise of marriage and the next generation.

A ball is the driving force in the Cinderella story. Everyone is going to the ball except Cinderella, the outcast who has been shunted out of her rightful place in society by her stepmother and ugly sisters. She longs desperately to go and by magic she is given a dress and a carriage and little glass slippers. Once there, everyone is amazed by her beauty and charm and no-one recognises her, so transformed is she from her ordinary, ragged self. It is there that her destiny is changed forever when she dances with the Prince and he is impelled by his love for her to search for her throughout the kingdom.

Henry Higgins in *Pygmalion* wagers that he can transform Eliza Doolittle from a common flower girl into a Duchess. The embassy ball is the climax of this comedy of manners – will Eliza pass the test or will she be unmasked as an imposter? This ball is where the great and the good gather, the beautiful gowns of the women and the gloriously handsome outfits of the men, their finery and style and charmed etiquette – it is implied - all manifestations of their inner greatness and goodness and worthiness. Can this other outcast, the coarse and vulgar girl picked up from the streets of London - with all the venality and badness and unworthiness implied in that – really become someone else, more beautiful and glorious on the inside as on the outside, merely because other people at the ball take her for who she presents herself to be?

Going to a ball – not just any ball, but an Oxford ball – was an integral part of this idea I had about who I should be. And beyond that, not just a single ball but many balls throughout a life that would be beautiful and glamourous and successful. But it was already the second year and I had not been to a single one.

There would only be this chance now – and one last one in my third and final year.

Many of my girl friends had already been to balls in our first year. And they were already preparing for the summer balls this year with their boyfriends. They checked out all the flyers and posters and compared the different balls. Who was the band? The Trinity ball had a fun fair – would there be rides or just shooting galleries and candy floss? Which college had the better layout for multiple marquees? Students who had inside knowledge through friends of friends who knew one of the organisers would spread the word and speculation fuelled everyone's excitement – there would be hot air balloon rides at Christchurch, Viennese waltzing at Somerville, a masked theme at Queen's. Each clique of friends had to reach a consensus to avoid rifts and individual breakaway couples: which one could they all agree on to go to?

And Josh had still not asked me to any one of them. It infuriated me, this having to wait for the man to ask. To take charge. To be the one in control. Why couldn't *I* ask him?

I don't know where or when I learnt that it was the man who had to make the first move. That a girl couldn't do the asking, couldn't be too forward. But Jane and I and our other girl friends used to talk about it. Did that particular boy like us? Why hadn't he made a move yet? How could we encourage him? What were the best ways to make the first move so that he thought that *he* was making the first move?

So I had to broach the subject obliquely, lay the breadcrumb trail. And all the time, I felt hurt. Why didn't he want to come to the ball with me? Didn't he want to see me dressed up to the nines, looking glorious beyond the every day, and spend a magical evening with me? Didn't he love me like those other men loved those other girls, ready and willing to escort them through one of the most significant romantic rituals of life?

It turned out he didn't like the idea of himself in black tie.

"They just look like twats, those Hooray Henries in their penguin suits," he said, making a face. "I'd feel like an idiot."

He always moaned when it came to dressing up. He was most comfortable in a rugged look – jeans and a simple shirt, occasional ethnic beads around his neck. *Sarongs* were fine as they had a traveller's worldly aura about them – although I teased him for wearing patterned *batik* ones which were meant for women: Asian men wore simple checked designs.

But I knew I would be able to win him around – it would take time and effort but somehow I would get my way. Like the White Evening. He had been reluctant at first when some of his friends invited us to dinner in Hall at Brasenose on the night of a full moon – the only condition was that we all dressed in white. He had grumbled about it. "Why get togged up in white? I don't know… shall we go?"

I had been excited, of course. "But it's a brilliant idea! We have to go."

"Maybe you could go… I might bail…"

"They're your friends, I can't go on my own, silly. Anyway, it'll be fun!"

"Why can't we just wear something smart? Maybe I could wear my blazer and tie…"

"No, Josh, you have to dress in white like everyone else. They're planning this special evening for us all. It's a full moon and it'll be amazing seeing everyone in white in the moonlight…"

His uncertainty surprised me. If anyone could pull off wearing white, it would be him – with his tanned skin and dark curls, he could wear anything and look amazing. In the end, he gamely dug out a set of white clothes including a white silk tie. He had no white shoes so wore his smart black pair, polishing them up till they shone. I wore a flowing white skirt with a pastel blue and pink hem. Over a netted camisole that was almost transparent, I threw a silky white shawl that occasionally slipped off my shoulders. My shoes were white pumps with a pastel trim to match my skirt. Underneath my suspenders and silk stockings, I had on a pair of bright red panties.

There was Emma and Richard, our hosts, moneyed and I think even titled; Francois and Marie-Louise from Paris, older graduate students, worldly and glamourous; Miles, Josh's best friend I had paired together with Lizzie to even out the numbers; and Josh and me. After dinner, we strolled out across the cobbles, past the Radcliffe Camera and onto George Street, our clothes shimmering in the moonlight. Like a faerie troupe, we laughed and talked, glowing phosphorescent amid the historic landscape.

Within our gliding flotilla of white, we mingled as we walked, sometimes clustering in groups, sometimes in pairs. As I strolled with Lizzie for a while, arms linked happily, I could see Josh laughing with Richard and Francois, his stride strong and confident. We would not have had this same conscious delight in ourselves if we had been dressed in our usual smart blazers or jackets or pretty party frocks. I was happy that Josh had not given in to his uncertainty. With all of us gleaming blue-white in the moonlight, the deliberate choice created a sense of drama that heightened the intensity of the evening. We were both spectacle and our own audience and the infinite reflections of ourselves lit up our evening like an electric charge.

Lizzie and I would usually hang out in jeans and a sweatshirt or jumper, makeup-less and casually slouchy. Tonight, as we walked arm in arm, I had a sway in my walk, kicking out my hips so that my full skirt swished around my calves. In my shallow white pumps, it was easy to sashay along, even as the pavement felt cold and hard beneath their thin soles. She kept pace with me in her plain white dress, still the girl she had always been. She was not wearing make-up and her simplicity, so different from my deliberate femininity, felt charming. She skipped along in a light skittish walk, like an excitable pony, giggling with delight at the other-worldliness of it all.

I found myself thinking of Josh and me, unpeeling our clothing in the dark. Even as we touched each other's naked skin, the feminine sensuality of all my clothing would stay with me and gave my body a flowing, writhing, sighing power. At first, our intimate moments together had been tentative and self-consciously restrained, sometimes awkward, sometimes pleasingly competent. But over time, I had cast away the schoolgirl I used to be along with the sexless blouses I used to wear. With my gossamer tops and floaty skirts and slinky silk stockings, I would let the ghost of Winnie move my body as she wished, fulfilling the promise hinted at by those garments.

Our clothes made us who we were that night, gave us a sense that we had created not just ourselves but everything the night had to offer. In the same way that my gold lamé leggings and tan stilettos had conjured Winnie, and my floaty skirts and bright jewellery had sculpted me into a Bright Young Thing, my naked but conscious sense of the woman I wanted to be, tonight our theatre of dress made us into immortals in a mythic landscape.

We floated our way through the well-lit streets and eventually out along a tree-lined avenue towards the University Parks. We came to a giant set of iron work gates, with ornate black and gold lattice work, their bars reaching up high into the infinite sky. They barred the way into the Parks. Richard and Francois tried them.

The main ceremonial gates were locked, as was the small side entrance for pedestrians.

"Let's go in," Francois said in his distinct French accent.

Richard and Josh joined him, looking over the iron bars and hinges to find a way in. The dark wilderness beyond seemed to provoke their sense of adventure.

"*Mais, c'est impossible…* " Marie-Louise began, looking doubtfully at the heavy bolted locks.

Francois laughed. "It's easy." That voice, with its Parisian disdain, made everything seem easy and effortless.

He was lean and muscular. He reached up to one of the bars, hopped up onto a cross bar and within moments he had scrambled over the gate, dropping like a cat onto the other side.

The other men were suddenly energized. They turned to us. "Come on, girls, we can do this."

Richard scrambled up the gates, calling down to Emma. "It'll be fine. We'll help you over…"

Josh looked over at me. I could see his impatience. He wanted to go over, too, but a sense of loyalty kept him this side of the gate. He glanced over at Miles for his support but Miles just puffed languidly on his cigarette, not caring either way.

We girls still hung back. Uncertainty flitted about us.

I wanted to join Francois and Richard. The men had made the climb look so easy. I wanted Josh and me to go over together. His restlessness made me anxious. I was conscious of my little pumps – would they slip on the iron railings, fall off if I pushed upwards on the balls of my feet? My skirt, which had made me feel so glamourous and beautiful all evening, suddenly felt like an encumbrance. Why couldn't I have been wearing trousers and solid shoes like the men?

"But our skirts…" Emma said. We all looked up at the tall spikes at the top of the gates. "How can we climb …?"

"And my shoes…" Marie-Louise indicated her heels.

I looked over at Josh. He was keen for adventure, too, I could see. He was looking at me with a frown. Would we girls ruin the evening with our wimpiness?

I stepped towards the gates and handed my shawl across to Francois. I gathered up my flowing skirt, rolling the material together high above my thighs, and up towards my waist. I tucked the folds into the back of my panties. In the bright moonlight, my suspenders and the tops of my stockings were clearly in view, the red of my underwear glowing black.

There were whoops and cheers from the men. The girls gasped, horrified and disapproving.

I said to Josh, "Help me up..."

Laughing, he lifted me and I pulled myself up to stand on one of the cross bars.

It was not too difficult after that to make my way slowly up using the lattice work and cross bars as steps. Francois, on the park side, directed me to the best holds. Josh stood below me ready to catch me if I slipped. I sensed them all watching me. I got to the top and bent over to hold on to the spikes. Carefully, I stepped one foot over to the other side. When I was sure I had anchored both feet on the upper-most cross bar, bracing my shins against the lattice work and spikes, I let go and stood up.

For a moment, I stood tall, high above them all, between earth and moon, the dark landscape of the parks ahead of me, my friends' upturned faces pale and small far below me. I wanted time to stop in that moment, to stay here towering above them all, seeing so far into the distance, poised between the structured stones of Oxford and the natural free forms of the parkland. This evening with its self-created theatricality would stay with me I knew, and this moment up here, alone, with my skirt hitched obscenely high, encompassed all my power and all my contradiction. I knew in that moment that I had Josh in my thrall and that he was already slipping away. That I was everything I had wanted to become and I was none of it. In my bold stance, I was seductress and tomboy, *pontianak* and child of nature, beguiling and guileless. I felt that I needed to choose only the one side, to be only the one singularity, like all the other women I knew. Lizzie with her girlish simplicity, Jane in her effortless femininity, Marie-Louse so poised and Parisian – they all seemed to be themselves so easily and without doubt. But me… who was I?

I felt the cool night breeze on my face.

And then I was over onto the other side, clambering down again and dropping into Francois's waiting arms. The men cheered. I untucked my skirt and let it fall, smoothing and fluffing it around my legs. I swung my shawl back over my shoulders and stood once again in a posture of flowing femininity.

The other girls reluctantly found their courage but none of them followed my immodesty, choosing to navigate the spikes as best they could in the fullness of their skirts. One by one the girls made it over, the men helping them and then shimmying over themselves, until all of us stood in the moonlit wilderness.

We moved across the open parkland as one single cloud of white at first but as the expanse drew us in amongst the trees and shadows, we dispersed, sometimes a thin thread, sometimes duets or trios of pale shapes in the magical landscape. Josh started off close by but I soon lost him in the myriad shades of blue-grey. He wanted to explore, to take in all the possibilities of the night and his sturdy shoes carried him onward, occasionally on his own, at times with the other men.

The grass beneath my pumps was uneven and the dew began to dampen my feet. The thin leather slipped against my stockings. I tried to keep up with Josh, with the men, but I walked awkwardly, my ankles kinking as my feet hit unseen dips in the ground. So I stayed apace with the other girls. Emma walked gingerly, concentrating on not turning her ankles in her high heels. Lizzie slipped off her shoes and skipped along in bare feet. Marie-Louise somehow remained statuesque and well, forever Parisian. Even as I chatted amiably alongside them, I felt a rising frustration.

I caught a glimpse of Josh ahead, looking out into the distance. He had got a bursary to go on an exchange year in Beijing, starting next October. He had told me excitedly about it – about learning

Mandarin and having the chance to study international relations from a Chinese perspective. It hurt that he had not talked to me about it before or told me that he had been thinking about applying for it. It hurt that his plans for next year did not include me. It seemed so easy for him – and for these men this evening talking over dinner – to make plans about their futures and their careers. They could go anywhere and do anything; as they were doing that evening, striding out across the moonswept landscape, while we girls followed in their wake.

I was in awe of Josh's certainty. He seemed like a man when he talked about his plans, with such understanding of the world. In those moments, I felt like a naïve schoolgirl all over again my head filled with stories I had read in books. I had no grasp of how I might engage with the world beyond Oxford. That world frightened me. What would be my place in it? Whenever I thought of that question, there was only ever one answer.

I wanted to be a writer.

I had always written stories as a child at home in Malaysia. At school, I had carried on with my own little stories outside of our required creative writing module. Here at Oxford, I had kept on writing in between my course work and the picnics and parties, tapping away at my typewriter some evenings when I had nothing to do and nowhere to go. But the stories still seemed childish. Lightweight. Fluff. I would start and then trail off after a few pages. I would jot down ideas for novels and never work them up into anything. There was no place for my attempts in the numerous literary magazines that were all over Oxford. The writing in those was cerebral, intellectual, and full of hard wit and brilliant ideas, the work of real *literati*. Mine felt like the work of a schoolgirl playing at grownups.

Others – Josh and our friends - talked confidently about becoming lawyers, bankers, accountants, diplomats, VPs in multinationals. To me, they were just words. I could not picture myself being any of those things and having a driving ambition for those careers like they all seemed to have.

Standing in the long grass that moon-drenched night, the dew seeping through my thin shoes, I wanted to capture that evening, not in images and not just as an anecdote shared with friends – but in words that would reach beyond me and beyond that singular moment. I wanted to write about it, to share with unknown others the smell of the earthy night, the surreal vision of that silver-blue landscape, the feel of the summer air on our skins – to transmit across time and place its magic and its desolation.

In those rare moments when I let go of the construct of who I should be, this secret treasure of my heart would emerge. This impossibility, this daydream. In that unguarded moment, my heart cried out to me.

And I turned away as I always did.

To write about that night would mean writing about all of its self-conscious glamour and all of its contradiction, and to expose to scrutiny all my power and all of my fragility. To write – truly write – would mean writing about heartache and hope and longing, about the secret shadows beneath the gold lamé leggings and careful makeup, about the frozen crevasses that you could slide into as Caroline had done standing in the kitchen of our student house – as well as the moments of joy and breathlessness and enchantment, ghostly moments that I hoarded secretly and shared with no-one because of the shame they made me feel.

I knew that I could not open my heart nor allow myself to feel my own tenderness and failings.

So instead of striding out into my life beyond Oxford, I had a sense that I hovered uncertainly here among the picnics and parties and punting and evenings dressed in white. I followed the lead of others, stumbling along behind Josh and our friends, hoping that maybe – if I pictured myself hard enough into one of those roles, if I worked hard enough on the idea of me out there in there in the world – I would become an ambitious, successful lawyer or banker or diplomat alongside the rest of them.

And in those moments of turning away from daydream of

being a writer, I turned away from the person I most longed to be. In the shadows of that moonlit night, I again let another sliver of myself slip away like a ghost.

Now, cuddled in Josh's arms, I said, "You enjoyed the White Evening in the end, didn't you? Even though you didn't want to go at first because of wearing white…"

He considered it and said slowly, "I guess."

"Think what you'd be missing if you didn't come to the ball. I'm sure Miles would come with me but it wouldn't be as fun as going with you."

"You're good at these types of things. Me, I don't know…"

"It's just one night. And then you'll have done it. If you really hate it, you don't ever have to wear black tie again. But you might not hate it so much."

"Well…"

"Everyone else is going. You'll know the whole gang. Anthony's not a twat, nor Sam. It'll be just us hanging out – only all togged up and with a fun fair."

"Oh, all right," he sighed melodramatically. He was smiling. "You really know how to get your own way, don't you?"

* * *

It had been a risk having that *cheongsam* made almost a year ago in the long summer vacation. At that time, I didn't have a boyfriend - Josh had still been just a friend travelling in Indonesia, I hadn't been invited to a ball in my first year and there was no promise that anyone would invite me to a ball in my second year. But my mother had said, "You never know, darling. Just in case. What if someone invites you and then you have nothing to wear."

So I let her take me to Binwani's, a multi-storey cloth emporium. I used to follow her there as child, playing amongst the bales of fabric as she chose cloth for her own *cheongsams* and tailor-made dresses. I felt all grown-up going with her now to buy my own cloth. We chose a ream of scarlet silk with a light, hardly perceptible, pattern.

To make a good *cheongsam*, you need a tailor from Shanghai and my mother's Shanghainese tailor was the one that everyone went to. He had a waiting list of several months but because my mother was one of his best customers, he managed to squeeze us in at short notice. The *sifu* – master - was a lean man in his late fifties, who wore a singlet and shorts in his hot, tiny shop on Imbi Road. He seemed in a bad mood, speaking only when absolutely necessary and even so in reluctant grunts. He measured me up, made a few indecipherable marks on a piece of scrap paper and we were done.

As we left the shop, I said, "Do you think there'll be a dress ready when we come back in three weeks?"

"He doesn't look like much does he?" Mum laughed. "But you wait and see."

The *cheongsam* is Cantonese for the iconic Chinese traditional dress, also known as the *qipao* in Mandarin. It has the high Mandarin collar and buttons that drop down from the left collarbone across the top of the right breast down to the side of the body. The sleeves might be three quarter length, capped or sleeveless, with a light concave scoop to show off more of your shoulder. The evening version is long but there's also the day version, which stops at the knee - made famous most recently by Maggie Cheung in Wong Kar Wei's steamy movie, *In the Mood for Love*. The lower half of the dress flows inwards – and in the day version gives you a pencil line shape down to your knees. In the evening version, the soft cascade continues ever narrower down to the ground, giving a sense that you disappear into nothing but air where your feet might be. Long slits on either side open up your freedom of movement again in contradiction to the restraining shape of the dress – and it is that tension that creates the breathless allure of the *cheongsam*.

Yet this dress with its high Mandarin collar that has become

Draping on Josh

so identified with Chinese identity began its heritage as a symbol of servitude. The styling of the collar came to China with the Manchurians when these invaders from in the north-east swooped south and overthrew the Ming dynasty in 1644. Up till then, the Han people – the dominant majority in China - wore gowns that were similar to the kimonos that we now associate with Japan, with a collarless judo-style, wrap-across gown, and flowing, capacious sleeves. One of the ways that the minority Manchurians exerted their dominance over the vast country they had conquered was to require, on pain of death, all Chinese men to wear their hair in a long braid – the queue – and all Chinese peoples to dress in the Manchurian style, with the high, closed collar. Under these Qing dynasty sumptuary laws, the ancient Chinese practice of foot-binding for women was also banned.

Over the centuries, as the Qing dynasty embedded itself and its customs into China, the Manchu collar and style of dress became part of Chinese identity. Both men and women wore the high collar on their tunics and gowns, which were loose-fitting and free. The figure hugging shape of the *cheongsam* that we know today emerged in the 1920s and '30s in Shanghai, when the closer fitting fashions of Western women spiced up that thriving and colourful international port city. Modernity was the all the rage and an explosion of Western influenced creativity fired up the Chinese *glitterati*. Ibsen's A Doll's House captured the Chinese imagination, its story of a woman leaving her unhappy, constricting marriage for freedom taking on symbolic meaning for an emerging socialist consciousness – inspiring many local plays featuring 'Chinese Noras'. The crooning music of Billie Holliday and Western blues divas translated into a mellifluous East/ West sound sung by beautiful Shanghai lounge divas in shapely *cheongsams*. The dress took on hints of Bette Davis and Lauren Bacall, evolving square shoulders and worn calf-length with the chunky Western high heels of that time. Over the course of the 20th century, its shape shifted with international fashions and the slits shrank or elongated with the tastes of each decade – or the daring of its individual owner.

Three weeks later, when I tried on that dress for the first time and saw myself in the mirror, I saw a woman, not a girl. As the *sifu* moved nimbly around me, nipping and tucking, and my mother beamed into the long mirror from behind, I stared at the stranger looking back at me. I saw her self-conscious stance, not quite knowing what to do with her feet, her half smile of pleasure and pride, her questioning eyes. I also saw her womanly shape, the elegant way the dress made her hold herself, the tentative thrust of her hips and breasts.

I saw in that mirror not just me and the woman I could be but also my mother in her *cheongsam* and my grandmother in hers, my great-grandmother in her *samfu* – a Chinese tunic and soft, loose pantaloons - and all the mothers who came before us in their Manchu collars and long gowns, and before them, those other Han mothers in their *Hanfu*, going back for generations to time immemorial. And I saw also the generations of daughters to come, girls who might one day look like me or my mother or grandmother, standing before a long mirror somewhere in time, seeing me at once beaming at her from behind and as a ghostly ancestor watching her from her familial past.

This dress placed me in a tradition that was beyond this individual moment, beyond going to an Oxford ball. Looking at myself in the *cheongsam*, I understood for the first time the idea that my mother and grandmother and family had for who I should be. I was one of them. I belonged to our history and I belonged to our future. In this dress, in the stark contrast between the schoolmarm-ish primness of the high collar and the almost obscene openness of the slits below, I was all that they were and all that I could be - a mother and a wife, a daughter and a woman, a matriarch and a lover.

And so, on the evening of the ball, I brought out the dress from my wardrobe where it had been waiting with such hope. Here it was, a soft river of scarlet in my hands, my 'just in case'. It struck me that I would never have worn anything else to a ball. Not the bell-shaped, wedding cake dresses with frills and taffeta that was the fashion at that time. Not anything Western that was cut to the sturdier shape of a European woman. Not that modern styling that hid my legs but revealed my shoulders and cleavage. In my imagination, whenever I had dreamed of going to a ball even as a child, I saw myself in this dress, this *cheongsam*.

On that summer evening, as the setting sun cast the mellow stones of Oxford in burnt umber, my friends and I in all our finery walked up from Iffley Road across Magdalen Bridge towards Trinity.

There is something about the severity of the high collar and the unforgiving close fit of the *cheongsam* that requires a sternness in your upper body as you wear it. You cannot slack if you are to keep the cloth from creasing over your belly or pulling up over any untoward bumps and crevices. You must be sleek and slim - and curvaceous, but only in the right places, which is why the dress has to be tailor made for exactly your shape and cannot be bought off the peg. When you sit, you must do so elegantly or the harsh Manchu collar will throttle you as the back of the dress pulls downwards. You cannot bend from the waist to pick something up because there is no give in the cloth so you must bend from your knees, legs demurely together, keeping your body straight and proud. You cannot take a wide stance because of the tight fit at your hips and so you remain always a long, flowing, feminine silhouette.

Then there's the wantonness of the long evening dress, with its alluring double slits from the floor up to just below the hips, that promises so much more in counterpoint to the strict coldness of the upper half. The slits mean that the dress has two long flaps, front and back, and if you're not careful in the way you walk, you will look as if you are a warrior in an extended loin cloth, your legs marching either side of those flickering tongues of cloth. You have to walk along an invisible line right in the middle of the dress, planting each foot carefully one in front of the other and in that motion, your hips sway and your bum flexes and the dress hardly seems to move. The aim is to reveal as little as possible despite the openness of the slits – so that in the moment that something is revealed, it is heart-stopping.

It took a lot of effort to walk in that dress. And in the stilettos that went with it. Placing each foot where it should go, letting my hips and bum twist with the motion. Trying to float effortlessly through the evening instead of galumphing awkwardly onward. I could feel the uneven pavement threatening every step, the thin soles like cardboard against the hard cement. I clung on to Josh's arm to steady myself. I felt helpless, like an old woman, or an invalid. I was terrified of misplacing a step, twisting my ankle and sprawling face first onto the ground, my immaculate shape crumpling into flailing humiliation. My back was already

Josh and me

beginning to ache with the effort of holding my torso so elegantly and with the strain on my legs from the steep angle of the shoes. Beneath my smiles and laughter and flirtatious manner, I felt tense and anxious and in pain.

I had poured so much effort into becoming this idea of me.

This moment promised so much for Josh and me. Despite his initial reluctance, once he had dressed and the gang were all together having drinks and admiring how we all looked, he had gotten into the spirit of the occasion. In the photos from that evening, he and I stand confidently, conscious of how good we look. He is wearing his grandfather's dinner jacket and we are striking poses for the camera. In contrast, our friends wear their outfits as if they were casual clothes, enjoying the evening without the need to preen. Josh stands boldly or sits with easy elegance. In most of the photos, I drape myself against him, my body delicate as a flower, decorative and demure – but in one, he is channelling

James Bond and I allow myself a bolder Bond girl posture, playing to the camera.

This moment promised so much and it was already coming to an end. His gaze had moved on, beyond me, to a wider world that was waiting for him. Beijing. International relations. A glittering career in the diplomatic corps or a multinational. He seemed to have such purpose and clarity about what he wanted for his future.

And I wasn't part of it.

To everyone around us, we seemed like the perfect couple, especially tonight - good-looking, clever, confident, always laughing and having fun and surrounded by a bubbly gang of friends. In our intimate moments together, there was a physical chemistry and we took pleasure in each other's bodies. It looked like a perfect relationship on the outside. And yet…In my heart I knew why I was not a part of his future.

I had put upon him the burden of becoming my rescuer. He would give my life meaning. I had given up on the truest dream of my heart – the one thing that gave me a sense of purpose: being a writer – and I wanted him and a life with him to define me instead.

He was *my* rescuer. It did not occur to me that he might have needed me to rescue him, to give him a safe haven, a warm hearth from where he could see the best of himself. I could not champion him as a loving partner should. I did not know how to love him while he soared. I did not know how to let him be the hero in his own world. Because I was too anxious making him the hero in mine.

I never showed him the me I was with Pippa and Lizzie and Jane, the one who could be loud and slobby, bossy and tomboy-ish, uncertain and afraid. I never showed him my anxiety about my future, never asked him to help me work out what career might suit me. I never talked about my writing or gave him any of it to read – he was supposed to be the man I loved and I never shared with him the treasure of my heart.

We never spoke about any of this – what words could encompass such unknowable, intangible things? But he sensed it in my neediness, in my wanting him to play his part in these self-conscious evenings. It was there in my intense focus on surface perfection: on creating stylish gatherings and choreographing witty dinner parties, my hypervigilance about my feminine appearance in mixed company, my obsession with my image and how I appeared – and compared - to others.

I had lost myself.

In that red *cheongsam*, in those gorgeous, tortuous shoes, floating through that Oxford evening, I was a ghost. How could he love an apparition?

Stilettos

BOUND FEET BLUES – THE STORY

Some Enchanted Evening

[As an eight year old, with Malaysian voice]
I'm eight years old. It's after dinner time in Malaysia. My sister
is five and my brother is four. We run into my parents' bedroom
and jump onto the bed. My Dad is reading a book and my Mum
is doing a crossword

We say

>   *Mum, mum, mum - Tell us a story*

And they both put their books down.

I say, [eight year old:]

>   *Tell us how you and Dad met.*

[Mum:]

>   *Well, I was a student at London University and one Saturday
>   night, my friends and me, we all went to a dance. It was at
>   Malaya Hall which is near Marble Arch.*

>   *I didn't know anybody so I was sitting by myself. I felt like
>   such a wallflower. The other girls there were looking so
>   modern - in their 1960s outfits. I was only half modern - I had
>   pointy glasses and my hair was up in the latest fashion like*

this, they call it a beehive. But your Ma-Ma, your grandma, my Mum, always said to me I must wear formal dress to this kind of dance. So I was wearing a cheong sam and I felt like an old maid.

Then I saw this young man across the room. He was so good looking, in his DJ. And he was also looking at me.

Waah, it was so romantic, just like that song in that film, South Pacific.

[eight year old:]

Mum, mum, mum - sing the song.

[Mum:]

Well, OK – I get myself ready first.... "Some enchanted evening, you may see a stranger, you may see a stranger, across a crowded room..."

We listen to her and we stare at her. And I think: this is what it is going to be like when I am a grown up woman.

My Dad says, [as Dad:] *Ya, I saw this kampong girl - this village girl - so old fashioned. So I took pity on her, lah.*

[Mum:]

Haiya, you are so rude

But I see them beaming at each other.

[Mum:]

So then he came over to me, lah, and we talked, lah

Then afterwards, we went for a walk through the London streets, late at night, it was so romantic with all the lights shining brightly. We walked from Marble Arch to Piccadilly -

it's a long way you know - me in my cheong sam and high heel shoes, tik-tok tik-tok like that. Aiyo it was so painful! I thought I would die, my feet hurt so much.

But I didn't care - because I was with your Dad.

Small Feet

It's the day after the ball in Oxford – Josh, me and our friends are hanging out in our student house. We're wearing T-shirts and jeans.

I am barefoot and I am so relieved. I can feel the carpet under my feet. I love being able to wiggle my toes. It's such a freedom. But a part of me feels ashamed.

I think of those women last night laughing and dancing in their high heels. They didn't seem to care that their feet hurt. Or maybe their feet didn't hurt. Maybe it's just me.

What's wrong with me? Why can't I endure the pain?

I feel bad that being with Josh is not enough to make me forget the pain. I feel like a fraud.

I walk across the room to get another drink. My feet are size 3 ½ which is quite small really by Western standards.

Josh follows me with his eyes. He says, almost to himself but loud enough for everyone else to hear – "Mmm, I do like small feet"

And I'm so embarrassed in front of all my friends.

But – secretly – I'm rather pleased. Because I'm quite proud of my small feet.

THE STORIES BEHIND THE STORY

For as long as I remember, my mother has been telling us stories. She would come back from going out to the cinema with my father and look in on us in the room that I shared with my brother and sister. We might still be awake with our *amah* – our Chinese nanny – or with Aunty Diana, who lived with us with Grandmother, my Dad's mother. We would clamour excitedly for Mum to tell us about the film she had just seen and she would change into her long nightdress and come and cuddle up with us. My Dad would join us in one of our beds or sitting up in the *rattan* armchair and she would begin.

She would take us step by step through the story, setting the scene, describing all the characters, building up the action. Her recounting was always so vivid, it would feel as if the movie was playing out in our bedroom. I will always remember *A Man Called Horse*, starring Richard Harris as a white man captured by Native Americans and treated like a horse. The harsh and powerful story stayed with me so intensely that in my twenties, when it came on TV late one night in England, it was as if I was re-watching the film a second time – apart from the violence she had edited out.

Or we would go out as a family to the 'flicks' as my Dad called it and if we fell in love with the film, we would make her tell us the story again and again - in those days before DVDs and instant home playback. Our favourite was *The Sound of Music*. We had the soundtrack album and knew all the songs by heart, and with the music like a map in our heads, we could remember all the scenes in sequence. At night, before going to bed, all of us tucked in and hugging our bolsters, she would come and lie down with us and tell us a bedtime story. It was a special treat if she did *The Sound of Music*. Because she would not just tell it – she would also sing all the songs.

She would only give us this treat sometimes if she had the energy or if we were particularly deserving of this special bedtime performance. Even so, sometimes she would cry out in desperation – part mock, part real - at the dreary, boring prospect of having to do the whole thing yet again. But she would give in to us and brace herself for another show.

And we were a relentless and demanding audience. If she skipped a bit or got the sequence muddled up, we'd get her to do it right. Sometimes, she tried to cheat and jump some scenes or cut stanzas from the songs but we'd spot it and cry out to her to do it all word for word as she had done it the first ever time.

There were some nights she would fall asleep half way through a song out of the sheer tedium of it. And whoever was closest to her would nudge her. "Mum, mum, wake up, you didn't finish the song…"

It wouldn't be just movies – Mum told us the stories of the books she was reading. I grew up with Alistair Maclean, Barbara Cartland, Isaac Asimov and Arthur C. Clarke through her re-telling of their novels. And when I was old enough to read grown up books, theirs were the first books I turned to. It felt grand to be at last reading first hand for myself those tiny printed words that had excited and moved her. And perhaps that is where my dream of becoming a writer came from – to write down on paper words that could thrill her and touch her and give her that same spark in her eyes whenever she re-told those stories from the books she loved. It was a fine moment when she accompanied me on my book tour in Malaysia and Singapore for my first novel, *The Flame Tree* – beaming at the back of the room and embarrassingly cornering everyone to tell them, "That's my daughter, you know".

She told stories from her childhood and her *pak tor* days – courtship days - with my Dad. It's strange and fascinating to imagine your parents not as your parents but as young, carefree individuals falling in love and hanging out with their friends. Mum would go up to Cambridge to see my Dad at weekends – "I wasn't clever enough to get into Oxbridge-lah so I only went to London U. *Wah*, it was so exciting that this Cambridge boy, so clever, so handsome, wanted to go *pak tor* with me." And it was she who described the picnics and punting with their gang of friends, going to parties and balls and driving out into the countryside in a hired car.

"And his friend, John, this English fellow – he was so tall and hunky, he thought I was like a cute little doll and he would pick me up and carry me and run across the quad. I would be screaming-lah and he thought that was so funny. He's a judge now, you know."

My Dad mock-groaned, "*Haiya*, your Mum, you know-lah, always screaming about nothing. Still the same now – what to do to get some peace and quiet, ha?"

And we would all laugh at silly Mum, who was not very clever and tiny like a doll and who squealed like a girly-girl at the smallest things.

She enlisted my father in her stories. He had always been a quiet man, an introvert to her extrovert, but she made him take up his part on cue. "And I thought he was so cultured and clever. When he asked me to go to the theatre with him – *wah*, with his English accent… Dad, do, do, do – do your English accent!"

Mum and Dad, Cambridge

My father would look embarrassed. "No-lah, you tell the story-lah. Why must involve me?"

"Do, do, do," she insisted. "Go on-lah, show the children…"

Reluctantly – but also with a shy look of pleasure – Dad would put on his English voice from all those years ago and say, "Would you like to go to the thatah with me?"

"Thatah, you know – just like those English fellows! Of course, I have to say yes-lah, how to say no to that?"

None of us could escape her enjoyment of the story of our lives. She wanted to know everything that happened at school

Dad at Cambridge

or on playdates with our friends. She listened to us excitedly retell shows we had seen on TV – The Three Stooges, Gomer Pyle, Zorro, the Carol Burnett Show. If we played out a scene or laughed at a catch phrase, she remembered our impression and before long, she would be demanding that we do it again.

"Do, do, do – do Gomer Pyle!"

"Dad, dad – look at this" she would cry. And to us, "Go on, imitate, imitate Carol Burnett…" or Curly, Larry and Moe or Sargent Garcia.

In a school play at prep school in England, my brother did a vocal impression of Margaret Thatcher – it was before his voice broke and he captured that slow, careful enunciation she had, like a foreigner trying to speak in an upper class English accent. For ages afterwards, until his voice became a deep baritone, Mum would beg him, "Imitate, imitate Margaret Thatcher-lah. It's so funny!" and he would rail and moan and complain – and then do it for us all.

She wanted to know everything that happened. Sitting round the dining table at home, the ceiling fan swirling overhead and passing round curry or stir fry or rice, we would tell my parents everything that happened at school. Later, from boarding school in England, I would write her long letters on blue aerograms several times a week, giving her long accounts of my days. Even now, I would email her detailed accounts of my daily life – and in particular, if I'm on holiday or doing something especially unusual or interesting, I would send her despatches from the front. When we all get together round a meal, my siblings and I in our forties and fifties, with our partners and my nephew, Mum (now known by all of us as Granny) and Dad in their seventies, Granny would tell us about the latest novel she'd been reading or the movie she watched on the plane from KL, and we would take turns giving accounts of our recent lives.

It's an odd thing. I never saw it before. But as I've been writing all this down, I've suddenly seen it. Of the many gifts in my life, this gift from my mother – her love of storytelling, of mimicry and performance, and her love of hearing the story of her children's lives – has been the gift that has shaped me more than anything else. It has been the driving passion in my life and the fire that has sparked every major choice for happiness I have made.

* * *

For a long time, I thought that a writer was something that you become – like a doctor or a lawyer. So, in the same way that other children – and later on, my Oxford friends – wanted to become surgeons or bankers or diplomats, I wanted to become a writer.

But this afternoon, looking through an old folder full of writings from my childhood, I realised for the first time, I never needed to *become* a writer. I have always been a writer. In the folder are school exercise books, A4 notebooks and loose sheets of paper overflowing with stories, most of them written in blue or black fountain pen, a few typed up onto foolscap sheets. The exercise books go back to 1973 and 1974 when I was ten and eleven. I churned out story upon story after school at my desk in the bedroom I shared with my sister and brother. They romp along, action/ adventure stories like the ones my mother told us from Alistair Maclean and Sarah Gainham novels, with very few corrections in my surprisingly neat longhand. They often land you straight in the middle of the action, setting up a striking – and intriguing scene – which is then opened up and deepened through flashback. As you read on, you learn who the main players are, their relationship to each other and how they came to be in the nail-biting opening scene.

I had a favourite fountain pen that I used, with a deep green plastic body and gold metallic trim. All the stories are annotated in pencil in my mother's handwriting, correcting spelling and grammar – and occasionally, sentence structure for better flow or greater drama. And all of them are graded – A or B+ - like creative writing exercises and followed by notes and exercises she gave me about use of language.

Young writer at work

Some of the stories on the loose sheets are bundled together by a folded A4 sheet on which I had written 'BAD'. Across the pages of one exercise book, I had annotated each leaf of a story 'Blah', 'Forget it', 'No good'. At the top of one story are the words 'Could be improved'. The typed up stories were the ones I felt were good enough for a print version and they are edited and tidied up stylistically from the earlier longhand first drafts. Even as an adolescent, I was already critiquing and editing my own work as all writers should do. Many of the stories on those yellowing pages have drama but that lack of realism and depth of characterisation that we see in TV adventure series – you know the ones, where clean cut Americans with immaculate hair and stylish clothing find themselves stranded on a remote island and somehow manage to remain well-groomed and only mildly perplexed by their predicament. There is very little attempt at real emotion or psychological portrayal in them – not surprisingly, given my age at the time.

But when I have a go at something more personal, there is a distinct shift in the narrative voice. You can see my attempt at psychological depth and a sense of trying to immerse myself in the time, location and context of the story as well as a growing confidence with pacing and handling the shifting needs of the narrative.

I was thirteen in the long, hot summer of 1976 when I first began to tell the story of my family in a novel that I kept coming back to over decades but never finished. All I managed to write was five pages in a school exercise book. I set them out here as they were written, the words flowing without pause – verbatim and unedited.

Ancestral Voices by Ooi Yang May

Chapter I

It was a dark, still night in the mid-1840s. The Opium War was sweeping across China, bringing grief and fear into the lives of the people. They not only feared the war, they also feared the bandits who terrorised the countryside and raided the villages, pillaging and destroying whatever they wished. Every night the villagers locked and bolted their doors, going to bed with terror in their hearts. But what good were locked doors against a gang of strong and ruthless outlaws?

A noise like distant thunder rolled across the rice fields, never ending; its volume increasing as each moment went by. Finally, tiny specks of light could be seen on the horizon and faint cries could be heard over the thundering of horses hooves. The lighter sleepers of the village sat up, rubbing the sleep from their eyes. Some staggered to the windows to see if it was raining, others to confirm their fears. They were right. "The Long Haired Brigands" were on the way to another looting.

A cry of terror awakened the sleeping inhabitants and within moments, confusion reigned. Men rushed around grabbing scythes and kitchen knives, at the same time telling their families to hide. The older boys grabbed sticks, eager to face the enemy and unwittingly, eager to face death. Women scurried about, searching in vain for a safe place for their children to hide, especially their teenage daughters. Youngsters and babies began to cry, sensing the fear in the air. Fathers hugged their children and wives once more and stepped out onto the streets to face the brigands.

It was a pathetic scene as the brave men were cut down like wheat by the merciless riders. Some riders were knocked off their steeds and battered by excited youths. These youngsters were hacked out by the foe and died without knowing what had happened. Bandits entered the little houses, slaughtered those who resisted and left with what treasures they could find under one arm and a struggling maiden under the other. Boys of nine to eleven were captured to be trained in the ever-growing army of "Long Haired Brigands".

"If you come any closer, I'll kill you!" warned a young boy, standing in front of his family a little carving knife in his hand.

"That's the spirit, young one, we need boys like you!" laughed a hairy outlaw, pushing the boy inside and beginning to look for precious things.

"We have nothing," said the mother of the boy, her voice shaking and her hand tightening on her children's shoulders.

"Is that so?" The outlaw towered over. He raised a hand to stroke her daughter's hair.

"Leave them alone!" cried the boy and lunged the man.

Luckily, before the man could turn on him, the robber chief came in. Grabbing the boy, he led him outside to let the outlaw do what he wished.

"What's your name, boy?"

"Kee Kwee Sin," replied the boy defiantly.

"And how old are you?"

"Ten."

The screams of his mother came to his ears and turning, he started to run into his house. The chief took a stride and caught him by the scruff of his neck. In this position, the screaming and struggling youngster was hauled away from the life he had known to the violent and terrifying world of the bandits

~

Kwee Sin entered into the routine life of the Long Haired Brigands with hatred in his heart. At first, he rebelled at every opportunity, ran away whenever he saw the chance that the outlaws caught him each time. Worn out by their severe punishments, the boy seemed to submit to their orders but deep in his heart, there burned a desire to kill the chief of these men and the hairy ape who had done his family so much harm. One day, he would avenge his kin but until then, he would learn the skills of fighting with a weapon and with his bare hands. Until that yearned for date, Kwee Sin would learn the tricks of the trade and then turn the tables on the bandits.

The band of robbers were always on the move, stopping for no more than a week at any one time leset danger lurked around the corner. If they were not trailing behind the men in the wagons, the boys would be wrestling and duelling with sticks under the strict surveillance of a number of men. They were taught to forget the life they had led and obey orders. Kwee Sin listened attentively but absorbed nothing. He built up an iron wall around him so that none of the outlaws' threats could frighten him. A plan was beginning to form in his brain and slowly, it became clear what he must do.

The years wore on and Kwee Sin grew from a boy to a well built a young man. His boyish features changed to become more precise and resolute; his plumpness disappeared and in its place came muscles of steel and a sinewy body; his appearance changed but in his mind remained the urge to avenge, no longer burning but the cold and ruthless. Unlike the other young men, he remained distant. While they were outlaws and plundered and killed with the older men as if they had never had a peaceful home in a quiet little village, Kwee Sin lurked in the shadows pretending to murder but letting his victims escape.

Now that he had a horse, KS could accompany the main body as they galloped into an unsuspecting village. It seems so long ago when he had been one of these youngsters, running about and trying in vain to protect his mother. The site of the still and silent villages before panic took over brought back heartrending memories of peaceful nights when he had lain awake, listening to the solitary sound of a night bird. Beside him had been his parents and beyond them his younger sister, their breathing steady and undisturbed. How he longed to go back to those unharassed days, to feel the arms of his mother around him, to hear his father's deep voice conversing with his friends, to romp around with the other boys but time was merciless. The thought that most of the boys he had admired were dead and his playmates were no longer laughing boys but cold blooded murderers did not surprise him.

It was now, on the eve of his twentieth birthday, surrounded by shrieks of terror and illuminated by the flickering light of hungry flames as they devoured the little village houses, that KS sat motionless on his powerful steed like a menacing statue waiting to come to life when the time was right. His dark eyes searched the mass of frantic people for his target. The leader of the bandits had a little boy by the scruff of the neck, laughing at the child's futile struggles. KS turned his horse and started to trot up to the two, slowly increasing speed till he was galloping as fast as the animal could go. His sword went up high above his head and as he passed, the weapon plunged down on to the helpless man who had turned but too late.

"Run, boy, run!" said KS through his teeth and as soon as the words were out, headed towards another horseman. With a fierce cry, the sword cut down yet another victim. KS did not slow down but headed away from the village where the other outlaws were shouting, "Stop him!" and forgetting the villagers, started to pursue the assassin.

Having a head start, KS soon left the Long Haired Brigands behind. He now had to cross the rough terrain of East China to arrive at a port where he would sail away to another land. Then only would he be safe from the dangerous grips of revengeful bandits. There - wherever it was - he would start life anew, become a respected man and probably get married and have someone to love who would love him, who would take care of him and their children. He would have children who would be strong and fight for what they thought was right and be leaders.

All this seemed so far away. They were just dreams but they could be fulfilled if he survived this journey, if he managed to evade the outlaws, if he found a ship to take him to a suitable country. So many ifs, so many uncertainties, so many problems. No matter, it was worth it. He had done what he had to be done and his kin could rest in peace.

Curiously, KS had felt nothing when he was doing the gruesome task, not even satisfaction. The years have hardened his heart and dulled his memories. He found it hard to recall the faces of his family distinctly. The images were hazy and sometimes the features of different people appeared on the shoulders of someone he was trying to picture. How he longed to for some means of retaining his loved ones images if not retaining them alive and well.

There are clichés in the phrasing and over-dramatic adjectives as well as a strong tele-drama flavour to the scenes. But for the first time, there is an emotional intensity as well as a sense of rhythm in the language and pacing to the storytelling. The Bandit Boy was revered on my mother's side of the family as the 'first ancestor' to a dynastic family, like Abraham in the Old Testament. The Bandit Boy was the man who came from China to Malaya and became the first father to the clan that brought into the world my Grandpa Lim, my mother and now me. His story –our story – in my young mind, needed a grand canvas and seriousness of undertaking, and you can see the attempt to rise to that task in the writing.

The bare bones of the story passed down through the family are that he was captured as a boy when a bandit band raided his village and when he was older he escaped to board a junk to Malaya as an indentured labourer.

There are so many questions in that single sentence. What was that like to be kidnapped from home? What happened to his family? How did he survive those years as part of the brigand gang? How did he escape?

Those questions intrigued me as a child. They still do.

In my adolescent telling of the tale, I tried to imagine myself into those questions. And the Bandit Boy I conjure is a hero. Of course. He is no murderer or rapist or pillage. He is decent and noble as all heroes are meant to be. As the family history needs him to be.

We see ourselves descended from a noble hero. It gives us a sense of pride and destiny. We are here because of him. We have within us his nobility and decency, his courage and defiance, his ruthlessness against evil and compassion for the weak.

But what if he survived not through honourable subterfuge and courage but by becoming one of them – like those other boys I describe in the story, murdering men and brutalising women? Or if he was weak and timid, a victim himself to brutish, invasive assault? As I express these thoughts out loud, and even only in the form of questions, I feel a queasiness in my gut and an anxiety of sacrilege. What would my family say, reading this!

I have always been a writer. But I have also needed time – and courage - to *become* a writer.

It's easy to write in clichés, those tried and tested well-worn words that others have used. It doesn't take much to write stock scenes and stock emotions. It's comforting and safe to follow the conventions of a given genre. It feels lovely to type out your thoughts as they come to you, without thought for style or structure or precision of language, without the rigour of editing, and call the volume of words a book and yourself a writer. But there's more to writing than that.

In life also, it's easy to follow the tried and tested path, well worn by previous generations and expect that what they have always done will bring you the happiness that they so want for you. It doesn't take much thought to do all the stock things that map out a conventional life – go to university, fall in love, get married, have kids, move to a bigger house, do well in your career, become a grandparent, retire. It's comforting and safe and feels lovely to fit in with what everyone else seems to be doing. But, of course, there is much more to living than that.

It's like the marriage vows. When we promise out loud before God and our gathered friends and family to be bound to each other "to have and to hold, from this day forward, to love and to cherish, for better, for worse, for richer, for poorer, in sickness and in health, forsaking all others until death do us part", we may feel a swelling in our hearts at the lovely, beautiful words and the familiar cadence and rhythm of the phrase. It's that feeling that makes us go "Aaaah." And it means nothing more. We move on quickly to appreciate the lovely flowers, the lovely reception and the overall lovely day. That's living life as a cliché, on the surface of things.

If we truly hold each part of that familiar phrase in our hearts and reflect on what it really means to be there for your spouse for better and for worse, it is a huge and magnificent commitment. For richer and for poorer. In sickness and in health. Forsaking all others. Are we prepared to do all that – no matter what storms and battles come - for the rest of our lives? How do we handle all those mundane, cumulative tragedies – arguments, failure to get that promotion, clashes with in-laws, forgetting to put the cap back on the toothpaste? And the dark, terrifying ones – losing a job, long term ill health, stroke, cancer? To see each other's gifts and flaws, our beauty and darkness, our triumphs and shame – to see it all and to accept it all regardless? Can we remember each of those vows for the next fifty years or more of our lives, day after day, and to fully commit to them in the worst of times as well as the best of times?

Or we may live our lives beyond such spoken vows, preferring to hold each other in a quiet place where no words need intrude. To be able to look into each other's eyes with an unshakeable belief in the other, to hold that gaze without tiring for all the years of our lives together, to love them even when sometimes we hate them. If we love outside of the familiar chant of marriage vows, is our love any less for being without words? Can we hold in our hearts the same promises of a husband and wife - though unsanctioned and unwitnessed - and remain steadfast in the face of all that life might throw at us?

If we can do that, then the words of the marriage vows move beyond cliché to becoming a part of our living, breathing souls.

So although I've always been a writer, it has taken me a lifetime to learn what that really means – to be able to write, and to live, beyond clichés.

My great-grandfather, the Bandit Boy, might have been a hero and he might also have been a coward. My mother, in her stories, plays up her dumbness and girliness but she is also smart and strong. In writing and in my life, I want to be my own hero – strong, courageous, funny, compassionate, loving – and at times, I am any one of those things. But I am also at other times vain, foolish, fearful, mean.

Our stories tell us – and the listeners gathered around us – who we all are. Or perhaps more truthfully, who we want to be. So in our family, when we tell each other the story of the Bandit Boy, he will always be noble and heroic and a man of action.

But for me now, in writing this book, in telling these stories, I have to make a choice to move beyond those kinds of clichés. To write about not just the funny and brave and glittering things that show me in a good light, but also those things that are hard for me to talk about – my loneliness and shame and anger and sadness. To express those things that are without words, that live in that quiet unspoken place and to let you see my fragility as well as my strength, my failings as well as my triumphs.

Because then those stories can be truthful to who we all are, my mother, my family, all those others in this story - and you, too, and me. We are all light and dark, brave heroes and cowards, loving and mean, vain and generous, angry and compassionate, ashamed and accepted, funny and wise, broken and whole.

* * *

My mother always wore the latest fashions. In the family photo albums, you can see her strikingly beautiful and glamourous, posing elegantly in the style of the season amongst the plainness of the rest of the family. She had the beehive in the early 60s, then a Mary Quant helmet cut, back to the semi-beehive with long ringlets of the early 70s, followed by long New Seekers style hippy hair which morphed into Farah Fawcett flicks and finally settling into a short, loose perm. On Sundays, we would all go the bookshop upstairs at Weld Supermarket and after browsing for books, we would cross over to the magazine kiosk, where my father bought the latest *Time* and *Newsweek*, we kids chose our Archies, or Snoopy or Superman comics and Mum found the latest Vogue and Harpers Bazaar. She pored over those magazines, thrilling over the newest looks and took them to her tailor with a sketch she had made, adapting her favourite dresses from the photos to her own taste and for the hot tropical climate. So in those photos we see her in short day *cheongsams* on special occasions but also day to day, in wide Grace Kelly skirts, pencil line shapes, Twiggy-style mini dresses – and after a few months spent in the Philippines where my father was working with a bank, a whole wardrobe of kaftans just when they were all the rage in the 70s.

Her morning ritual would begin seated at the triptych mirror of her dressing table. Laid out in front of her on two shelves was everything that made the magic happen: face creams, foundation, cotton wool, cotton buds, lipstick, eyeliner, eye shadow, eye brow pencils, brushes, blusher, hairspray, perfume. In the drawers on either side was the backup – a range of different coloured lipsticks, eye shadows and face powders for different occasions and different looks. When they were fashionable, she had a variety of false eyelashes. There were tweezers for her eyebrows, bottles of nail varnish in a range of reds and pinks, cuticle softeners and sticks. And not to forget – all the liquids for the reverse of the process: removing the makeup and nail polish as well as lotions to be applied before bed. One drawer was dedicated to curlers and hair pins to maintain the perms and in a rattan wastebasket to one side of this altar to beauty was her hairdryer, plugged in and ready to blast. And finally, the hand mirror which she would pick up at the very end of it all and examine herself close up and also reflected back in the triptych.

After doing the laundry in the early dawn and seeing to our breakfasts and sending my father off to work and us to school, her own day would begin here at the triptych. Often during the holidays, I would follow her into the bedroom and loaf on the bed while she dabbed and brushed and painted and combed and sprayed and examined. I might read a comic or we would chatter away. My brother and sister might be there too, playing on the wooden floor or joining in the chat. Sometimes, in the afternoons, I sat on her stool in front of those mirrors alone in my parents' bedroom and looked at myself as she would, turning my head this way and that. I peered at all the jars and bottles, picked up the different brushes, held the hand mirror up to my face and made odd shapes into it with my mouth, my breath steaming up the glass.

Beyond the makeup and clothes, what my mother loved most –
and still does – were handbags. And shoes. She has a handbag for
every occasion, and shoes to match. She has a handbag for almost
every outfit, and shoes to match. These days, in her seventies, she
has settled for a range of flat soled shoes but her wardrobe is full
of a lifetime of high heels and small, feminine shoes from strappy
sandals and wedges to elegant court pumps. On hot afternoons,
when we were feeling bored, sometimes, my sister and I used to

Mum in one of her *cheongsams*

raid Mum's wardrobe and play dress up in her shoes, our childish feet in her high heels, tottering precariously, pitched forward and clumping along, a handbag swinging in the crook of our arms.

Mum would laugh and show us how to walk properly in high heels, enjoying the excuse to sort through her shoes and put on different pairs for fun.

"You watch the models on the catwalk and see how they walk. One foot in front of the other like this-lah, in one straight line. Then your hips can sway. Very *chiew hay* – very flirtatious."

It was a special occasion when my parents went out in the evening for a smart function. Scrubbed clean and in our pyjamas, we would pile onto their bed and watch them dress. The air conditioning would be on to keep the room cool and the mosquitoes out. My dad looked handsome and dashing in black tie and his hair slicked back with Brylcreem. My mother was transformed as she put down the hand mirror and stood up from the triptych in her long, brocade *cheongsam* and stiletto heels, smelling of exotic flowers. A last minute check of her lipstick and a snapping shut of her finely textured clutch bag, and she was ready. Her heels clicked across the wooden floor – *tik-tok, tik-tok* - and it felt as if we were seeing them in their courting days again, about to step out of the bedroom onto that long, long walk from Marble Arch to Piccadilly.

I used to think: one day. One day, I would sit down at a triptych dressing table of my own and I would magically know what to do with all those paints and potions and lotions. And I would pick up my hand mirror and turn my head this way and that, checking my makeup and hair and then when it was all just right, I would stand up. And in that moment, I would be transformed; no longer a child but a grown woman, unrecognisable, like Cinderella at the wave of her fairy godmother's wand.

And yet, it seemed all so inconceivable. I didn't really want to powder and paint and buff and comb and brush. I didn't want

Mum and Dad all dressed up

to wear high heel shoes. I didn't want to walk one foot in front of the other in a straight line. I didn't want to puff and blow and curl my hair. I didn't want to wear skirts and dresses and bother with carrying a handbag. I wanted to run around, barefoot or in flip flops, pull a brush once through my hair, wipe my nose on my sleeve. I couldn't imagine getting so excited about handbags and shoes as my mother did. Flipping through her magazines, I didn't understand what absorbed her so much in those pictures of skinny women in pretty dresses.

But one day, I kept telling myself, it would happen for me. I would turn eighteen and become an adult. At the stroke of that midnight on my eighteenth birthday, all these things that I didn't want right now, I would suddenly, miraculously, want and I too would rise up from that three-mirrored altar, fashionable and beautiful and glamorous.

* * *

My mother's mother – my Grandma – always looked regal and elegant whether she was wearing *cheongsams* or casual slacks. She carried herself with a quiet upright authority that made whatever she wore look smart and sleek. Her hair was always immaculate, in its neat Vera Lynn style and the only sign of the changing decades on her face were her glasses that evolved with the fashions of each period. She sat elegantly, worked in the garden among her beloved orchids elegantly, played with us children elegantly. Seeing me slouching in a chair or slumping as I walked, she would look at me commandingly and pull her shoulders back to indicate I should do the same.

I wish I could say that I was an obedient granddaughter who hastened to do as I was told. But regrettably, I can't. Instead of straightening myself up at these commands, I would scowl and roll my shoulders inwards even more into a deeper hunch. And she would sigh sadly at my disobedience.

One day. In the same way that one day at eighteen I would miraculously and without effort become just like my mother and love of pretty, girly things, one day when I turned fifty I would become like Grandma, upright, distinguished, graceful and regal.

One day.

It was a hope and a longing; that these things that were expected of me would one day come easily and naturally. That I would be able to fulfil the destiny that my family had in mind for the girl I should be and so make them happy and proud of me. But for now, dark-skinned from hours playing in the sun, scrawny and unruly, my short hair combed to one side out of the way, I could still be free.

Grandma had a prominent mole on her upper lip, just to one side of centre. Sideways on, it sat dark and round like a smooth prominent raison on her profile. It might have looked ugly to some people. Occasionally, when photographs of her came back from the photographer's shop in Taiping, the small town where my grandparents lived, she would find that the mole had been made to vanish in a gesture of thoughtfulness by the print developer. But that mole, in our family, like that of the unmistakeable birthmark

Grandpa and Grandma Lim at their wedding, their birthmarks
erased by the kindly photographer

on Grandpa's forehead was an indication that she – and he – had been marked for greatness by the gods. So we would all laugh at the silly photographer who had thought he was doing her a favour in touching up the pictures.

If you looked carefully at the side of her head, you would also see that beneath her carefully brushed hair, there was a frightening scarred patch of bare scalp behind her ear. She would show it to us sometimes, gently drawing her hair back like a curtain and we would stare at it, fascinated and a little squeamish.

"No need to be scared," she said. "It's just a scar. It happened when I was young, five years old. It was in China. We were very poor - I always like that saying 'poor as a church mouse' because my father, your Great-grandfather Quek, was a pastor and we were all like little church mice. My mother had to manage the house by herself and there were so many of us, my two older brothers – they were always studying - and the three younger kids who were still so small. Me, I was the eldest girl so I help her in the house and in the kitchen, even though I was only five years old at the time.

"So that day, I was making porridge for the family, and I was so small, I had to stand up on a stool to stir the big pot on the stove. I don't know what happened, but when I lean over to stir the big boiling pot with the long wooden spoon, I slip and fall. Aiyooooh, it was so terrible, I fell down into the hot congee and everything fell down. The congee was all sticky and we couldn't get it off quick-quick - so it stick to my head and my hair and it burn me. Tsk, tsk, haiyah, so terrible… Lucky, it was just my head on the side here, not on my face. Thank God, my face was not burned. I am very blessed, so lucky."

I couldn't imagine the terror and agony of that moment. I couldn't imagine being let near the stove, with all the boiling pots and the sizzling wok; or helping round the house, being a little grown up before my time. We had a cook and a maid and an *amah* – a nanny. We were kept safe at home and when we were in a public space, kept within sight of a trusted adult. I couldn't understand at that time how it was that Grandma felt she had been so lucky in that terrible moment.

I couldn't imagine being such a *kwai noi* – such an obedient daughter. To do what needed to be done to help my family and to do it without complaining and without thought for myself. To set aside what I wanted – to play and read and write my stories, or just to slouch on the sofa staring into space – and instead do the dutiful thing, whether that was fetching a drink for my father or studying at my school books or standing up straight when my Grandma asked me to. I would throw tantrums and sulk and stomp around and slam doors. I would talk back to the adults and fight with my brother and sister. And Mum would have to drag me screaming to sit in the bathroom until I cooled off. She never locked the door on me - just shut it and walked away - but I knew I had to stay in there till she came to let me out.

In the echoey tiled bathroom, I would shout and scream and throw the plastic tooth mug at the walls, watching it bounce off the tiles. I crushed and twisted the foil tubes of toothpaste and smeared them on the mirror and walls. But I never broke anything, never really destroyed anything. And when I calmed down, I would wash away the white minty splatter.

I liked the quiet and cool of the bathroom, its isolation from the rest of the house. For a few hours, this was my space. All mine, and mine alone.

I couldn't imagine standing so upright in the world, with a mole right there on my face where everyone could see and a horrible bald scar on my scalp, so serene and authoritative, so grateful for the hard times as well as all the good in my life, and with such pleasure and confidence in who I was and in the family that surrounded me.

Here in the bathroom, just me by myself, I could be small and angry and naughty and disobedient and scared and sullen and hunched. There was no-one to see me but me, no-one to be with but me. And it was nice.

Grandma used to tell us the story about how she and Grandpa met. When she was twelve, her father Reverend Quek was sent with his family to Singapore by the Presbyterian Church to minister to the parish on that bustling port island. The Quek family settled there and when Grandma was in her early twenties, she started medical school at Singapore University. In her class was a stocky, athletic young man, who had a loud coarse laugh and a cheeky grin.

"Everybody knew Swee Aun," she said, still dreamy even in her 70s, whenever she spoke about Grandpa. "He had this big birthmark on his forehead, just to one side here, and we all call him Scarface. There he was with his pipe and always joking around with his gang of friends. There were not many of us girls studying medicine and the boys, they always play jokes on the girls-lah. One time, my friend, Siew Mei, she put her hand in her lab coat and she started screaming the whole place down! *Aiyoh*, it was so funny, and so shameful – the boys, they put a man's part in her pocket, you know, from the dissection lab where we all had the cadavers to cut up…!"

It was funny to think of Grandma and Grandpa – well, before they became Grandma and Grandpa. We loved leafing through their photo album and seeing them so young and fresh-faced, Grandpa in those baggy '30s style trousers and Grandma in pretty *cheongsams* and chunky high heels of that time. It was odd to see them in our minds as two young medical students, hanging out with their pals and horsing around in such a scandalous way. It was odd to see a photo of Grandpa playing rugby and running in a race, looking hunky and sweaty, his Brylcreemed hair flying in the wind.

"I would go and watch him play matches-lah," Grandma said coyly. "And then he notice me always there and he came over and talk to me…"

When he proposed to her, they were walking up on a hill overlooking Singapore. He gave her a ring he had found in the street. "It's just for now," he had said. "I don't have anything of my

Grandpa and Grandma Lim with my mother

own now. But one day, I promise you, I will give you diamonds."

It seemed to me, listening to Grandma tell her stories, that for her and Grandpa, their love story was about more than just their individual lives. When her story and his came together on the edge of that rugby field, they became part of a larger, multi-stranded single story – the story of our family. Their love story, as simple as it was, like so many sweetheart stories of boy meets girl at college, was also about dynasty. Not in the sense of kings and power and empire but dynasty in the sense of a family in the continuum of time, of knowing where we have come from and a passing on of ourselves to the next generation.

I hold in my hand a delicately ornate necklace, sparkling with scores of diamonds. It is one of the many gifts of diamonds that Grandpa promised Grandma. With it, in the box padded with shining cloth, there is a little note in her handwriting bequeathing it to me.

In contrast to Grandma in her beautifully shaped *cheongsam* that she made herself, I remember my Great-grandmother Quek always dressed in *samfu* – a loose white starched tunic with the Chinese collar and side buttons and baggy black silk pantaloons. She and Great-grandfather Reverend Quek lived with Grandma and Grandpa. They had their own set of rooms at the far end of the colonial wooden longhouse. They spoke only Teochew, a dialect of Chinese that my brother and sister and I didn't understand. They seemed to have stepped out of the history books and my childish mind imagined a long line of old people looking just like them going back into the mists of time in a China I had only seen in Kung Fu films, unchanging for a thousand years.

It was difficult to imagine them as having been young once and in love, like Grandma and Grandpa had been, and like my Mum and Dad, too. Great-grandfather Quek, Grandma told us, had been a young man studying to be a pastor at the Presbyterian seminary in Swatow province. He was tall and good-looking and, in my mind, I added a pair of round gold-rimmed glasses like the one Great-grandfather Quek always wore now, and a *queue* – the long single plait of hair that all Chinese men were required to wear under the Qing dynasty, the last imperial family to rule China. One day, he was out walking with the other novices from the seminary and they came to a stream. There at the water's edge was a group of young women, washing clothes, chattering and laughing together. He noticed among Great-grandmother among them – or rather, the young girl who would become Great-grandmother.

In my memory of this story, he didn't go up to her straightaway but would walk back by the stream many times over the next little while with his friends. The girls would notice this group of shy but persistent young men and they would blush and giggle and pretend to ignore them. Until finally, Great-grandfather plucked up enough courage, perhaps with the egging on of his mates, to approach the group of maidens and start a conversation with the pretty one he liked. And now, here they were, together still, loving and solicitous to each other into their nineties, enjoying their children and grandchildren and great-grandchildren in a hot, humid country far away from the home they had once known.

It felt impossible to imagine in those moments when I felt small and hunched that my own story waited for me somewhere out there beyond the cold tiles of the bathroom, beyond childhood, beyond my family. I longed for it – for a story of meeting The One, of his story and mine flowing into the continuum and of bringing up daughters and sons of my own, just as all these women before me had done. And to do it with the same pride and devotion and sense of being a part of something greater than myself as they had done. It would happen, surely. It had to happen. In the same way that I hoped that one day, when I became an grown woman, I would miraculously love pretty things and high heels and know what to do with make-up, I hoped also that I would become the kind of woman that a man, a husband – my husband – would notice across a babbling stream, across a rugby field. Across a crowded room.

But in those moments, alone in my own space, all I knew was that I wasn't like my mother and my grandmother. I didn't know how to be pretty or poised or obedient or dutiful. Dimly, I had a sense that even as I wanted all those things, to be part of the dynasty going forward into an endlessly flowing future I also knew deep down in a quiet wordless place, that I didn't want the same things as they did.

* * *

It didn't happen miraculously, my transformation into a grown up woman. When I was in the sixth form, my mother taught me how to put on make-up, sitting at that altar at last in my own right. I took off my glasses, peering at my face in the triptych of mirrors. I put on the cloth hairband to sweep my hair out of the way. Mum stood beside me, talking me through this rite of passage. I learnt about moisturizing and foundation cream, applied with the tips of my fingers. She showed me the base powder and how to pat it on all over my face with a small round sponge, blending it gently into my neck and throat. Next came the rouge but it was only to be applied lightly below the cheekbones and on the forehead. She showed me how to brush a light vertical line of the blusher down my nose to the chin, make a thin outline along my jawbone and finish with quick hardly discernible strokes down my throat.

"You don't want to have a different colour face to your neck, like a clown, so you must blend it all in," Mum instructed.

Then came the hardest part: my eyes.

First, I had to learn how to hold the eyeliner pencil in my right hand, while pulling down one lower eyelid with my little finger. My left hand held the hand mirror focused in on my eye as carefully, I drew a dark line along the rim of the lower lid. The pencil scraped uncomfortably along the lashes, bringing tears into my eye. It was a strain to keep the line of it straight as my little finger threatened to slip from under the lid. The result was a bit wobbly but not bad for a first attempt. The top lid was easier as all I had to do was close that one eye and draw as if I was drawing on a piece of paper.

But that was not all. After the pencil, came the two-toned eye make-up, a dark blue for top lid nearest lashes and a paler highlight to sit on top. Chinese eyelids lack the definition of the upper ball socket of European eyes, our lids sitting flush with our eyebrows. The two tones created the effect of a slight indentation between my eyebrow and the eye socket and made my eyes a more prominent feature of my face.

And I had to do the same again for the other eye – and make sure both looked even, moving the hand mirror to the left and to the right, touching up here, rubbing out there. When they finally matched in tone and colour, I felt immeasurably pleased.

The final touch was the lipstick. My mother often used scarlet but I opted for a more muted rusty shade. The unscrewing of the stick to reveal the crayon-like colour felt like the ultimate feminine action. She showed me how to stretch my lips in an 'O' to apply the colour, and then 'mmm' my lips over a tissue to remove the excess. And when I unwound the stick again, snapping the cover on – in that one action, I felt I had passed through an initiation into the world of women.

I pulled off the hairband and put my glasses on. There staring back at me in the mirror was a younger, skinnier version of my mother.

It was about this time that I got my first perm. *Charlie's Angels* was all the rage and no-one wanted to look like Kate Jackson, the one with the straight dark hair and sharp, intelligent face. It was Farah Fawcett or Jaclyn Smith who were the ones that caught the gaze of the men with their bouncy, flicky, curly hair – so, that was the hair that all the girls and women wanted.

That was also about the time I got my first pair of high-heeled party shoes, a light brown strappy pair. Looking back, the heels were not that high but at the time, they seemed to arch my feet into an impossibly painful shape and so felt precariously grown up. Wearing them with a new pencil skirt and a silky striped blouse, my hair all bouncy and flicky and curly, I felt grown up and sophisticated – like my great heroines, Bette Davis and Lauren Bacall.

When I went back to school after that holiday, I had my own make-up bag and a party outfit, ready for any sixth form dances that might be on the horizon.

There was a dance in the gym with a disco ball and coloured flashing lights by the sound system. Boys from a nearby all boys boarding school were bussed in and under the watchful eyes of both male and female teachers, we all bopped and shuffled and tried to seem more grown up than we were. The cool girls looked pretty and glamourous in flowing dresses, some showing off their shoulders, all with bouncy hair and high heels. They seemed to be so comfortable with the boys and know what to say to them, how to flirt with them. I still felt like a nerdy four-eyed square in spite of my girly shoes and pencil skirt and make-up, hanging back against the wall with some of the other goody-goody girls.

But I did get to dance with a boy, awkwardly bumbling along on the dance floor and making painful conversation. I can't remember exactly how it happened but I think some teachers sent a knot of gangly, shy boys over to our knot of gangly, shy girls and told them to ask us to dance.

Later, we went outside to look at the moon. Away from the loud music, we chatted about books we liked to read. He seemed sweet, and rather good looking. I said I was cold and he took off his jacket and put it over my shoulders. It was just like in the movies!

The door behind us opened. It was one of the teachers.

"You shouldn't be out here," she said.

So we went back inside.

After that night, I never saw him again though we exchanged a couple of letters. I don't remember his name. But I'll always remember that gallant gesture. It is a grown up gesture that a man makes for a woman. Did this boy thrill inside with an awareness that in this moment he had taken on the role of a man, protective and strong? Had he learnt such gallantry in the movies or watched his father do it for his mother? For me, I felt the thrill of possibility and hope – in that moment, I was not a shy bookish brainiac in his eyes but a woman. And I might yet be - in a few years' time, when I turned eighteen and took my place in the world as a proper grown up – the kind of woman that a man might notice on some enchanted evening.

* * *

I never thought of myself as having drive or focus. I hated having to do my homework and I often daydreamed at school. I had no particular ambition to be anything – not a doctor like Grandpa and many of my uncles and aunts, not a lawyer like my Dad or an English teacher like my Mum, nor an engineer or accountant like others of my relatives. Despite having a reputation at school for being a brainiac – due mainly I suspected to always having my head in a novel - I did middling to well in exams, studying just enough to get B grades. My family – uncles and aunties and grandparents – who had all achieved straight A's in their youth, worried for my future. What would happen to such a lazy girl who had no ambition and who seemed to be filled with such apathy when it came to schoolwork? All I wanted to do was read my books, watch movies and scribble my little stories. What was the good of that?

But, looking back, I had – have – more drive and focus than my family gave me credit for. It was just that I channelled my energies into things that were not what they wanted, like being top in my studies or exams, but into what *I* wanted above anything else.

The transformation had begun in front of that triptych of mirrors. And now at Oxford, I wanted above everything else to be like all the other girls – and more. To be more desirable, more attractive, more woman than any of them. I wanted to be the kind of woman that men noticed. Anywhere, anytime. And I set about completing that transformation with what I have come to recognise as my characteristic determination and single-mindedness.

It was not the hoped-for miracle of my childhood fancy that made me into the slinky young woman in the red *cheongsam* and it did not happen automatically that I began to love pretty clothes and learnt to care about feminine shoes and bold earrings and necklaces. It was an act of will.

I watched and observed and read what I needed to learn from magazines, talked girl talk with my friends. If I was going to do this - achieve the life that was expected of me and that I expected of myself - I was going to do it better than all the other girls. And it was working.

With all those parties and picnics and friends to hang out with, punctuated occasionally by tutorials and short stints writing essays, there was little time to be alone. I liked it that way. On the rare occasions when I found myself with nothing to do in my room, tired of reading Shakespeare or Coleridge or Dickens, my housemates all out, I would get my coat and go and find someone in College or cycle up to see friends across Oxford – anything

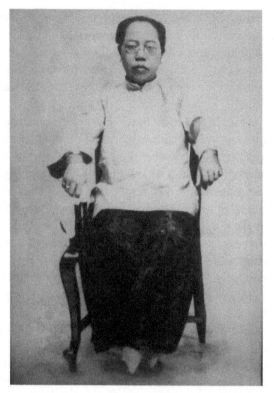

Great-grandmother Ah Mooi, with bound feet

to resist the pull into the quiet stillness. The woman I wanted to be did not have a cold, tiled bathroom waiting for her in the silence. She had no emptiness within, no uncertainty, no doubt. She was what she presented to the world in her finery that was impenetrable as armour and her make-up as unwavering as war paint.

* * *

Grandpa's father, Great-grandfather Lim, had been a hospital orderly as a young man in Taiping, at that time a thriving tin-mining town several hours north by train from the capital Kuala Lumpur. He was the son of the Bandit Boy, the older of two brothers, a square-faced, charismatic man whose appetite for women shaped the history of our family.

One day, at the hospital, he came across a young woman with bound feet. She was sweet and demure and refined. We don't know what the illness was that had brought her as a patient to the hospital or how long she stayed until she was cured. But we do know that he fell in love with her and helped to nurse her back to health.

Later, to show her gratitude for his solicitousness, she cooked him a special cockerel soup.

"It's the special soup that a young bride is supposed to make for her husband," Grandma said. "So it was her way of telling him that she liked him-lah."

The significance of the soup was not missed by Great-grandfather and he took this quiet young woman to be his wife. She became *Tai Ma* – Eldest Mother and Great-grandmother No. 1, the matriarch of the soon to be extensive Lim family.

Mum asked, "How did this bound foot woman come to be in Malaya?"

We were sitting on the verandah at my grandparents' house in Taiping. It was the hottest part of the afternoon, just after lunch. Grandpa had gone back to the surgery where he still worked as a GP after retiring from politics. My brother and sister and I were playing on the cool wooden floor while my Mum and Grandma sat in rattan chairs. We sipped ice-cold fresh passion fruit juice, the glasses damp with condensation in the heat. Cicadas hummed and the red hibiscus flowers flamed in the bright glare beyond the shaded verandah.

Grandma said, "We don't know for sure. But she would have been very brave to come all this way on her bound feet by herself."

"What is bound feet, *Ma-Ma?*" I had stopped playing with my toys and was listening intently.

"In olden days in China, little girls used to have their feet bound to make them small. They start from young when the little girl's feet are still small and they bind them up tightly with bandages to stop them from growing. It was very painful. Imagine tight, tight bandages around your feet. That's what happened to *Tai Ma* when she was young."

I had never known *Tai Ma*. She had died long before I was born. I always pictured a little old wizened lady but in the only photograph we have of her, she is a young woman, small and round with a little round face. She is sitting in an upright Chinese chair in her best *samfu*, neatly starched and ironed. She wears a pair of delicate drop earrings and we can see bangles and rings on her hands and wrists where she rests them on the arms of the chair. Her tiny bound feet, little triangles of white, peek out from beneath her shiny, silk pantaloons. Close up, she has an earnest look in her face and behind her wire-framed glasses, her eyes are serious. From a distance, I can see my mother in her – and obliquely, my own face in repose.

Might that have been me, had I been born, like her, in another time?

"Tell, tell, tell – tell about *Tai Ma*." I wanted to hear her story. To step into her life – into her shoes – in my imagination and to feel what it was like. I wanted to understand. "Why did she have bound feet?"

Mum said, "Well, in China, they used to think that small feet were beautiful. So to marry a good husband, you have to have small feet."

"Ya, that's true. Now, *Tai Ma* –we only know her story from after she came to Malaya. Before that…" Grandma frowned, trying to think of what she had been told. "She was married before, I think. But we don't know what happened to that first family and how come she was in Malaya by herself."

It was all very unsatisfying, not having a story about *Tai Ma*. And it didn't make sense. In that photograph of her, she didn't look particularly beautiful, with her round, plain face and round, plain shape. I cocked my head, thinking hard. Those tiny little triangles poking out from her pantaloons didn't look especially beautiful either.

I looked at Grandma's feet in her embroidered slippers. "*Ma-Ma*, why don't you have bound feet?"

Grandma smiled. "My family, we are all Christians. We don't bind our feet. Only the traditional old-style families in China used to bind the daughter's feet."

"There's no bound feet here, is there, *Ma-Ma?*"

"No, here overseas, no need for bound feet – and anyway, better not to have because here, everybody, women also, got to work-lah. And nowadays in China after Chairman Mao, foot binding is no more, thank God."

My mother gestured to me to come to her and I climbed up onto her lap. She held my feet, examined them, stroked them, counted my toes. "Such beautiful feet. How did those mothers do it, *hoh*, Mummy?"

Grandma sighed and shook her head. "*Sum tong-ah, chun hai* – heart would ache, truly."

My feet are very small. Perhaps that was from evolution, I pondered, sitting in my mother's lap - because Chinese women for generations in China had had their feet compressed, Chinese girls now are born with small feet. Maybe for modern girls, if they still had foot-binding, we would not need to have our feet bound because they would be already naturally small through natural selection. We would all be beautiful and be able to find husbands without going to all that trouble and pain. It was only later, when I was older, that I realized that I'm the only one with small feet among the women in my family. My mother's feet are size 4, my sister's size 5 – as were Grandma's.

That afternoon, I looked at my feet in my mother's hands and wiggled my toes. She laughed and I was glad that we were Christians and lived in the present time in a modern world. It was hard to imagine having bound feet. I had once squeezed my feet into an old pair of trainers, feeling my toes crammed hard into the tips as I was just about able to force my heel into the canvas. It was so uncomfortable I couldn't stand up.

What would it have been like to live your whole life unable to walk without pain? Why did girls need to have their feet bound to find a husband? It didn't make any sense. But many things about being a girl didn't make sense to me.

Lotus feet

BOUND FEET BLUES – THE STORY

The Concubine

[As Storyteller:]

Once upon a time, in China, 1,000 years ago – there lived an Emperor. He had many concubines. One of them was a pretty dancer. She was his favourite.

She had small delicate feet and one day, she bound them up and danced on point, like modern ballerinas do, and her feet looked even smaller and more delicate.

And the Emperor said, "Mmm, I do like small feet."

All the other concubines flew into a jealous rage - they wanted small feet too. So they began to bind their feet. Everyone could see how dainty and elegant small feet could be. And the dukes and princes and courtiers all said, "Mmm, we do like small feet."

These women with bound feet were considered feminine and desirable. They walked in a swaying, delicate manner which all the men in the kingdom found charming. They could not move quickly and had to take tiny baby steps. These women were considered a class above those dirty, ugly, vulgar peasants with their big, horrible, masculine feet.

These women with baby feet were the ones who found the best and richest husbands.

So more and more women began to bind their feet.

And their daughters' feet.

Till all the women in the land had small, dainty, elegant feet. These bound feet became known as Lotus Feet. Little Lotus Feet like the bud of the lotus flower.

But when all the women have small feet, how do you distinguish yourself, be the special one that the prince or duke or rich man will notice – like Cinderella - and take to be his wife?

You make your feet even smaller.

So the greatest prize of all, the most treasured, most perfect foot was one that was 3 inches long, the tiniest that a human foot could possibly be. And this was known as The Golden Lotus.

A MOTHER'S LOVE

[As bound foot mother:]

As a mother, you want the best for your daughter, don't you? You want her to have a good life and to be chosen by the best and richest husband. You look out there and see all those women with small feet and you know it's a competitive market.

So you call your daughter to you. She is four years old, the best age to start. You explain to her what you need to do and why you need to do it.

You start gently at first. You curl her toes over and tie her feet loosely with ribbons. It hurts her but only a little. And she must learn to go about her daily life with her toes curled over.

She used to be able to run and play. And now she can't. She is so small as you watch her. She hobbles slowly like an old woman; but when she wants to go somewhere fast, she crawls. And you think she is so resourceful.

Then she tries to take off the ribbons but you chide her and remind her it's so she can find a good husband. And she listens to you and learns what it is to be an obedient girl.

But her feet keep growing. So you tie the bandages tighter. And her feet keep growing, as she grows taller.

She is five years old. You slice the bottom of her foot, cutting through muscle and tendon. And you fold her foot over and tie the bandages tight.

She screams. And you weep.

And you remember what it was like for you at that age. How you screamed and struggled and tried to run away. But how could you with your feet cut in two?

You are not angry with your Mama, for doing this to you, no, no you're not - you are grateful to her – you are grateful to her, because look – you have this good life and this good husband you know your children will never go hungry.

But your daughter's feet keep growing.

She is six years old. And you break her toes. And still her feet keep growing.

She is seven now. And you break the bones in her foot.

And still her feet keep growing. So you keep breaking the bones and tying the bandages tighter and tighter.

She is ten now and after six years of this ritual every week, every month, she no longer tries to run away. She can't. She submits. She knows the value of having tiny feet – yes, she does. After 6 years of this ritual every week, every month, she is obedient, she is passive, she endures – all these are good qualities that a desirable Chinese wife should have. However her husband treats her, she will endure. You feel so proud of her. And you break the bones again and tie the bandages tighter and tighter till there is nothing left of but two tiny little stumps.

That are 3 inches long.

The same size as your feet.

The prized Golden Lotus.

THE POWER OF THE GOLDEN LOTUS

[As bound foot mother:]

That night, you're lying in bed, naked, your feet unbound. Your husband is kneeling at the end of the bed, holding your tiny foot in his hand.

He is naked, ecstatic, erect. He is gazing at your Golden Lotus, adoring its delicate beauty. And suddenly you know it's all been worth it.

You may not be able to stand in this moment because without the tight bandages, your feet would just collapse under your weight. But you don't need to stand, you are where you should be, your husband at your feet, worshipping their soft, contorted shape.

You are aware that some people - Westerners - think these feet ugly, deformed. Their missionary women come to your country and want to stop foot-binding because they say it's cruel. These big Western women with their big bosoms and big masculine feet - they dare to tell you that natural feet can be beautiful!

But look at their own culture. Their women will do anything to be more feminine and desirable. If they had the skills to do it, what cutting and slicing would they endure to enlarge their breasts, tie up their intestines and break their faces, break their noses, break their teeth and reshape them according to their standard of beauty?

So you make no apology for the Chinese standard of beauty, that has endured for 1,000 years and will endure for 1,000 more.

As a wife – with your tiny feet and your beautiful embroidered gowns – you don't need to walk about freely, you stay where you belong, bound to the house, bound to your husband.

A woman who moves about freely like a man - with natural

feet - is an abomination. She knows nothing of obedience or submission and cannot be controlled. Men may use her as a servant. Or they may use her as they please but they would never marry her.

It makes you angry to think of the ruined lives of these women. It's their mothers who are to blame. Their mothers were weak and pitied their pain and did not break their feet enough. But you – with your obedience and submission and endurance – you achieved the 3 inch Golden Lotus. It is you who deserve this man.

This man – so powerful, who could have any woman he chooses, chose you to be his wife.

And he is here kneeling at your feet, caressing them, kissing them, loving them.

This is your only power. This power makes sense of everything you have endured from the moment your mother first curled your toes over. This was the only power your mother had, and your mother's mother before her, going back forty generations.

So the next morning, you take out a fresh set of bindings and call your beloved daughter to you again.

THE STORIES BEHIND THE STORY

For a long time, I believed the story my Grandma told us about how foot-binding worked – that tying bandages tightly round a little girl's feet stunted their growth so that while the rest of her grew up into adult size, her feet stayed tiny like a child's. Inside those little pointed shoes I saw in photographs, I imagined perfect baby feet, soft and chubby and sweet. I thought that the pain of walking on bound feet was like the pain of walking in shoes that are too tight.

I don't know if Grandma told this version to spare us the terrible truth of foot-binding or whether, coming from a Christian background where none of the women in her family had bound feet, she did not know what the process really involved.

Last year, when I first started researching how women bound their feet as I was writing *Bound Feet Blues*, I almost vomited in horror.

In the show, I map the foot on my left hand. I curl my fingers over to illustrate the first step of curling the child's toes over. I fold my hand down at the knuckle joints to denote the folding over

My left hand stands in as a bound foot, Conway Hall

of the foot when its sole is sliced in two. Then I crunch my hand into a fist at the next stage when the foot is broken and further compressed. Each step along the way, I can sense the audience cringing. I see some people cover their eyes with their hands. Others look horrified, their faces collapsing in sympathetic agony.

Finally, I deform the shape of the fist using curled and twisted fingers, allowing only the thumb to stay loose and visible representing the intact big toe.

I present the finished stump with the back of my hand to the audience as if I am holding a revered trophy for all to admire. Only the thumb is visible and small stubs of fingers are just hinted at.

The audience by this time is exhausted, weak from the imagined torture.

And then, I turn my hand so they see the grotesquely twisted fingers clenched into my palm.

In their minds, the audience sees the misshapen, hideous foot, toes gnarled and crushed into the sole. And the final horror of it sinks in.

"The golden lotus", Conway Hall

It was an irreversible process that belied the dainty, gorgeously embroidered slippers that the women always wore. Beneath the beauty and the delicacy was an unspeakable and relentless violence. It was inflicted by mothers upon daughters out of the greatest love and the most immoveable cruelty. It was a cultural norm that defined feminine identity and – literally - kept women in their place.

But there was no Foot-binding Handbook, or any classes you could take, or any specialist practitioners who might offer their services in a clinical setting. Each mother would bind her daughter's feet the best way she could, perhaps with the help of her own mother or that of her mother-in-law. There was no anaesthetic. And no antiseptic. How would you do it? How would you break her feet? Which of the kitchen knives would you use to slice through the sole of her foot?

Step by step, month by month, year by year, that mother would have to improvise, break the bones any way she knew how, slice and fold and bind as best she could.

Sometimes the open wounds would become infected and exude pus. If the toes were bent too sharply, circulation might be cut off and gangrene would set in. The aim was to make the foot narrower and more contained as well as shorter so it might also be folded length-ways and the rotting flesh scraped off to minimise its shape. For the young girls who did not die from the infection or gangrene or trauma, lotus feet had a characteristic smell – of rot and sweat and infection combined with the scent infused into the bandages and powder that might be used to keep the feet dry.

I used to think it was a one-off thing – that all a mum had to do was tie up her daughter's feet in a set of tight bandages at a young age and that would be it: daughter would grow but her feet would stay the same kiddie size so that after the initial pain of the bandages squeezing your feet, it was then just a matter of learning to balance on tiny feet.

But of course feet don't stop growing just like that, the process

Presenting to the audience the "prized golden lotus", Conway Hall

would take much longer. It would take as long as it took for a girl to grow into her adult size – that is, aged fourteen or older. So it might take up to ten years or more.

What would it have been like to have been a girl growing up within such a culture? To have experienced your entire childhood through this one obsessive, implacable violent act, repeated again and again? Inflicted upon you by your mother and grandmothers in a turmoil of love and harshness of heart. To live your whole young life in agony as bones are broken and healed and broken again. With no escape, no excuse, no alternative, however how hard you might scream or struggle. And ultimately, accepting it, no matter how much dread or fear or anguish you might have; giving yourself over to the process, steeling your mind and heart to allow what had to be done to be done.

What kind of woman would you become after ten years or more of this process through your most impressionable and formative years? What would make you do this same thing to your own daughter? You know the horror and agony of it and your instinct as a mother is to protect your daughter, to love her above your own life. And yet, you do this unspeakable thing to her.

What kind of woman are you?

* * *

Nicky sat reading on a bench in Victoria Park in North East London on a glorious summer day in 2013. Around her, there were people picnicking on the grass, children playing tag, couples strolling. She was wearing a summer dress, the sun warm on her bare shoulders. Her bright mahogany hair was let loose and its bushy curls were wild and unruly in the sunlight. After the winter months in shoes and boots, she liked the freedom of wandering through the summer in flip-flops and today, as she crossed her legs, one rubber sole hung freely from her toes.

She was aware for a moment of someone speaking to her.

"Ooo, ooo," a young man's voice said. "I really like your feet."

She looked up. He had stopped in front of her.

Taken aback but registering that his remark was a compliment, she said, "Ummm… thank you…"

"I'm a real foot man. I look at a lot of feet, and your feet…" His words tumbled out, almost as if she had not spoken. "Your feet are great, the best feet I've seen. Could I just see… could you take them out of your flip-flops? Could I have a closer look?"

Nicky stared at him in shock. "No, not really. No."

"I'm twenty-five. I really like older women. Are you single? I'd really like to take your feet out."

"It's really kind of you to flatter my feet – but, no, thank you very much."

He lingered but not menacingly. There was something child-like in his enthusiasm for her feet. He gazed at them, commenting as much to himself as to her.

"They're the best I've ever seen. They're lovely. Mmm, yes, very nice. Just great…"

Every time he asked Nicky to let him closer to her feet, she said no.

She felt uneasy. The encounter was surreal and a little creepy.

But she did not feel threatened. In fact, it was oddly amusing. She found herself writing up in her head her Facebook update about this moment.

After a while, he wandered away.

She had been chatted up by men many times before, often in bars and pubs but not in a park. They had often glanced at her breasts, either openly or surreptitiously, but this was the first time her feet had been the centre of anyone's attention.

It struck her that this young man's manner had been gentle and polite in contrast to those other encounters. The ploy of the men in pubs would be to insult her or put her down - which was meant to be form of teasing flirtation, she supposed. Or as a power play, a way of making her feel unsteady about herself so that she would want ingratiatingly to gain their approval in some way. Whatever the purpose of it was, those men would just annoy her.

Many men just didn't know how to get it right with women, she thought. There were the more sensitive ones and usually, with those, things would start off pretty well. They were interested and listened as much as they talked. They were considerate and funny. But just as she felt herself relaxing and warming to them, they would misjudge the next step and lean in for a snog. Power and sex. That's what it seemed that men wanted in these superficial encounters.

If that was all she knew, she would have a skewed view of men. But she had been in good relationships with lovely men. She smiled to think of one of her boyfriends, whose hair had been longer and wilder than hers. He had been a model and would sometimes wear more make-up than she did. He had been kind and gentle and funny. He loved her for who she was – unruly, messy, wild. Like her hair. She laughed. They had had good times together, she recalled fondly. She had gone out with him because he was different and interesting – not the stuffed shirt, solid type that a lot of women would prefer.

She thought suddenly of Gena, her best friend from a long time ago. She and Gena had been a pair! They had both been a bit wild, with unruly hair and dressing up in anything that took their fancy. They had been Goths for a bit, tried out baggy men's suits, done the glam thing.

And then at some point, Gena had decided she wanted to find a man and get married. She changed everything about herself. She started to dress like a corporate wife, became straight laced in how she acted and moved and talked. She married a rich man and lived in a big, corporate lifestyle house. Nicky winced thinking about the time Gena had invited her round for dinner. They sat at the dinner table for a formal meal and made conversation. This was not the friend she had known.

They lost touch. Later, she heard that the marriage had ended in divorce. But she and Gena had never been able to pick up their friendship again.

Power and sex. It's not just men who want those things. Women, too.

For some women, marrying a rich man is a giddying power play. What he can give you can be a form of aphrodisiac. As men chatting up women in pubs are drawn to cleavages and breasts and young men in parks may see only women's feet, women, too, turn men into objects of desire for their wealth and status and power. What is it like to be a man who is married for his money or his title or the influence he can wield over others? What is it like to see a woman do anything – even change the very core of who she is – to make you choose her above all others? Would you be aware of it? Would it matter to you?

Nicky got up and headed back home through the park. She played over in her mind the odd incident with Foot Man.

She was more than her feet, she knew that for certain. But did Foot Man know that? Did he care? To him, it was almost as if who she was didn't matter. It had been her feet that he had wanted to go out with. She couldn't help but laugh at how bizarre that sounded. And who was Foot Man really – as a man, a person? Would she ever know?

She thought about the post she had started composing for

Facebook in those creepy, uncomfortable moments when he was talking so lovingly about her feet. Had this been her way of turning him into an object as he was making her into no more than her feet? In that moment, he was just a funny story to tell her friends, no longer human, no longer a person she needed to feel anything about. It had helped diffuse her discomfort as only laughter can do.

He was of course more than his foot fetish but she had never got the chance to know him, the person, because he had put her feet in the way.

* * *

In Chinese tradition, *yang* is the male principle and *yin* the female. *Yang* is associated with an active energy, masculinity, a vigour that takes you out into world. *Yin* is passive, feminine, a form that rests at home. *Yang* is the sun, bright and invigorating. *Yin* is the moon, soft and yielding. *Yang* energy rises, *yin* descends. And yet, *yang* is of the earth, solid and powerful, and *yin* is of heaven, transcendent and ethereal.

At the Ming exhibition at the British Museum in 2014, there was a throw-away line in one of the little notes alongside an exhibit explaining that it was the fashion of the time (in the late 1600s) for men to look bulky. So they wore many layers of robes to increase their build and girth. In paintings of emperors and men of importance, they are seen seated on a throne-like upright chair, legs and arms held wide to increase that sense of stature.

In contrast, women are depicted in soft, flowing robes, slim and delicate, their tiny bound feet peeking daintily out from beneath their gowns. Women were meant to glide, like heavenly creatures, unsullied and floating above the stolid, drab earth.

But in making love, men take their place above, dominant, powerful, conquering while women yield and succumb below, heaven submitting to the will of the earth.

These principles are as potent in today's world as they were in ancient China.

The ideal of manhood for us is a physique that is bulky and muscular, with broad shoulders and strong torso, thick, chunky legs and arms. He is active and strides out in the world, takes charge, doesn't back away from a fight. Think of James Bond or any action hero in popular culture. Think of sturdy boots and solid, manly lace ups.

The feminine ideal is slim and willowy, small shouldered and tiny bodied, with long, svelte arms and legs. Thanks to feminism, she is more active than passive and takes her place in the world as much as in the home. But the heart and emotions remain her prime domain and in the art of love, we see her more passive than active – for a woman to bestride the man in any popular movie is shorthand for the wild, outrageousness of her character. Think Audrey Hepburn or any popular female star, all of them skinnily beautiful. Think high heels.

Divine. Heavenly. Ethereal. Though these words can sometimes be used to describe men – most probably George Clooney – they usually conjure images of women.

Powerful. Strong. Heroic. You see a man, right? Even though the words can apply equally to a woman.

We have ideas about what men and women should be like – even in today's modern, democratic, equal-rights and diversity valuing societies – and these ideas are not dissimilar to ancient Chinese principles that were based on rigid Confucian teachings.

Women want to be feminine. There's nothing wrong with that – and there's a great deal to love about it. How glorious it is to revel in our bodies – our softness and suppleness, our curves and gentleness, our long hair and how beautiful we look in make-up and flowing, feminine clothes, the way high heels make our feet look sleek and sexy. How joyous to love our children, love the homes we make, to create pretty things and to take care of the men we love.

But we are also capable and powerful, strong and active, hard and aggressive, logical, intelligent, leaders, scientists, warriors, selfish, single-minded, destroyers, rageful and butch as much as bitch. We are masculine as much as feminine.

There is an anxiety about being too masculine. Which is why so many of us fear being called a feminist. We might as well be called a man-hating bitch. Because a feminist supposedly hates men. But a feminist doesn't hate men. She wants to stride through the world in the fullness of who she is – both soft and hard, yielding and assertive, leader and follower, logical and emotional, sun and moon, feminine and masculine.

And what would the world be like if a man could do the same – be able both to engage in the world and in creating a home, to discover all of himself in his strength and fragility, heart and head, gentleness and power, control and submissiveness, masculine and feminine? To express the fullness of who he is?

There is so much anxiety, however, in our culture around men being too feminine and women not being feminine enough. This anxiety of being too much like the other keeps us in its grip still. So, while individual men and women in cosmopolitan melting pots such as London may dress and behave as they wish, we all of us play out our lives within the expected gender roles of the wider culture.

And it is a culture of shame.

Effeminate men are ridiculed – or worse, beaten and even killed. Boys must be boys and play with manly toys. Heaven forbid that a young boy should want to wear pink or play with dolls like a girl.

Magazines and the media peddle a single global ideal of feminine beauty and she generally looks like Elle Macpherson in her prime – tall, slim, blonde, high cheek-boned, large eyed, young, glamourously made-up. Any variation from that is policed through shaming.

It is big business for paparazzi to shame female celebrities in unflattering photos – you can see those fuzzy pictures in magazines with an inlaid zoom or a big red arrow pointing to the fat rolls on their tummy or the cellulite on their thighs. There is a glee in pointing out these women's ugliness as they are snapped without make-up or looking dishevelled and frumpy. A Cambridge professor has been described as being 'too ugly for TV' for her long, grey hair and make-up free, lined face. Normal sized women are perceived as overweight and there are very few larger women seen on film or television or in the public eye. And very few older women, too, who are unafraid of flaunting their grey hair and wrinkles in the media. A woman is considered brave if she shows her face publicly without make-up, leading to a social media viral meme of young girls posting 'no make-up selfies' of themselves, accompanied by much soul searching and angst in their status updates alongside these photos – and much affirmation of their courage in the responding comments. High powered women in high profile roles are routinely referenced as mothers or grandmothers - and their hair and outfits are as much part of the commentary as their policies or achievements.

In schools and colleges, girls learn to keep quiet and let the boys shine so that they are not vilified for making the boys look stupid. In board rooms around the country, men dominate by numbers – and also by vocal presence as in most mixed gatherings, men will speak more than women. We fear being called bossy or a bitch so we shy away from leadership and assertiveness or cloak it all with indirect language and mannerisms so we can still be liked. Women who are outspoken have to deal with threats of violence and rape designed to force us into silence – as in the case of the female journalist campaigning for a Jane Austen bank note who was viciously trolled on the internet.

So we learn that we must be always attendant to our looks – because if we are ugly or fat or dress badly, we will be ridiculed and our views dismissed. We must also attend to ourselves in relation to men – because if we are not mothers or grandmothers, we may be mistaken for ball-busting, man-hating, irrational feminists and all our opinions and achievements will be seen through that lens and be easily discredited. We must be silent and embrace the status quo, let men take the limelight and always agree with them – because otherwise they will bully us into submission to make sure they continue getting their own way.

Not all men need to silence women, not all men are bullies, and not all men are sexist. Not all women shame each other, not all women fixate on being thin and beautiful, and not all women care about pleasing men.

In the same way that not all women in China had bound feet. Nor all fathers wanted to see their daughters live through such pain and mutilation. Nor all men consider women inferior to them as taught by Confucious.

But the prevailing culture of any time sits upon its people like an invisible miasma, permeating the air we breathe and the thoughts and values we live out through our relationships and the lives we lead. It is so ever-present that we are not even aware of how it shapes our thoughts and anxieties.

How much of you is you – and how much created by the values of our times?

How do you hold yourself at work? Do you let men speak more often? Are you less direct than a man would be? What values are you passing on to your daughters? Do you buy them only girl toys? What about the men in your family – are they allowed to show weakness or emotion?

As a woman, are you afraid of being called bossy? A bitch? Do you tell people you are not a feminist but you believe in equal opportunities? Does it worry you that you might be called ugly? Or fat? Do you worry about your weight? Your age? Do you – will you – colour your hair to disguise the grey? What kind of shoes do you wear? Would you ever wear flat shoes to a glamourous function or a business meeting? What kind of woman are you now, in this culture, in this time you live in?

What kind of woman would you be in ancient China?

I would like to think that if I had been born in ancient China, I would have been the kind of woman who would have refused to bind my daughter's feet out of love and compassion for her and in defiance against a cruel, misogynistic cultural practice.

But I don't think it would have been so easy.

For one thing, as a woman within that Chinese culture, I wouldn't have any clue about misogyny or feminism or equality as concepts – or even possibilities. I wouldn't consider the practice of foot-binding a cultural construct that one was choosing to uphold – and so could be unchosen. Foot-binding and the role of women within Chinese society – that was just the way things were, and had been for generations since the time of William the Conqueror. All this questioning and placing of an individual life as central to our concerns, this idea of personhood above family and community and culture – all this is a construct, too, albeit a modern and Western one. And even so, the segregation of *yin* and *yang* still remains woven into the fabric of the norm.

It is not easy to step outside the norm.

Big hair, the norm during the '80s

At Oxford, I liked to think of myself as forthright and capable of speaking my mind – but I worried that people would think me a bitch, so I tempered my opinions with indirectness and gentle words.

As a young lawyer, I wanted to believe that I had the skills and talent to lead but I worried that I would be called bossy. So I wrapped my statements with ingratiating smiles and tried to seem less powerful.

I wore little dainty shoes I hated so that I wouldn't be dismissed by men or looked down on by other women. I had to become more feminine, more noticeably desirable than other women to overwhelm that ever-present feeling of not being beautiful enough, not woman enough - not good enough.

And, even so, when I met an immaculately feminine woman in high heels, who was closer to the global ideal than I ever could be and who seemed to carry her beauty so effortlessly, I would feel my self-worth plummet as I compared myself to her.

In my mind, I have an idea of myself as a bold, strong woman who dares to speak my mind, who can proudly call myself a feminist. And yet, I have an anxiety around the pages I have just written. Will people think me a ball-busting, man-hating dyke for writing all this? I feel I want to justify: some of my best friends are men, I don't hate men, really I don't. I want to plead: I am not a shoe fascist either, I am not advocating for women to throw away their high heels and only wear flats, really I am not. I want to placate: please don't hate me criticizing the norm, for questioning it.

And I am horrified that I am so easily susceptible to the power of this internalised shame.

It is not easy to step outside the norm. It is much more comforting to embrace it. There is so much to gain by staying within the norm, so much to revel in.

So the two scenes in the show, *A Mother's Love* and *The Power of the Golden Lotus*, are spoken in the second person singular – 'you'.

On stage, I am the mother and wife with bound feet, speaking to each woman in the audience with an unwavering certainty: if you were in my position, living in the same time and place, you would do the same.

You would not question the norm. In fact, you would uphold it and glory in it. You are proud of your culture – and beyond simply being a part of it, you are at the supreme pinnacle of your world. You are the most beautiful wife and mother that you can possibly be, achieved through your mother's love and your own endurance and will.

You are the envy of your social circle. Other women with bigger feet do not have a patch on you. They try to hide their how they feel but you can see it just under the surface. They may have married well, too, but their houses are not as grand or lovely as yours. They may put their hair up just like yours or copy the way you wear your beautiful embroidered gown but they can never be as beautiful. Their feet are just not small enough. So their husbands are B-listers. But you – you have the David Beckham, Prince William, Charles Saatchi of your time. In your company, they know they will always be second best.

You – you have no doubt, no shame about who you are.

And because you love your daughter, you want her to have the best, just like you have had. But even if she might not have been able to achieve the Golden Lotus, the very least you can do is to protect her from the shame of being outside the norm. In practical terms, you don't want her to suffer the ignominy of being unmarriageable or the horror of being a spinster or a servant or a prostitute. But at a deeper level, even if your husband were wealthy and compassionate enough to let her live at home for the rest of her big-footed life, you wouldn't want her to be ridiculed, to be considered a lesser woman – or worse, a mannish woman. You wouldn't want her to feel the shame of those big protruding feet sticking out from under her beautiful gown or to sense the disgust that others would feel seeing her galumphing gait.

Because this life, in this time and in this place, is all you know.

* * *

Samiel was going to become a successful model. Still at high school, at sixteen, she had started her professional career already at a modelling academy in Buenos Aires, learning how to hold herself, how to walk, how to apply her make-up, what clothes looked good on her. She was tall and willowy at 5' 8" (1.75m) with large dark eyes and fine cheekbones – a Latin Princess Di in the making.

You are so beautiful, her family and friends would say to her, you should be a model.

She was a straight-A student, bright and determined. So far, she had achieved everything in school that she had set her mind to. This was going to be no different. She approached modelling as she approached everything else – with quiet focus and drive. She wanted to make her family proud of her. She had always been a good daughter and now, she was going to succeed at this as much for them as for herself.

This morning, she was learning how to walk in high heels, along with the other girls in her class. They were all tall, all beautiful, all with the same drive to be the best. She squeezed her feet into the shoes. They were too small so that her feet could look more elegant – one of the tricks of the trade. As she stood up slowly, the pain in her feet intensified as her weight pushed the flesh and bones against the already too tight leather. She swayed slightly, trying to find her balance on the high heels. These were the highest heels that she had ever worn – were they 5 inches (13cm), maybe more? Her feet were pitched sharply forward, her ankle taking the strain. Her toes felt crushed and contorted. The intense pain seemed to travel up her legs and spine and burst across her brain.

"No, no, Samiel, no frowning," Her teacher, Tini, called from across the room. Tini was an elegant woman, an ex-model, and Samiel loved everything about her. She wanted to learn so much, to know how to carry herself with the same poise, to command a room with such beautiful presence. "It must all look effortless.

You are serene and lovely – no pain, there is no pain."

They began to walk around the room, Samiel and the other girls. Many were ungainly, awkward. Some found a natural sway. Others teetered gingerly. Samiel worked hard not to grimace or wince, not to let the sliver thin heel slip and send her tumbling.

"No-one must know your pain. Hide it well. With a smile. A calm gaze. You are beautiful, that is all that matters." The gentle words floated above the girls. "Think of how you dance with a man, how he moves you, turns you, pulls you towards him. Your shoes are your partner through life. Learn to dance with them. Get to know them, move with them. What do they like? What do they not like?"

Over the weeks, they learnt how to dance – and for each girl, the rhythm and music of her shoes were unique. They learnt how to hold themselves a little forward, taking their weight off the decorative heel and walk on tip toe. They learnt how to ignore the pain, transform it into beauty. They found a small point of balance within their shoes, precariously between forward and back and not too much to the side. Here in this small space, the shoes gave back to them the reward of all the weeks of hard work like a dancer holding his partner tight and close and strong. Here in this perfect moment of the *pas de deux*, they could be poised and taller even than their natural glorious height, slim, sleek silhouettes of perfect womanhood. But if they moved a fraction out of this safe haven, the shoes would fling them aside with contempt – and they would be vulnerable again, wavering, and uncertain in their stance.

It is in this suspension between stillness and danger that the allure of women in heels lies. In one moment, they might tower over you – over any man – all legs and intoxicating perfume. And in the next, they need you. The world for them is dangerous – a misstep and they will fall, they cannot walk fast or far. You offer your arm and they must take it or they will have to stay forever rooted to the spot. You offer your hand to help them out of the car. They take your hand to glide up and down the stairs. The world that is dangerous to her is a bold arena to you – it is your world, made for you, harsh and hurried and boisterous, and no place for the fragile vulnerability that is woman.

Samiel learnt over the years that in this world of beauty, nobody cared what she felt inside or what she thought. Nobody cared about the pain. The only thing that mattered was her beauty.

But there was a problem. No. There were many problems. Problems with her beauty. Beauty. Could she even describe herself as beautiful? Compared to the other girls, maybe she wasn't really so beautiful.

Sitting in the high chair in front of the huge, neon lit mirror, she listened to the make-up artists talk about her as if she wasn't there.

"Look at those eyebrows. *Tsk, tsk,*" one of them said, shaking her head.

The other leaned in. "Ah, yes, I can see it. One is higher than the other, no?"

"It would be better if they were lined up like this." The first one drew a finger across Samiel's brow.

They both turned to the mirror to look at the wonky eyebrows. Then the second one said, "Oh dear, you see that nose. It's crooked."

Their two heads hovering above Samiele peered into the mirror. Cocked to one side to weigh up the evidence in front of them.

"Oh my God," the first says. "How this girl can be a model? Look at that bump there in the middle of her nose, and how the whole thing slopes to the right."

Samiel wanted to explain. She had broken her nose as a little girl playing too boisterously in the school yard. You could hardly see it. Or could you? She squinted into the mirror. She had not noticed that bump before. It looked huge. And her face that she had seen thousands of times before gazing back at her looked suddenly ugly, with its misaligned eyebrows and misshapen nose.

At the wardrobe fitting, Samiel stood in her underwear while the designer eyed her up and down. He walked round her like a man might walk round a car in a showroom, appraising the bodywork, looking for faults. Normally, she stood confidently. She liked her body. But something in his manner made her feel awkward. She felt herself hunching in a little. He sighed and tutted. "It's going to be difficult finding something for this shape."

"What do you mean?"

"You're size 8, right?"

She nodded.

"See, you're too fat." His tone was contemptuous.

"What?"

"And, look at these." He reached out and grabbed her breast. Squeezed. She recoiled, drew her arms up to fend him off. "You call these breasts? There's nothing here."

He circled her again. He snorted. "Too fat with no breasts. You need to be a size 6 if you're going to make it in the big time. And get a boob job."

She was a failure. How was she going to face her family and friends? Everyone one was so proud of her, so excited for her. She had made it so far – she was a model! It was a big deal. And now, everything she had dreamt of hung on a thread. She was too fat and it would damage her career. She would never make it as a world-class model. There were so many other girls skinnier, with more perfect features and bigger breasts than her. They would get the calls, the best jobs, become the face of international products. While she…

She could not bear to think of the alternative. She felt so ashamed. She could not speak about it to anyone. But she knew that there was one thing she could do. And she would do it well, just as she always did everything well. With her drive and focus and clever mind, she was going to ace this. She would will herself into becoming a size 6.

It began innocuously enough. Samiel cut down on her portion sizes at meal times, eating a little less than normal. Then she started eating only half of what was on her plate. She started to lose weight.

But the half full plate felt shameful to her. It would upset her mother, she knew, if she did not eat it all. Her mother was the nurturer, the provider of comfort and nourishment. Not to eat her food would be an insult. And she did not want to hurt her mother. So she would hide the food in her napkin. And later, flush it down the loo. Or she would eat the whole meal and find the chance afterwards to throw it all up again into the toilet.

She continued to lose weight. She checked herself in the mirror obsessively. And each time, she saw a girl who was still too fat. Her energy flagged. She was missing out on opportunities because she was too tired. Too tired to perform, to stand tall and glowing, to float in her beauty with ease.

It was all going wrong.

One day, she visited her doctor for a routine checkup. It was nothing out of the ordinary. But when she got home, her mother was waiting for her.

"The doctor just called. She says you have anorexia."

"I can't believe she called you!" Samiel was furious. How dare the doctor interfere in this way! "I don't have anorexia. That's ridiculous."

It was a horrible, shameful label. Anorexic. Anorexics were sick people That was not her. She wasn't sick. She was a model. She was beautiful and successful. Models are meant to be skinny. She was doing what she needed to do to be better at her job. Why couldn't they all see that?

But something inside her knew that the doctor was right.

She found a therapist and worked with her over a period of time. In a little while, she started eating more and more again. She put on weight and her health returned. She gave up her modelling career and studied Industrial Design at the University of Buenos Aires.

Today, Samiel Carolina Rodriguez Barros is founder and director of Dare to Glow, a training and consultancy service. In her work, she guides women to express their inner beauty and discover their primal power as mothers, mentors and nurturers of the next generations.

"It's not about *looking* beautiful, it's about *feeling* beautiful," she tells me over Skype from her home in Geneva. At forty, her dark hair is peppered with grey. She doesn't appear to be wearing any make-up. She is in a soft grey sweater. She is beautiful.

Her journey from modelling to anorexia and back to full health informs her life and work. She says, "Typically my clients are professional women who feel out of balance in their life. I help them to reconnect with a deeper part of themselves. When they can feel their higher purpose beyond just surface pre-occupations, they can move forward towards their dreams feeling grounded and authentically empowered."

She speaks passionately, reflecting back on the pain of excessively high heels. "That pain goes straight up your spine from your feet into your brain. How painful it is to be a woman. I am in pain but still I have to perform. How does your brain function when you have that pain at the base of who you are, where you have your roots?"

Emerging from an industry fixated on looking good on the outside, she has dedicated her life to firing up the inner glow that burns within us all. True beauty, she says, comes from within. And in contrast to the isolation and competition between women that characterised her experience of the modelling world, she brings women together in Women's Circles so they can support each other, share their stories and create community.

"I wear clothes now that make me *feel* beautiful. Not what's fashionable. What is comfortable. If I am comfortable, I feel powerful and at ease with my body."

I ask her what shoes she wears these days.

She laughs, throwing her head back. "I love high heels! But not high, high heels. Not if they give me pain. High heels that look good but not crazy high. Anyway, where I live, we are near the countryside so I wear flat shoes most of the time, old boots, anything comfortable. And in Geneva, the streets are old and there are cobblestones. I take public transport everywhere. I choose shoes that are comfortable – so I can walk my own path, on my own terms."

* * *

In 1644, the new emperor of China and the progenitor of the Ming dynasty, a Manchurian who had taken power by violence and invasion, banned foot-binding. It was part of a set of laws that dictated what the Chinese people wore, mandating *queues* for men and the Manchu-style tunic with its high Mandarin collar for both sexes. While those latter laws came to be obeyed and over the centuries even evolved into symbols of Chinese identity, foot-binding continued for almost four hundred more years. It is a testament to the will and defiance of generations of Chinese women.

Manchu women did not have bound feet. But the allure of the tiny bound foot that the indigenous Chinese women had was so powerful that over time, even they wanted to have dainty little feet. I believe that some Manchu women bound their feet and their daughter's feet. Others wore a version of high heels that gave the impression of tiny feet beneath their long gowns.

These Manchu shoes sat on top of a small pedestal that acted like short stilts at the centre of the sole. The slightly wider pedestal base acted as the surrogate foot, while the real foot in all its hugeness was balanced a few inches above, hidden from view. These stilts would have made walking precarious and would have required the women to mimic the small, mincing steps of a woman with real bound feet. As with women with real bound feet, the fragile unbalance of these women in Manchu heels would have made them seem vulnerable and dependent. They would have needed help a helping hand, an offered arm, as they stepped out of sedan chairs and made their slow, elegant way up and down stairs.

Chinese women could have stopped foot-binding four

hundred years ago. They could have saved sixteen generations of women and girls from the horrendous violence of being crippled by their own mothers and grandmothers. Manchurian women need not have voluntarily signed up to this brutal practice.

And yet foot-binding bound them all in its thrall.

From my research over the last year, it seems to me that the whole of China was in a state of perpetual tumescence for centuries over the idea of bound feet. Tiny feet were the ultimate icon of beauty and it defined women's identities and roles and the institution of marriage. They also became a rallying symbol of nationalism during uncertain times and an index of economic success. An outpouring of art and literature were devoted to them.

I am indebted to a number of academic papers and books on bound feet for everything that is in this chapter. You can see the list of them the Sources section at the end of this book. I have relied primarily on Wang Ping's *Aching for Beauty* and Shirley See Yan Ma's *Foot-binding: A Jungian Engagement with Chinese Culture and Psychology*.

For a woman, it didn't matter if you were pretty or ugly, young or old, slim or fat. If your feet were small and delicate, you were the equivalent of Elle Macpherson. You were wanted and desired and could pick and choose your husband from a clamour of suitors.

Men adored these tiny feet. Beyond caressing and kissing them, they loved the smell of them – which I can only imagine to be the fragrance of rotting flesh, cheesy feet, perfume and powder. Connoisseurs of lotus feet categorized the different shapes and sizes, giving them a range of names – fragrant lotus and the like. Men loved holding the little shoes, drinking wine from them, placing the tiny feet against their penises. The slit across the middle of the sole looked like a vagina and men would long to penetrate it. The big toe, standing strong and intact, had the shape of a penis and men would long to be penetrated by it.

The idea of the women's pain and endurance made being with such a woman all the more intoxicating. To know that she had suffered such agony and yet held herself now with such poise and elegance, gave her a tragic, poignant quality that made men pity and love her so much more.

She would not be able to leave her father or husband's house without aid so she would never be able to flirt with other men or have affairs. She would never be able to walk away from her husband whatever he chose to do to her. To know also that over the years of endurance and pain, her spirit had been broken like that of a good horse, to know she would not defy her husband and would always be helpless, dependent, docile – in a Confucian culture where everyone had their place in a rigid hierarchy, it was comforting that a wife could be kept in her place not just literally but also psychologically.

This dependent, malleable, virtuous and beautiful woman, ever devoted to her husband, came to be a symbol of his power and wealth. She could not even move around the house without a handmaiden. She had to be carried everywhere beyond in a sedan chair. This precious doll had to have beautiful things around her. It took a rich man to give his wife all these things. And the smaller her feet, the more she would have suffered, the greater her value and so the greater his potency among his social circle.

These women inspired the eroticisation of purity and the Cult

Longing for love, Conway Hall

of the Exemplary Woman grew up around women with bound feet – specifically, wives with bound feet. These wives gave over their lives for the happiness, comfort and honour of their husbands. And it was the ultimate act of love and duty if a wife gave up her life following the death of her husband. The Chinese woman with her bound feet was seen as a civilizing influence and a symbol of China's cultural superiority over other countries. Some of the elite felt that if Chinese women were sent to aggressing neighbour states, the civilizing effect of their beauty and charm would diffuse the warring tensions in the region. Against the Manchu edict banning foot-binding, the practice flourished as a political act of defiance that was wrapped up in Chinese nationalism.

And at the same time, erotic art and literature flourished depicting women with bound feet in a dizzying range of sexual acts. The most famous was an erotic novel, Golden Lotus, which ultimately sees its protagonist die from exhaustion for having had too much sex with the eponymous heroine.

In this steamy brew of sex and power and desire and purity where woman's broken body came to represent everything that a culture valued and beyond that the entirety of its national identity, women who did not have bound feet would surely feel ashamed.

"Does my bum look big in this?" has been a comedy line from an old sketch show that has passed into our cultural history because it captures in one question all our anxieties as women.

Look at any part of your body you hate. Or feel ashamed of. Is it your bum? Your breasts? Your waistline? Your hips? Your chin(s)? Your wrinkles? Or Other? Or All of the above?

Take your shoes off and look down at your feet. Think about those beautiful embroidered slippers that the most delicate Chinese women would wear on their bound feet, so tiny and fragile, like those of a porcelain doll. Look again at your own feet – wide, flat, with five splayed and protruding toes. Look at those toes – long, thick, maybe with a few little hairs. Maybe you have corns or bony bits sticking out. Maybe your toes are bumpy or craggy. Maybe your nails are not as perfect as they should be. All that meat sticking out from under your legs.

Was that what women with unbound feet saw when they looked down at their natural selves?

Did they also see in their mannish, ungainly feet their failure as women? They existed only to serve those better than themselves, to run errands, to cook and clean and fetch and carry. Their bodies were no more than pissing pots for men on the prowl, despised for their unbound feet and yet desired for the relief they gave. They worked in the fields like men. They were part woman, part man, a horror against the neat order of Confucian hierarchy.

Women in ancient China who had natural feet would instinctively try and hide them from view, especially on special occasions where they might find themselves in the company of women with lotus feet. Some young girls would bind their feet themselves – if they were motherless or in a household where there was no older mother-figure to have done it for them. Imagine breaking your own feet, slicing through them, folding and bending them, with no skill or training - or anaesthetic – and only your own pure will to drive you onward.

Living within the miasma of a prevailing culture that shames women in our natural selves as ugly, old, fat, mannish, bossy, what would you – do you – do to take away the pain of that shame? As a woman in ancient China, would the pain of binding your own feet seem less than the pain of the psychic shame of enduring ugly, mannish, disgusting natural feet?

* * *

Bev woke up one morning and couldn't get out of bed. She was due to fly out to Dublin to interview a hot new rock band on the rise. It was a gig that would have been the envy of any music journalist. She should want to go. She should want it. She should want so many things she had in her life. And yet, she felt she couldn't go on with any of it.

She pulled the duvet up over her head. It was safe and warm here in this cocoon. She did not have to face anyone here. She did not have to go out into the world where everyone could see what a sham she was.

Here under the duvet, it was fuggy from her exhaling breath. But even the thought of pulling her face up out of its protective comfort to take in the fresh air in her bedroom was too much. She was going to stay here forever.

Was it only a few years ago that she had strutted into one of the trendiest clubs in London, a woman in supreme command of herself and the centre of adoration in the throbbing, strobing press of bodies? How had she got from there to this place? This fucked up place where she felt like she didn't exist and was worth nothing.

That night at Skin Two, a fetish club in a basement off Charing Cross Road, she had been the queen of the night, walking in with Rich in her six-inch heels. She was wearing a figure-hugging bespoke black latex dress with red trim, and lacing all the way up the back that revealed the cleavage of her buttocks. Her shapely legs were in sheer black stockings, the seams straight as riding crops up the back of her calves and thighs. She walked on tiptoe in the six-inch stilettos, stood on tiptoe, sat with her feet in tiptoe. Not many women knew how to walk in six inches but she had mastered it and despite the discomfort, she revelled in the sensation she was causing.

Other women flounced by in their three-, four- and even the rare five- inches. But they were nothing compared to her. And she could see that they knew it. They would glance at her feet and she could see the moment of their defeat in their eyes. She smiled a smile of triumph each time.

And the men adored her even more. Especially Rich.

She loved the way he looked at her in these moments of her supreme power – she loved his desire and subjugation to her enthrallment. She was twenty-four and at ten years older, he was her lover and mentor. Everything she did, she did for him – the dominating way she dressed, her razor-sharp stockings, the shoes that sent him wild. Everything she had become – sexy, sultry, powerful, adored - was because of him.

He loved being on his knees before her, calling her mistress, asking permission for everything. Here in this club, it was not only he who was her slave. These other men, in their black leather and latex, they wanted to be dominated by her too. And for a time, she luxuriated in her role, coldly ignoring their pleas for attention just long enough to whip up their excitement, dismissing them curtly when she grew bored, curling her lip in disdain at everything they did to try and please her.

It was around that time that she became famous. Or, rather, her foot did. In those six-inch heels, her ankles and feet contorted into an abnormal and almost unattainable beauty, her calves flexed into hard, round balls. They were objects of desire beyond any of the women in their lesser heels. For the shoot, the photographer got her stand on a high table in a brightly lit studio. The precariousness of the position gave the moment an added frisson as she towered over them all, resplendent in gleaming rubber and those impossible heels. Her foot made the front cover of Skin Two magazine.

But it wasn't Bev who wore those shoes and struck those latex-clad poses. It wasn't Bev who sneered and flicked her contempt at all these men. It wasn't Bev living this darkly powerful life.

It was Betty Page.

That was the name she had given herself. It was taken from Rich's favourite pin-up girl from the 1950s. Betty (sometimes Bettie) Page was the iconic figure of S&M, often seen in black stockings and suspenders, kicking up her high heels on beds and chairs. She wore lacy Victorian bodices and frilly gloves, her lips dark scarlet and her thick black hair in an oddly wholesome neat cut.

It was Betty Page whose by-line stamped the music articles that Bev wrote. It was Betty Page who was bad and wild. She partied hard, drank hard, took the hard drugs. She was the one who lived the rock 'n' roll lifestyle. She was the one who could thrive in this hard world.

Not Bev.

Curled up under the duvet, it was Bev who found herself unable to face Betty's life.

Somewhere along the way, she and Rich had broken up. In the past few years, she had carried on in the persona he had moulded her into, going to the clubs, partying as she had always done, only without him.

Without him by her side, the advances of the submissives in the club seemed more threatening. They pushed her to do things to them she did not want to do. She didn't want to whip them. Sometimes, she didn't even feel like playing at her dominatrix persona. And then they would be pissed with her, angry and aggressive that they had not got their own way. They were supposed to be subservient to her. She was the one who was supposed to be the powerful one, dominating them all.

But she wasn't the one in control if they felt they could rail at her like they did. Had she ever been as powerful as she thought she had been? Had *they* really been the ones in control all along, these men who were the so-called submissives?

The realisation shook her.

The next day, after Bev had stayed in bed two days running, her best friend Gill called. Remembering that period now, Bev says, "Gill made me go home and stay with my parents. I got myself signed off work with stress for a month. In all that time, only a couple of my music business friends sent me a card or got in touch or wished me well. It was as if I no longer existed for them. They wanted me around if I was the life and soul of the party but if not…" She makes a dismissive sound. "What happened that morning – it really made me think about everything – my friends, my life, who I was."

It took some time but she drew away from the fetish scene, shed Betty Page, stopped the drinking and drugs. And finally, many years later, she threw out all her high heel shoes. She tells me, "The crunch point came when I got terrible back pain and I went to see a specialist. He said I had a herniated vertebra. It was from all those years in those extreme high heels – the way they make you stand, make your spine contort, that's what did the damage."

Bev pauses, reflecting. "I don't regret any of it. It was fun and wild. And I did feel powerful and sexy. It was great! It just wasn't sustainable."

She smiles. "I live my life as me now. I'm still mischievous and up for a good laugh. But I feel grounded and empowered without having to dress up or pretending to be anybody other than who I am. I wear flat shoes and I think I look great in them."

* * *

Foot-binding in China slowly came to end over a fifty year period in the early part of the 20th century. An edict abolishing it was issued in 1911 and this time, unlike the edict of 1644, this new prohibition took hold. Revolution was in the air across Europe, Russia as well as the Far East. In China, new fashions, new music, new theatre – and new ideas - from outside were pouring in, especially through the major cities like Shanghai. This was the time of the suffragettes in Western countries and socialist ideals calling for equality and justice across all classes and genders. Modernity was exciting and sexy.

Sexier than bound feet.

Women stopped binding their daughter's feet in the cosmopolitan cities but it took another fifty years for the practice to come to a complete end across the vast country, especially among isolated, rural communities. There are old women alive today who still hobble on bound feet.

For women whose feet were already broken, they could not simply unbind them. It was an irreversible process that destroyed the shape, bones and muscles in the feet. Removing the bandages left the feet structureless – and useless.

So they have had to live out their lives in an age of freedom still bound to a tradition that had no more value. Worse than that, it was a tradition that came to be derided and in those decades of tumultuous change, it was a new shame they had to face for bearing on their bodies this symbol of an outdated world. In the violence that came with the communist uprising, their feet gave away their aspirational sentiments and elitist values immediately, whether they were rich or poor. And on those tiny, broken feet, they were the ones who could not run from the raging masses in this ideological revolution.

* * *

Most of what we know about foot-binding – its allure, its political and nationalistic role, its role in creating the Exemplary Woman – comes from the voices of men.

It is men who are the writers of the erotica, the categorisers of the different shapes and types of bound feet, the pontificators on the civilizing influence of foot-binding, the champions of the Exemplary Woman.

The women who bound their feet and their daughter's feet for a thousand years remain largely silent. They spoke about it – if at all - only in private, in words that were passed from mother to daughter, vanishing in the moment they were said out loud. Their voices were ephemeral, passing like a moment in time, even as their feet were destroyed for eternity. How many thousands? How many hundreds of thousands – millions, even – of women had bound feet in a nation as vast as China in a time span of a millennia?

The silence of all those women, their acquiescence, their utter belief in it and attachment to it for all those generations – it leaves me awe-struck and filled with terror.

What destructive traditions keep us mute? What self-imposed limitations do we acquiesce to? What unforgiving norms do we utterly believe in and remain attached to?

Today, it is modern women's voices who have kept the image of the bound foot in our consciousness. Writers like Wang Ping, Shirley See Yan Ma, Lisa See, Jung Chang. And me.

There remains a fascination with bound feet in both East and West. Lisa See's novel *Snowflower and the Secret Fan*, about two friends in 19th century China with bound feet, became a bestseller and hit movie. People remember vividly the section in Jung Chang's *Wild Swans* describing foot binding. Photographer Jo Farrell's project to photograph the last women in China with bound feet was splashed across international news and magazines. The mere mention of the title of my show – and this book - piques interest.

The fact that foot-binding is a defunct practice takes away the urgency and rage that we might feel in the face of an ongoing practice like female genital mutilation. We recognise in bound feet a powerful symbol for the price that women pay for beauty and acceptance. And that, as a symbolic metaphor, can allow us to reflect what it means to be a woman – whether in the context of the West or in other cultural traditions across Africa and the rest of the world.

At the same time, the allure of the sex and violence inherent in bound feet remains. The obsession of the men discomforts us as with any fetishization. The silence of the women lures us in as with any mystery. And despite all that has been written about it by us modern women – us outspoken, big-footed, independent-minded modern, un-Exemplary Women who stride about in the world thinking ourselves equals of men – with our ideas about the social, psychological, economic, political, genderised, historical and a myriad of other reasons that foot-binding occurred and lasted for a thousand years, there remains at the core of it all, the enigma that continues to beguile us. Even as we may understand all those reasons intellectually, we still find it difficult in our beings to understand why all those millions of women clung so single-mindedly to such a brutal manifestation of their womanhood.

* * *

I perform *Bound Feet Blues* barefoot. Although it is subtitled *A Life Told in Shoes* and different types of shoes are mentioned throughout the show, as they are here in the book, no actual shoes are presented for the audience on stage. This creative choice emphasises that the shoes – and feet - are a metaphor. It becomes intensely powerful in the three scenes that start this Chapter as both metaphor and literal image. When the audience sees my bare feet, the vulnerability and fragility of feet – their own feet as much as mine - become more poignant, especially in contrast to the contortions that my left hand goes through transforming into the Golden Lotus.

In rehearsals for the show beyond the Conway Hall scratch night, director Jessica Higgs put me through a process known as "hot-seating" to help me find the character of the bound foot mother in the scenes that start this Chapter. We gave the mother a name, Mei. Jessica would ask me questions and I was to answer them in the persona of Mei, the bound foot mother.

Sitting upright and still, as Mei, I felt her to be an aloof, aristocratic woman who had married well and was certain of her class and her world. She was the queen of her household domain, the envy of her social circle, a good wife and mother. In the first hot-seating attempt, I – or rather, Mei – experienced Jessica's questions as impertinent and invasive. In my mind, we were living at the turn of the century with a new world order of motor cars and railways encroaching on the old ways. Out of nowhere, I - Mei - had decided that this person asking so many questions was of a lower class and had come into my home, this symbol of decorum and all that was right in the Confucian world, to criticize and demean it for a modern audience out there who did not understand or value my traditions and the traditions of generations of my family. I was dismissive, defensive and refused to answer any questions.

It was curious. Even as I, Yang-May, wanted to take part in

this hot-seating process for the sake of my performance and for the sake of the show, Mei had decided she was having none of it. Neither Jessica nor I understood her defensiveness at this point.

We tried again. This time, Jessica suggested that Mei, with her good breeding and perfect manners, would make this person feel welcome and want to help her understand Mei's life. Things went along better. Mei described her life in her beautiful house, embroidering, arranging flowers, creating a beautiful life for her husband. She talked about her children and the need for discipline and focus. I sat in an upright chair, with my bare feet tucked under me. Jessica sat opposite also in an upright chair. She was wearing shoes.

As her questions turned towards my – Mei's - feet and foot-binding, I suddenly became very aware of my naked feet. I felt a surge of emotion take hold of me. Tears welled up in my eyes. I couldn't speak. I did not want to. This was none of her business. I didn't want her looking at my feet. I wasn't going to talk about foot-binding. I pulled my feet further under the chair. I felt shame, as if the questions had reached into my jeans and were probing the most intimate part of being a woman.

Jessica stopped the exercise. Mei's instinctive defensiveness made sense now. No matter that the questions were neutral – sympathetic even – she had experienced them as invasive. It was almost as if I, the modern woman, had understood something at a primal level that I had not grasped intellectually before. Mei had needed to protect herself. Her feet. Her nakedness. Her essence as a woman.

Had we touched ephemerally at the core of foot-binding? Was this why these generations of women continued the practice even as they lived out their lives as voluntary cripples and their daughters shrieked in pain? And why they stubbornly carried on even when imperial edict declared it should be stopped?

It was beyond anything rational or logical. Beyond making a good marriage, beyond fitting into the norm, beyond economics or nationalist fervour. Beyond all those reasons that we might think or hypothesise or analyse.

Their very identity was bound up in their feet. For Mei and those generations of women like her, their delicate, beautiful, contorted tiny feet had become the essence of who they were as women. They felt about their feet as you and I might feel about that most private part of our bodies, where our womanhood resides in all its warm, moist intimacy. And to make them unbind that part of them, to lay it bare for all the world to see, to claim that that most integral part of who they were was just like a man's – would have been an annihilation of their very selves.

The experience transformed my performance. The ambivalence that I had personally felt about foot-binding and my own sense of horror and distaste was gone. In its place, was a certainty and confidence in the Confucian world view and my – Mei's – role within it. In the writing, I had given voice to her and all those silent women from foot-binding's golden age. In the performance, I let her reveal and revel in her pride and power - as a mother and wife and a sexual being. And more than that, she is an advocate for her culture and the choices that she and the generations of women before her have made. Because she is not just Mei – she is not even just me – she is all of us women, claiming our lives as best we can within this time and this place, wherever we may find ourselves, in this the only world we can ever know.

For, if we were wrong about the choices we have made, if the person we have suffered so much to become is no more than a construct, an idea, a whim that could be given up in an instant – what then? Who are we then?

Kok-kok shoes

BOUND FEET BLUES – THE STORY

TOMBOY

[As ten year old:]

I'm ten years old in Malaysia.
At home, I don't like wear shoes. I love to feel the warm wooden floor in the bedroom, the cold tiles in the hallway and the prickle of grass in the garden.
I have short hair. I like to play soldiers. I have a green helmet and a canteen and I love my toy gun
I'm Bruce Lee...
I'm John Steed with his bowler hat and brolly.
There's Emma Peel – with her long hair and catsuit and knee high boots.
I don't want to be Emma Peel
I don't want to be a girl.
I want to be a boy.
I should have been a boy.

[As adult me looking back:]

In my family, there's a story that everyone knows. This is how my Aunty Diana tells it.

[As Aunty Diana:]

So, May-May, in Chinese tradition, when a man and woman get married and they want to have a son – and every Chinese family wants an eldest son - on the wedding night, they get a young boy to roll on the marital bed. That way, his boy essence passes to the bed and when the newly married couple go onto the bed to, you know – the boy essence passes to them and that is how you make a son.

You don't believe me? It's true!

So on the night of your parents wedding, there is a big party at your grandparents' house. I am nine years old and your Aunty Leng is eleven and we are so excited to be at the party with all the grown ups. The party comes to an end, late at night and it is the job of your Great Aunt No. 3 – your *Sahm Koo* – to be responsible for this significant ritual. She finds a baby boy, one of the nephews – he is all sleepy - and she picks him up and carries him upstairs to the marital bedroom. All the guests follow to witness this significant ritual.

We follow also *lah*. We are so excited to be part of this ritual. We push through the legs and we pop out in the bedroom, in front of *Sahm Koo*.

And there is the bed, big and empty, waiting for something to happen.

So we jump onto the bed – we are so excited, and we are giggling and rolling around.

But the grownups are like: "Aiya, get off! No, no – we don't want girls. This is not for girls! You spoil it all, you spoil it all! You are so naughty and disobedient. So shameful for girls to be on the bed." And they shoo us off the bed and we are crying and we feel so ashamed.

Sahm Koo puts the baby boy on the bed but it's too late. The ritual is spoilt.

[As adult me looking back:]

So I was born, eldest daughter instead of eldest son. When I am three years old, my sister is born. And then when I am four – yes, my parents had to wait four long years –my brother is born. He was the precious boy and he became the eldest son. Two girls, then a boy. See – the ritual does work!

It's when I am four that I know for the first time that I should have been a boy.

[Adult me looking back to being a four year old:]

I've got pigtails and I'm wearing a fluffy white dress. I'm wearing white socks and little white shoes with pearl buttons on the side. I look at myself and I see this girl, this worthless girl. And I feel ashamed. I'm a disappointment. Everybody is over there fussing over my brother. Nobody sees me.

But I know I'm not worthless. I can't be worthless. I can't be just a worthless girl

I am the eldest son. I should be the eldest son. It's just that they can't see me because I'm dressed like this stupid girl.

So the next time my mother tries to make me wear a dress I scream and struggle and try to run away. I want to be like a boy, with short hair and boy clothes and boy shoes. My mother is weak and she pities my pain. And so she cuts my hair and lets me wear boy clothes and boy shoes.

I love my boy shoes. They are strong and sturdy and they have these fantastic laces. They go *kok kok kok* when I walk. Just like my Grandpa's shoes. Everybody respects Grandpa, with his smart suit and pipe and kok kok shoes that give him power and glamour and authority.

But the family – Grandpa, Grandma, my uncles and aunties – when they see me, they are angry with me: it's so shameful for a girl to dress like a boy. You are so naughty and disobedient.

I don't understand. I thought they wanted an eldest son. Look, I want to say, I'm here, I'm your eldest son.

But I don't have the words.

PONDAN

[Adult me looking back:]

By the time I am ten, I'm wearing boy clothes at home.

But at school, I have to dress like a girl. I have this navy pinafore thing but its ok because at least I don't have to wear girl shoes. I can wear my white rubber shoes – you know, like sports shoes.

There's a woman who works at the canteen at school. She is big and fat and has short hair. She wears man's clothes and man's shoes. We are having lunch, me and my school friends.

One of them says, "Eeee, look at that *pondan* – the queer. You don't go near her. I hear stories – you go near her and she touch you down there-one. We go, Eeeey, so shameful."

And the woman must know we are staring at her and laughing at her.

Another one says, "*Geelllee* – makes me sick. So shameful for a woman to wear man's clothes. There must be something wrong with her. They should put her in that hospital for all the mad people, Tanjong Rambutan, and never let her out."

I don't know if what they are saying is true or not. But it doesn't matter. They think it's true.

But all I see are the woman's sad and lonely eyes.

I stay sitting with my friends. I listen to them laughing. I think about my family's disappointment and shame when they look at me. Is that me, there, that *pondan* with short hair and man's shoes?

So over time, I give up my *kok kok* shoes – and all the power and glamour that they mean to me. I give up Bruce Lee and John Steed.

I hide my shame and I bind up my spirit of rebellion and defiance. With obedience, submission and endurance, I bind up my tomboy energy and I break its bones, cut down the eldest son and bind the bandages tighter and tighter till there is nothing left but a heart that is tiny and broken.

And over it all, I put on a beautiful, embroidered disguise. I'm twenty-five. I'm in London. I'm a lawyer. It's the 80s. I have incredible, amazing power hair. I have beautiful clothes and beautiful *tik-tok tik-tok shoes*:

A pair of navy Gucci pumps, red wedges with white trim, white wedges with blue trim, delicate Italian slip-ons in a two toned black, tan sling backs with killer heels and - knee high boots like Emma Peel.

All the men in my social circle see a woman who is feminine and desirable.

And this is my power.

These lovely young men who are good looking and tall - they are lawyers and bankers and have CVs that would make my family swoon. We go to the theatre and the opera and host dinner parties together. They can cook and keep house and they are kind and sweet. They would make such perfect husbands.

And every moment is an agony.

It is her they love, the China Doll – with her beautiful hair and beautiful clothes and beautiful little shoes.

I see my life stretching out ahead of me for so many long, long years. How many tiny painful moments does it take to make a long, long life?

How will I endure it?

I cannot scream or struggle or run away. My world is so tiny now, bound up inside this disguise.

Looking out from this broken place, I wonder – will anyone ever see me?

Will I ever dare let anyone see me?

THE STORIES BEHIND THE STORY

The revolver was heavy in my hands, heavier than I expected it to be. I had to use both hands to steady my aim. Even then, the gun wavered as I tried to line up the sight.

We were in scrubland somewhere outside Taiping, the old colonial town where my Grandpa and Grandma Lim lived. It was late afternoon and the hot tropical sun was giving way to the cool evening. The hills that embraced the town were a misty blue in the distance. Here, the jungle had been cleared for tin mining generations ago and now the sandy husk of the depleted landscape was being reclaimed by tropical grasses and shrubs.

It was the school holidays. I was thirteen. It was December 1976. We had come to stay for a few weeks as usual with my mother's parents in her old hometown. My uncles and aunt were there and my baby cousin as well as my parents. With everyone there in convivial mood, this Christmas as a special treat, Grandpa had brought us out here with a collection of his guns to give us a taste of shooting. We did not know then that it would be the last Christmas we would have with Grandpa.

I fired off a shot and the recoil kicked the pistol up and back. The shot reverberated across the empty bushland.

I had missed the old bottle Grandpa had set up on a ridge of rubble and sand.

We all took our turn. It was exciting to hear each gunshot crack the still afternoon, its rolling boom echoing out across the old tin mine. I wanted to have another go, keep trying till I could hold the gun with ease and shatter the Coke bottle with one unwavering bullet.

After the revolver, Grandpa brought out his rifle. It was slender and sleek in my hands. But again – so much heavier than it looked. He showed me how to load the next round, pulling the hand grip on the barrel towards me – there was a satisfying *ka-chunk* just

Shooting with Grandpa Lim

like in the movies. And then I was lifting it up, my left arm thin and spindly in front of me, my right arm awkwardly kinked as I tried to hold the stock against my shoulder. The barrel swayed this way and that the longer I worked to line up the two sights, my arms tiring too easily.

Blam!

Missed again.

But the power of the rifle in my hands, the recoil against my shoulder, the explosion of sound and the ringing in my ears... It was thrilling!

Grandpa and his brothers, my great-uncles, and their sons all went shooting for snipe and other birds in the jungle around Taiping. Between them, they had an array of rifles and shotguns. Grandpa had a pack of black Labradors and he would pick his favourites to go on those outings with them, the dogs leaping eagerly into the back of the old station-wagon. My brother was still too young to go with the men folk on these trips. My father went along once but was too much of a city slicker to enjoy trudging around in the swampy heat.

If I had been a boy, at thirteen, I would have been old enough to go hunting with Grandpa. I would have been man enough too, I was sure of it.

Inside, I was Clint Eastwood, six foot tall and chomping on a cheroot, swaggering into desert towns in beat-up cowboy boots that *chinked* with spurs as I walked. I was William Shatner, golden bronzed and broad chested, boldly going where no man had been before, a maverick led by his passions.

But to everyone outside, I was just a rebellious teenage girl. I lived in a pair of old white Bata trainers. I had a lanky bob and square gold rimmed glasses, a gawky stoop to hide my breasts and a gangly, awkward manner.

So I had to stay home.

At dinner time, as we nibbled at the fresh, tasty meat of Grandpa's birds in soy sauce and spices, I would see the jungle and vines and hear the gunshots felling these little trophies that should have been mine.

* * *

Grandpa loved playing rough and tumble with us when we were little kids. As soon as we had any co-ordination, he would hold our feet in one hand and balance us like an upright skittle in front of him while my mother freaked out quietly in fear that he might drop us. He held us up on his shoulders, carried us there like sacks of rice. He hung us upside down as we squealed and giggled. Sitting in an armchair, he bounced us in the hammock made by his checkboard *sarong*. He would lie on the floor and make us walk along his spine on his bare back, our tiny feet giving him a gentle massage. It made him laugh to let us have a suck on his pipe, the smoke sweet and acrid at the same time in our mouths, the bowl comfortingly hot in our cupped hands. He would grab us and cuddle us, giving us wet, tobaccoey kisses on our cheeks as we struggled and shrieked with laughter.

He was the essence of everything male and powerful and vigorous.

Gun dog Sally with my mother

There is an old black and white photograph of my mother taken when she is about five years old. She is grinning widely in a white fluffy dress and a giant bow in her hair. Beside her is a perky black cocker spaniel. "That's Sally," my mother would tell us. "She was my dog. She was loving and faithful and such a good dog. We all loved Sally."

She was one of Grandpa's favourite hunting dogs. The brightest and most loyal, always by his side on his shooting trips and the fastest to retrieve his game.

On one hunting trip, Grandpa did not come home as he

usually would have done just after sunset. It was a familiar story but my mother would tell it again as we looked at that photo of her with Sally – and we listened to it again, like a comforting litany. Grandma, and the whole family, waited up anxiously for him. "We were all so worried, don't know what can have happened. And then when he finally got home," my mother said, "It was late, late at night. He was soaking wet all over and he was crying."

It had been the last shot of the day. It was getting dark and they were heading out of the jungle back to the car. Sally had leapt into a river to retrieve the bird. The water was fast flowing and swirling, more so than usual. He had seen her bobbing head for a moment and then she was gone.

He raced up to the water's edge. She was nowhere to be seen. Without a thought for anything beyond Sally, he plunged into the river, shouting for her. Again and again, he dived into the dark, rushing water, swimming down into the depths, desperately looking for her. As the sudden night of the tropics fell, he stayed on in the water, drifting downstream, diving, shouting, hoping against hope to find Sally, his loyal companion, his daughter's beloved dog.

During the war, when the Japanese invaded Malaya, he had joined the medical corps. Leaving Grandma and their two little girls - my mother was a toddler at that time and my aunt still a baby – he would disappear for months. "I was so frightened," Grandma would tell us, sitting on her verandah as the blazing afternoon turned mellow ochre. "We didn't know where he was, whether or not he would come home safe."

Then late at night, he would be at the door, a stranger with a beard, gaunt and tired, home briefly before taking off again. We have no stories of what he did in all those months away, where he was, how many men he tried to save. Did he speak of that experience to Grandma, lying in her arms, clean shaven and fresh again? Or did he hold it all inside because careless talk cost lives and because to speak might be to open heart wounds that needed to remain sutured?

A few years ago, I was packing up my late uncle's house. He had died too early – my mother's youngest brother, the baby of them all – and just a year short of the age that Grandpa had died. I was his executor and I spent weeks after work in his tall empty house in Pimlico sorting through everything he had in the house, late into the night. He had become the custodian of all the Lim family papers and memorabilia after Grandma died, twenty years after her beloved Swee Aun. The attic was piled high with boxes. There were letters, cuttings, Grandpa's awards and plaques, photo albums, diaries, files. Sitting amongst these boxes of history, I pulled out a roll of canvas.

It was heavy. There seemed to be long thin items inside, like chopsticks rolled into an apron. In the yellow electric light, the canvas seemed khaki in colour and stained in brown. I undid the cloth ties and unrolled the canvas there on the wooden floorboards.

It was a set of surgeon's tools – scalpels and strange instruments I did not recognise. They gleamed, clean and bright in this London evening, oddly shiny against the old, battered canvas. For a moment, I stared at them blankly. And then I knew what this was. It was Grandpa's medical kit from "Japanese time", as Grandma called the Japanese Occupation of Malaya. The khaki was Army khaki. And the brown…I realised then that it was blood, soaked into the material. The blood of soldiers he had tried to save.

I pictured him at home, after the war, cleaning and polishing his instruments and carefully sliding each one into its proper place in the resting place. Rolling up that blood stained kitbag, tying the ties and putting it all away. And rolling up with it the wounds his hands had dug into, the faces of the men he had worked on, the noise of gunfire, the cries of pain, his own fear and loss and not knowing if he would see his family again.

So many stories.
And there was only silence in that drafty, wintery attic.

* * *

One of the few stories we have direct from Grandpa is the story of the Bandit Boy. On the hissy tape recording of his voice that December of 1976, the story he tells is an epic that spans generations. He is careful to note the names of the ancestors clearly for us. He knows he is recording this for posterity. He speaks deliberately and there is a hint of Churchill's gravitas.

All the other stories we know about him come from Grandma or my mother. It is the women who are garrulous of the heart. The men speak and laugh but their hearts are silent, protected.

In Chinese tradition, only the eldest son can worship at the ancestors altar and be the conduit between the living and the dead. In this way, a family remains connected through time for generations upon generations. The dead taking a protective interest in their living descendants, negotiating with the gods, working the back channels of the unseen world to bring good fortune to their children and grandchildren and great-grandchildren. In return, the living pay their respects to their ancestors through offerings and prayers and riches sent through to the other side. And it is the eldest son who is the high priest of these transactions. It is he who holds the two worlds together.

That is why the Chinese are obsessed with having a son. Because without a son, the ties between the past and the present are severed. The dead are trapped in the other world, lost and diminished in their power without the gifts and prayers. They become dispossessed without the regular care packages sent from the living. And the family comes to a literal end. After so many generations of men, a single generation of daughters drops them all off a cliff. A daughter cannot carry the family name. She marries out into another man's family and is lost forever to her own. Her existence is not recorded in the family records. She has no voice, no right to speak – and certainly not to the dead.

And yet, it is us daughters who know how to speak from the heart. We are the ones who carry the family stories as we carry its children. Tears do not frighten us. An aching heart does not incapacitate us. We notice the little things – another's mood, small charming moments, what someone wore, the food they like to eat. We make stories out of anything and everything. We dare to shed tears. We dare to cry and lay bare our aching hearts. While our men have been taught to be afraid of sorrow and pain and to shut themselves into silence for fear of them. They learn to be all *yang* – analytical and rational and in their heads, quoting stats and staying on the hard surface of things. For some, they may be lucky enough to find a woman who can create a safe haven for them to undress their silent hearts and it will be only to her that they will reveal their tenderest, most fragile selves. But for others, they may not be so fortunate or trusting and for them, there can only be safety in silence.

What do all these eldest sons say to their ancestors? Kneeling there at the threshold of the dead, joss sticks in hand, how do they use this opportunity?

I think of those weekly calls home from boarding school to my parents in Malaysia. And all those calls now from my home in London to them back in Kuala Lumpur. My mother and I will chat away and share all our news from the important stuff to the inconsequential and small tender moments of the heart. And then she'll say, "Here, talk to your father."

And he'll come on the line and we'll stare into the awkward silence across the thousands of miles.

"So…" he says after a while, "How's the weather?"

I imagine all those eldest sons, dutifully at their ancestral altars, waving the incense in their clasped hands, kneeling down before their fathers and forefathers in a posture of the greatest respect. I picture them thinking anxiously: at least as the younger generation, it's not for us to speak first and we can wait here in silence.

And out of the void, the ancestral voice of the males of the clan speaks at last. "So…" it says, "How's the weather?"

Sit us at the crossing place between our two worlds, we mothers and daughters both alive and dead, and such stories we could tell! How we would weep and laugh and speak of all the things that men would leave unsaid, the important stuff and the small tender moments of the heart.

But perhaps that is why we chatty women are banned from this ritual of ghostly communication. Perhaps if an eldest daughter were to kneel before the ancestral altar with her questions and chatter about hopes and joys and tenderness, it might upset the tranquil order of the world.

In response to the ancestral enquiry, the eldest son might give a review of the weather fronts in the last month and speculate about the coming frost. Ancestor and descendant might discuss the stock market, how Manchester United is doing, what's in the news, the long view of the family: births, deaths, graduations and the like. And they would feel a sense of continuation and kinship across the void. But put a daughter there asking about feelings and what it is like over the other side, the ancestors might have to look at their own deadness and the loss and grief of infinite separation. There would be bound to be tears and confessionals of some nature or other. And it would all be horribly awkward.

At that time, aged thirteen and hunching angrily over my growing breasts, angry at my period pains and heavy bleeding that made it clear why it was the Curse, angry at my acne and oily hair, angry at not being allowed to wear *kok-kok* shoes, angry at having to put on a frock every Christmas, angry at everyone and everything, I did not see that tears and pain and an open heart could be my trophies, that words and talking and stories could be where true power lay.

I saw only what I could not have.

Only men could smoke pipes, as Grandpa and my uncles did. Only men could stand with their legs apart and sit with one ankle up on the other knee. Men took up space in the room. They were listened to, deferred to. Seen and heard.

When the boy cousins came of age, they were allowed to hike

with the older men through the jungle to the grave of the Bandit Boy to pay their respects on the Feast Day of the Hungry Ghosts, an annual Chinese ritual to honour the dead. "It's dangerous for girls," the family would tell me when I pestered them to take me, too. "It's far away from anywhere, very difficult to get to-lah. Bad people can come there."

I loved the succulent meat of chicken legs but I had to make do with the bland white breasts. "Legs are for boys, one, because they walk out into the world," I would be told. "Girls have the breast meat because they take care of the little ones." That never made sense to me other than as a good wheeze to give the best cuts of meat to the men.

In family chatter round the dinner table, I would throw in my thoughts and no-one would hear. Then my brother would chime in saying pretty much the same thing and suddenly, everyone would be amazed at how clever he was. "But I said that first," I would cry and it would be like bird song in the wind.

Only the boys would carry on the family name, their identity remaining unchanged whether they married or not. They belonged to no-one. They owned who they were and passed on a part of themselves into history. I could only ever be someone's daughter or someone's wife or someone's mother.

But then I found that in my little adventure stories in those old exercise books, I could become a Someone.

Many of those stories were in the third person, about beautiful young women and handsome young men entangled in murder, mystery, adventure and suspense. But there was a special place in my heart for the 'I' narrator. 'I' was always a young man who could shoot a gun, win a fist fight, protect the heroine and outwit the villain. 'I' was broad shouldered, muscular, strong, bold. Many years later, when Matt Damon whizz-banged his way through the Bourne movies, it was like watching that old 'I' come to life before my eyes.

My stories were an escape and a becoming. For the few hours that I sat at my desk by the window, looking out at the flame tree

Soldier "boy" with my pal from next door

in the garden, I could escape my gangly, weedy female body and my sense of being a stranger in strange land. I was no longer 'just a girl', no longer that lazy, naughty, disobedient disappointment to the family. I was the person I wanted to be – someone one who laughed with his gang of friends, who was loved by a beautiful woman, who loved deeply in return, who was confident in who he was, who knew what he wanted, who could win the day. Someone who wore sturdy boots and tough shoes he could run and kick and fight in. They were stories about men like Grandpa – only younger, before they became fathers or grandfathers. They were *Boys' Own* stories – but written with a girl's heart.

In my stories, 'I' and I – we could hide in plain sight.

* * *

The only other story I remember Grandpa telling was the story of the kidnapping and how he came to own a revolver.

It was during the Emergency, that period after the Second World War when communist factions in Malaya were fighting to overthrow British rule which had already been destabilized by the war and the wobbly economic climate of the post war years. They used guerrilla tactics, emerging to create havoc and fear and then retreating into the safety of the jungle. Most infamously, the British High Commissioner was killed in an ambush on his convoy on a winding road to the hill station, Fraser's Hill.

Those others who thrive in chaotic times also took advantage of the instability, especially with the armed forces and police distracted. There were shootings and assassinations of rivals, armed robberies and kidnappings.

Grandpa by that time was a prominent member of the community in the small town of Taiping. He was involved in local politics and a well-respected GP with a thriving practice. It was clear that he was well off, with a large extended family - including his own immediate family, his father and his father's several wives, his siblings and their children – all living in a large extended house. The family owned property and land and an orchard of *rambutan* trees.

One morning, Great-grandfather – Grandpa's father and son of the Bandit Boy – sat in the orchard watching the many children from his many wives picking the small, red hairy fruit from the trees. Some of them were up in the branches reaching the topmost fruits, others on the ground with gunny sacks gathering up clusters from the grass. They were laughing and chattering and life was good.

Suddenly, armed men emerged from the surrounding forest and rounded up the family.

"Come here!"

"You don't run or I shoot!"

"Don't move!"

The children and young menfolk of the family clustered together, circled by the men. Great-grandfather sat on his stool, a gun to his head.

Uncle Willie, a small wiry teenager then, watched it all from high up in one of the trees. He had been trying to reach a cluster of *rambutans* just too far up. The men did not see him, hidden amongst the thick leaves. He climbed slowly down and slipped away in the shade of the dark trees. He ran the several miles back into town, weeping in terror.

"*Tai Koh*! Eldest brother!" he shrieked as he burst into Grandpa's surgery.

By the time Grandpa reached the orchard with the police, Great-grandfather was gone.

In the version of the story I remember, the whole family waits at home together, anxious and not knowing what might come next. The police hunt down information from informants and known gangland contacts. And then a masked pair on a motorcycle zip by, throw something into the compound.

It contains instructions for the ransom drop.

There is a chase and shoot out through the seedy side of town. How does that come about? Perhaps the police zoom after the bikers. Perhaps the informants turn up a lead. The police run down the suspects in the tight, dark alleyways, feet racing through the shophouses, gun fire and bullets ricocheting off grimy walls. Grandpa follows them, he needs to be there, cannot sit at home.

A gang member lies bleeding in an upstairs room of a shop house, fatally wounded from a police bullet. Grandpa pushes past the officers. Is the man still alive? Grandpa bends over him, instinctively and always the doctor honouring his oath to save a life. And as he works on the wound, he pleads, "Where is my father? Tell me, where is my father."

The man says nothing. He only screams and writhes in pain.

And then is still.

The ransom note tells them a time and place and an amount. Grandma, it specifies, must take a rickshaw and come with the money. Alone.

I see Grandpa there at home, covered in a dead man's blood. Distraught and anxious about his father but trying not to let it show. His father may never come home. And now they want his wife in harm's way. "I cannot let you do this," I hear him saying.

I see Grandma there, still and elegant in her day *cheongsam*.

Around them is his family – Grandpa's family. Her family now. Great-grandfather's three surviving wives and Grandpa's fourteen brothers and sisters.

She sees Grandpa's pain and his love. She sees his family's hope and their fear. She sees her own children – my mother and my aunt and two uncles, still kids.

She makes a decision. God will provide. And I imagine her saying, simply. "I must."

On a lonely road flanked by encroaching jungle, the rickshaw stops at the appointed place. I imagine it to be a straight stretch with a long line of sight so that the gang can see who might have followed her. I picture Grandma sitting in the passenger basket in her *cheongsam*, a battered black doctor's bag on her lap. The cash is inside. The rickshaw rider is a policeman. He stands by the saddle, smoking, tensely watchful. The sounds of the jungle swing and sway around them.

She waits. But no-one comes.

Somehow, later, the police track down the gang to an isolated shack somewhere in the jungle outside Taiping. Grandpa is with them, hoping against hope that this is the place where they are holding his father. There is another shoot-out. It is chaotic, loud, figures running and darting through the trees. Grandpa moves away from the squad cars, edging his way to the shack. Is his father in there? Can he get to him while the gang are distracted in the gunfight?

But when the smoke and the gunfire and the havoc die down, and the police burst into the shack, it is empty.

Grandpa stands in the dark hovel. He sees for himself the empty room. His heart lurches with horror and despair.

His father must be dead. They must have killed him and dumped the body somewhere. Or perhaps he is tied up in a place that no-one will ever find, waiting in the darkness forever.

Devastated, he heads back to the squad cars alongside the police officers.

There in the back seat of one of them is a bulky figure.

It is Great-grandfather, calmly waiting for his son, a beaming smile on his face.

In the chaos of the shootout, Great-grandfather had been left alone in the shack. So he got up and walked out of the door, making his way to the squad cars he could glimpse in the distance.

The police licensed Grandpa to own a revolver after the kidnapping. There were bodyguards for a while. But thankfully, they were never needed. Nor was the gun.

"No, I was never afraid, not for one minute," Great-grandfather would say to the family and anyone who asked him. "I knew my son would come for me."

* * *

It is the police chase, the shootouts, the whizz bang that we see vividly in this story. It is Grandpa as a man of action as well as a man of compassion and healing. It is the revolver that is the lasting artefact that we each were able to hold in our hands many years later.

Grandma's quiet courage is a minor plot point. But it is she who goes alone into the jungle with a solitary policeman, uncertain of the outcome. It is she who waits, exposed and vulnerable, in the flimsy rickshaw. She does it because it is the right thing to do. She trusts her life - and what that means for her children - to whatever her God will bring. Her stillness is heroic.

And it is only many years later, when I am grown up, that I see this power of the feminine.

As a child, battling against the failure of being a girl, I grasped after the masculine charisma that Grandpa had.

Grandpa and Grandma's story was the great love affair in our family history. He had the gruff, earthy manliness of Spencer Tracy and she had the handsome beauty and elegance of Katherine Hepburn, and just like that Hollywood power couple, their chemistry was palpable. As individuals, they were clever, capable and born to be leaders – Grandma within her Methodist church community and Grandpa as the head of his large, extended family and local networks. But together, they made history.

And I mean that literally.

After finishing medical school, Grandpa's first job was as a doctor at a leper hospital near his hometown of Taiping. Towards the end of their medical training, Grandma fell ill and had to step back from her studies for a year or more. By this time, they were engaged and she wanted to start a family so she decided not to return to college after her recovery. As Grandpa's new wife, she lived with him in quarters at the hospital and helped out – visiting with the patients and supporting them and their families in a non-medical capacity.

Later, after Grandpa set up his own medical practice in Taiping, they lived in one room of the large family house with the extended Lim household – Great-grandfather Lim, his three surviving wives and their children. Grandpa became active in local politics. Grandma led the women's community at church and conducted the choir. She volunteered as a prison visitor and at a boy's borstal. She hosted dinners and accompanied Grandpa on political visits. She translated his speeches into Chinese and helped him learn them in English, Malay and Chinese. He joined the Malaysian Chinese Association, a new political party formed in post-war Malaya as the country moved towards Independence. His role took him into national politics at a critical time in the nation's history. By the time, I was born he was the Minister for Commerce and Industry in the new cabinet on the eve of *Merdeka* – of Freedom.

Grandpa and Grandma moved to the capital Kuala Lumpur

and lived at the Minister's official residence near the *Agong's* – King's - palace. In the year that I was born, 1963, he was one of the six signatories of the Malaysia Agreement, a treaty with Britain that was Malaysia's Declaration of Independence. It created the nation of Malaysia and enshrined into perpetuity *Merdeka* Day on 31st August each year.

Representing Malaysia, developing trade links, encouraging inward investment, building a nation, Grandpa travelled across the country, across Asia and globally, Grandma by his side. He sat down with prime ministers, royalty, presidents. Grandma chatted with Eleanor Roosevelt and the Queen – and Imelda Marcos. She could hold her own at state dinners, seated alongside statesman and captains of industry. They were friends with the great names in Malaysian history - the father of the country and first Prime Minister *Tunku* Abdul Rahman and his successors *Tun* Abdul Razak Hussein and *Tun Hussein bin Dato'* Onn – as well as the King and the Sultans of the different Malaysian states. They played golf with the leaders of industry, business and politics. My parents' wedding in 1962 was splashed across the news and anyone who was anyone in the new Malaysian political ruling class was there.

He was the love of Grandma's life. They rarely spent a night apart. In her later years, she would tell us a little coyly that she would put a dab of lipstick on before going to bed so she always looked beautiful for him. She would fall asleep in his arms every night.

"If you argue," she would advise us, "You must never go sleep in another room. Always must sleep back in your bed together. Because why? You are angry at first and don't want to touch. Then at night, you are sleeping and you touch each other by accident – then you touch maybe not by accident, then a little bit, a little bit, you make up-lah."

She was happy to be by his side, to create the safe heart and home space for him to soar. She was proud of him, helped him in his work, made him shine, adored him. She made him possible.

The body language says it all – yes, they are both me

But it was he was the one with the accolades, the trophies, the title – *Tan Sri* (equivalent to the British "Sir") – and national and international respect. He stepped out into the world of work and action and making a difference.

Like my father, in his dark suit and tie, heading off to his law office every day to make deals, advocate, make his mark in the world. In legal circles in Kuala Lumpur, Dad made his name as a fierce, super-clever lawyer – known about town as the one-eyed lawyer who could make you tremble with a glare. He started out as a junior lawyer in a big corporate firm, built his experience in a small partnership and in an American bank and finally set up on his own. Today, he is one of the most respected senior lawyers in the capital, still working in his seventies and consultant to the major players in Malaysian business.

Wanting to be a boy, for me, was wanting all those things that I saw that the men in my family had. Without words, all I knew was that there was something desirable in the square angular look of men's clothing and their slow sound of their deliberate walk, their deeper voices, their short capable hair. I watched with the eyes of a child as the women focused on *them*, on *their* needs, on *their* glory. For the women, their whole world seemed to their husband. I watched as *they* in turn focused on their sons, saw in the boys their potential for glory. I knew they loved us, the girls and women in their lives, but it seemed like a different kind of love. It was as if in looking at us, they saw only their best and most glorious selves reflected back – just as when you look in a mirror, you don't notice the mirror itself but only the image inside it.

It felt to me, that when they looked at me, they did not see me and my glory. And I wanted them so much to see that glory that waited shyly in my heart. I wanted them to coax it out, to coo and fuss over it as they did for my brother and as my mother and grandmother were doing for them. And because they did not, a bloody-minded tit-for-tat in me refused to let them see their glory in my eyes.

So when they looked at me what I gave them was a broken mirror.

They could not see in my eyes the respect they were due. I refused them obedience and silence but gave them sullenness and answering back instead. I upset the natural order of things with my short hair and boy's clothes, demanding what they had even as I showed my contempt for it. "Girls are better than boys," I would declare loudly. And yet, I wanted to claim the space of the hero and not the heroine, John Steed instead of Emma Peel, Grandpa rather than Grandma. Unable to articulate what I longed for, with no language to ask for what I needed from them, my glory coiled and twisted in on itself only to explode in raging, prolonged tantrums.

No matter how much I might scream that girls were better than boys, in Chinese tradition, that statement could never be true. Girls were not even equal to boys so how could it be conceivable that they might be better than them? The culture of a thousand years and more was in my family's DNA – even though we were

"I love my toy gun"

largely Christian and modern and Westernized and educated and no longer practiced foot-binding or caning of children and my grandparents and parents and extended family loved me as a family should. My mother and grandmother and aunties, female cousins and generations of women before me all willingly accepted their roles, thrived and revelled in their identities as wives and mothers and daughters.

What was wrong with me that I could not? Would not.

* * *

I had never seen a woman like her before. She stands arms akimbo in a black leather cat suit that seems painted on. Her left hip is kinked out, softening the masculine pose. In that picture, you cannot see her feet but I know that only kick-ass boots that have a masculine sturdiness will have given her that strutting stance. The cuffs of long sleeves are turned up, forming sharp black wings at her forearms. There is a light star shaped tattoo just above her right wrist. Manly studded rings deck her fingers. A drapery of heavy chains and metal necklaces pour down her chest.

The cat suit is unzipped all the way down to her belly button, revealing a plunging V of her pale bra-less torso.

Her hair has the soft but slightly masculine androgyny of the '70s. Her strong eyebrows contrast with the delicacy of her feminine lips. Her large pale eyes gaze out of the poster with defiant confidence.

Suzi Quatro.

I had never heard music like hers before. I was eleven and she was The Wild One, All Shook Up Down in Devil Gate Drive. In those days before the internet and Youtube, I read up everything I could about her from the teeny-bopper magazines. She was from Detroit. She lived in England. She was only 5 feet tall.

Listening to her music blast out from the tape recorder by my bed and hearing that huge raspy voice belt through the thrashing, shrieking rhythms, I could see her in my mind thrusting and striding and dominating an arena full of screaming fans. Was she really not much bigger than me?

Here was a woman I could see myself being.

What was it about *her* catsuit and *her* boots that were different from Emma Peel's?

At that time, the usual music that I loved was at the other extreme end of the charts from Suzi Quatro. The lush orchestration of the Carpenters with the sonorous caramel of Karen Carpenter's voice gave me the feel of sinking into a hot bath. I bopped along to early ABBA. The haunting guitars and earnest poetry of John Denver and Gordon Lightfoot opened up the vast North

175

American landscapes in my mind. But most of all, I adored the romantic ballads and the breathy caress of Olivia Newton-John.

Aah, ONJ - as I used to talk of her with my sister and my friends.

I loved ONJ's blonde, blue-eyed girl-next-door persona, her wide smile against her tan. She was fresh air and faded denim and meadows in summer sunlight. I knew most of her songs by heart, sang along to the numerous albums of hers I had. Stayed up late to watch her appear on the Cliff Richard Show, tore out photos of her from teen magazines, plastered the walls with posters of her.

This was music that my family could love, too. On long car trips, when we drove up to visit Grandma and Grandpa in Taiping or wound our way down to Port Dickson for a seaside holiday, I would bring my tapes and a portable tape player and play my music in the back of the car. Sometimes, we'd all sing along. We would talk about the stories in the ballads. Why did the girl kill her lover on The Banks of the Ohio? Why was it a shame that the man in Sundown gets feeling better when he's feeling no pain? At these times, I would chatter excitedly about these stories that intrigued me, these singers whom I loved and the music that moved my heart. We could all share in the music together and I forgot my armour.

And then there was Suzi, whose crashing sound tore through the safe, easy listening comfort like a fury.

My family didn't understand why I liked 'that noise'. Her leather and metal look unnerved them. So I listened to her on my own, the volume turned up till the air seemed to vibrate with the shrieking guitars.

Suzi Quatro was not really, truly scary. Her butch persona was tempered by an underlying sweetness. She stayed on just the right side of feminine.

So how was that different from Emma Peel in her butch but also feminine catsuit and tough but womanly kick-ass boots?

Women who straddled the canyon of gender fascinated me. I caught an old movie one afternoon where a young Katherine

Hepburn disguises herself as a boy. With her strong cheekbones and handsome face, she is jaw-droppingly attractive as a young man – and also as an androgynous woman. Google *Sylvia Scarlett* and you'll see what I mean. Later, after I came to England, I stayed up one half-term at my uncle's flat just to see the infamous Marlene Dietrich movie where she swaggers across a smoke filled bar in white tie and tails to flirt with both men and women, ending the scene with a teasing kiss on the lips of another beautiful woman. She has the angular shape of a lean man, the long masculine stride – and yet, she remains a woman in drag throughout. And there was Julie Andrews, as *Victor/ Victoria* – by then I was at Oxford and determinedly feminine. She was less convincingly masculine but there was something about Maria von Trapp in white tie and tails that confusingly sent my heart a-flutter.

Emma Peel was about being and staying a woman. She put on a catsuit to show off the shape of a woman. Her knee high, high heeled boots were those of a woman. She did not venture close to the edge of the gender precipice. Her sexuality remained safe – strong and feline, but safe.

Whereas Suzi Quatro, Marlene Dietrich and even Julie Andrews channelled a streak of masculine energy that made their femininity electrifying. They moved like men. They held your gaze like men. They took command like men. Their sexuality was unsettling.

I could hardly understand my own feelings but looking back, I can see it now.

I wanted to be Suzi Quatro. But I wanted to have Emma Peel.

* * *

I was transfixed. In the cocooning dark of the cinema, the lovers are luminescent giants on the screen. They are in the sumptuous robes of a mythical pre-Manchu China in a landscape that is at once stylised and lush with period detail. Their world overflows with a cast of thousands, peasants and scholars, rich folk and poor, expansive as the vastness of China and contained within the visually stunning backdrops of the Shaw Brothers studio sets. Cherry blossoms float through the air, red barrel-tiled Chinese roofs peak out above the mock Oriental streets, the shiny black hair of the women are piled in elaborate shapes and dripping with jade and gold, the men stride along in boat-shaped black and white cloth shoes and the women glide like angels without feet. The evocative semi-tones of Chinese opera swirl and clash in my ears, the singing voices of the hero and heroine nasal and high-pitched snake around me.

In the packed movie theatre, we were all as one being, laughing at the playfulness of the lovers' friendship at the beginning, intrigued as their friendship turns to love, hopeful when the heroine's secret identity is revealed, heartbroken when it is clear this cannot end well, despairing as their unrequited love irrevocably leads the lovers towards death. And finally, weeping with joy and sadness as they are united again as butterflies in the afterlife.

I was nine, perhaps ten. *The Butterfly Lovers*, one of the great folk legends of China, had been adapted into a film, *Love Eterne*, which was taking Asia by storm. It was an operatic musical in Mandarin with songs punctuating the spoken dialogue. The legend is as famous in the Chinese speaking world as *Romeo & Juliet* is in the West.

A young girl disguises as a boy – with the blessing of her family – to study at a famous academy. There 'he' meets a handsome, sensitive young man and they become the best of friends. Only 'he' falls in love with his best friend but cannot reveal how 'he' feels. After three years, our heroine must return home and her best friend walks with her part of the way – as they walk and talk, she tries to tell him that she is really a girl but our scholarly but dumb hero misses all the hints she is dropping.

As they part along the road, our clever heroine then tells him that he should meet 'his' sister and playing up the role of matchmaker, she invites him to be sure to visit her at home. Some time later, our hero comes to visit and is greeted by his pal's sister – our heroine dressed as herself. He is instantly attracted to her. She reveals to him that she had been in disguise all those years at college and she is in fact his best friend. Oh joy! He realises that he has loved her/ him all this time and now, it means they can marry and be together for all time.

Only – she is now betrothed to another by a marriage arranged by her father and she cannot shame her family by running off with the man she truly loves. They part devastated. Our hero dies of a broken heart. She hears the news on the day of her wedding and collapses. But she goes through with the wedding as she is duty bound to do.

The wedding procession passes our hero's grave. A tornado whips up and they cannot progress. She leaves the wedding group and goes to the grave. As she kneels and hugs the tombstone, weeping for her lost love, the storm builds and everyone is swept to the ground. Only she remains upright, clinging to the tombstone. The grave opens up and we see a glimpse of our handsome hero looking at her with love. She throws herself into the grave.

The storm subsides. And first one, and then another - two butterflies emerge, dancing in the still air. They circle each other, bobbing and touching and parting only to return to each other again, and gradually float off into the sunset.

So far so melodramatic. Yes, there is the frisson of the cross dressing in first half of the story with its touch of Shakespearean mistaken identity. Yes, there is the heightened emotion, the impossible love, the death of two star-crossed lovers. Yes, you might think, of course this operatic movie is going to hold a young tomboy would-be writer like me transfixed. But there are plenty of over-wrought, heightened, sensationalist dramas with these kinds of themes – *Fidelio, Twelfth Night, The Merchant of Venice, West Side Story*… What's so special about this one? Why this movie?

Well, in this 1963 film version of the legend, the Hong Kong studio Shaw Brothers – the Far East equivalent of MGM – cast a woman as the male lead.

Ivy Ling Po, as the scholar, adopts the exaggerated masculine moves of the male characters in Chinese opera. In her grey, manly robes, she widens her body, takes up space with her strong stance, strides and swaggers, kicking out her leg as she prepares to kneel on one knee. She sits with her legs splayed apart, hands on each knee. Her gestures are jagged, staccato, angular. And yet, she is undoubtedly a woman. Without make-up and with sharp heavy eyebrows, Ivy Ling Po looks like a cheeky tomboy. In contrast, the actress playing the heroine, even while disguised as a boy, Betty Loh Tih, retains the mannerisms of a girl. There is a slight glide to her walk, her gestures are more fluid and feminine and she does not impose herself into the space with the same confidence. When the heroine returns to her identity as girl, there is little change in Betty Loh Tih. Just a touch of make-up brightens her lips, her eyebrows take on a lighter, softer curve, her hair is displayed in an elaborate headdress and her movements remain flowing and floaty in slender, gentle shapes.

There is no attempt in either actress to modulate their voices to the deeper registers, remaining always vocally two women. The musical style of the film played to this vocal limitation, derived as it was from *huangmei* opera, a form performed primarily by women and originating from local folk songs sung by women as they picked tea leaves.

So what I – and everyone else in Asia - saw on the screen were two women falling in love with passion and intensity, two women who were soul mates and yet could not be together in life because of family and duty and sacrifice, two women whose impossible love re-united them in death as butterflies. Two women for whom an entire continent hoped, wept and rejoiced.

In the dark theatre, I laughed along to the play on the mistaken identity. I held my breath as our heroine tries to tell the scholar who she really is. But it is when the two meet as their own selves that my heart stopped.

There on the screen is a tomboy flirting with a beautiful

woman. They were falling in love, holding hands, embracing. The beautiful woman is looking at the tomboy in a way that no woman should look at another woman. It was breathtaking.

And then they are weeping, torn apart by tradition and family expectation. And when the beautiful heroine swoons at the news of her true love's death, I felt a thrill of despair and longing.

I longed to be looked at like that – and loved like that – by a beautiful woman.

* * *

A tomboy remains attractive if she stays on the right side of feminine. A woman channelling her masculine energy thrills us – so long as she is still available to men. Katherine Hepburn as Sylvia Scarlett, Marlene in white tie and tails, Julie Andrews as *Victor/ Victoria* are no more threatening than heterosexual women in disguise. Ivy Ling Po as the lovelorn scholar continues visibly to be a woman throughout.

So long as we remain on the femme side of butch, we remain safe. The hint of transgression offers a frisson and no more. We return always to the fold. We stay where we belong.

But if a woman steps too far into the realm of the masculine, she becomes scary.

The woman at my school canteen was too butch, too manly. From her manner, it was clear she did not care for men. She had stepped across the canyon of gender into their territory. She was not one of us – not a girl, not pretty, not willing to give herself up for the delight of a man. But neither was she one of them. She did not have their strength or an inborn demand for respect. Despite her rolling, wide legged walk, she did not have balls. And yet she dared to overstep… She was the Other and a freak.

And so we laughed at her. I laughed at her. Laughter made the world safe again for us. For me.

It was just a phase, this tomboy part of my life, I told myself.

Like the ugly duckling, I would become a beautiful swan. Just like all those other tomboy girls – those sporty, loud, cheeky, unruly, un-girly girls that I could see at school and on TV and read about in books. Like Jo March and Calamity Jane, I would pass through this ungovernable phase and then settle down in a white dress with a man. Anything else was unthinkable and horrifying.

In my twenties in London, presenting to the world a persona that I had created from an exhausting, driven act of will, I often felt I was in drag. While I was in Oxford, there had been a playfulness about being Her, this slinky young woman who could be smug and glamourous or dumb as they come depending on her audience of men. It had been fun to create Winnie or a *pontianak*-like vamp, to show off my suspenders and knickers reaching for the sky over the University Parks, to cuddle kitten-like in Josh's arms. But now in my mid-twenties, Josh was gone and I had been through several more beautiful men with impeccable credentials and volumes of ambition. The novelty at playing a part had worn off. She would be who I was going to be for the rest of my life.

Yes, I still enjoyed the chase – the flirtation, the coy smiles, the making eyes over drinks. I liked the way they looked at me with desire, appreciating my wild womanly hair, my delicate neck, my caramel skin, the dark chocolate buttons of my nipples just glimpsed under translucent white blouses, my slim hips, my small feet shown off in tiny little shoes. I liked making love with them, too, and the way they watched me, as I moved with them, sighing and coiling and crying out with the pleasure of it.

But afterwards, I would lie awake as they slept. It's like that feeling you get when your boss's secretary calls you out of the blue. Your boss is delayed, he can't make that big meeting. He needs you to step in. All the parties are in the conference room and they are waiting. You haven't read the file, you don't know the issues. But you have to do it. Everything hangs on this meeting – the whole deal, the fate of the firm. Your boss's secretary hands you the file – it is so huge, you buckle a little under its weight. As you open the door and see the army of dark suits round the table, she says, "Oh, and he said to tell you: don't fuck it up."

Lying there next to my current gorgeous young man, I would feel the tension return to my body. And before long, there it was again, the knot in my stomach. My mind would be racing. I worried about my bad breath. How did my hair look, flattened and tangled? If I fell asleep, he might hear me snore. I was only little, I thought, not this grown up sexy woman he saw. I didn't really know how to be in this world. I didn't know what women were supposed to do in situations like this. How did they stay beautiful throughout the night and wake up the next day fresh and ready to be kissed again? Would he understand if I told him? I wanted to tell him so many things. I wanted to tell him that sometimes for no reason, even on the sunniest days and even when we seemed to be having great fun, I would suddenly feel sad. I wanted to tell him that I didn't know who I was.

I wanted to tell him how much the world out there scared me.

One night, I tried to talk with Andy. We lay in the dark and I said I felt depressed. I didn't know the reason, I just felt down. Maybe it was my job. It was too stressful. In the far reaches of my mind, the dark shadow of a dying swan flickered. But I looked away. He took me in his arms and kissed me lightly. I talked a bit more. Maybe I wasn't cut out to be a lawyer. He made all the right sympathetic noises. But he didn't really know what to say. He kissed me again. I could feel his erection. We kissed some more. I let my body take over, dropped my sadness like a night dress. Things might be all right after all, I thought. I was with Andy and he was kind and gentle. He loved me, didn't he?

Afterwards, he fell asleep. I lay awake, his semen drying on my thigh.

How did they do it, those other women? Could they talk to their boyfriends and husbands? Maybe I was just going about it wrong. Using the wrong words. Picking the wrong time. Maybe I wanted something he could not give me. Maybe those clichés were true – talking just wasn't a guy thing.

I wanted the magic that we all hear about. The chemistry. The electricity. The spark. That all-consuming, all-transformative passion. The whirlwind. The thunderclap. The moment when everything gets swept away. All my doubts, all my uncertainties, all my sense of not knowing – that fluttering shadow just out of my vision - vanishing in an instant. I wanted some enchanted evening – to see that someone and to know. That he was the One.

I wanted Andy to be the One.

And he might be still. Mightn't he?

I felt cold suddenly even as his arms wrapped me against his hot, broad torso.

Maybe no man would ever look at me the way I longed to be looked at. Or love me the way I longed to be loved.

I envied those friends of mine who never seemed to bother with make-up or trying to be feminine, and yet retained an air of girlishness about them. They never wore the latest fashions – just the standard, classic look of 'nice girls': simple skirts and blouses, a pretty sweater or cardigan and corduroy trousers, or a shapeless frock. They seemed comfortable in their plainness but certain nonetheless in their womanhood. And many of them had boyfriends.

Maybe if I didn't try so hard. Maybe if I just went for the simple, make-up-less look, I would meet a man who could love me for me. If I took desire out of the equation, maybe I might see in his eyes that love and acceptance I craved.

But when I looked at myself in the mirror, in a classic sweater over a plain blouse, flat pumps under my jeans, my face sallow and dull without make-up – I saw a mannish woman pathetically trying to look feminine in those little white pumps. I felt a lurch of disgust. Swapping out the pumps for a pair of trainers, I stood again in front of the mirror. That was better, more natural... But now I just looked like a fourteen year old boy with Marc Bolan hair.

To my surprise, there were a couple of men who fell in love with me during these few years. I would still doll up most of the time but I was less vigilant about not being seen in my sweatshirt and jeans. There was a freedom in it that energised me and a carelessness with Mark and Rhys that somehow made them pursue me more. They were skinny and witty and had something of Woody Allen about them. Unlike Josh or Andy or the other men I usually dated, they lacked physical beauty but I liked that they liked me. I was touched that they were enamoured by me. They made me laugh. And I could talk with them – about feelings and emotions and literature and writing. With Mark, we even encouraged each other in our writing and exchanged poetry. I wanted to love them back. But when I let them kiss me, I felt sick.

"I must be just a shallow lookist," I said to Lizzie, half-laughing, half-embarrassed. "I can only go out with good looking men."

We lounged on a grassy bank on Hampstead Heath. It was a sunny Saturday afternoon.

I had known Lizzie since Oxford. She had been part of our gang, been there at all our student parties, walked barefoot with us on the dewy grass on the white evening. But she had never been a close friend till now when we were all down in London. She shared a house with Jane and others from Oxford, all young women, all in high-powered jobs in multi-nationals. We saw each other at parties and picnics but also now met up for walks and movies, just the two of us.

She said, "Maybe you're just not in love with either Mark or Rhys." She didn't look at me, focusing on the daisy chain she was working on.

I watched her intricate interweaving of the small white flowers with larger yellow dandelions. How had she learnt to do that? It was what young, fresh-faced girls used to do in Ladybird books and Janet and John type stories and tales from Mallory Towers. I had seen girls at school years ago making simple linked daisy circles but I had never come across anyone in real life who had the skill that Lizzie had of creating a fancy chain or bouquet out of wild flowers every time we sat down in a meadow. It seemed such an old-fashioned, charming skill.

But then there was something old-fashioned and charming

about Lizzie altogether. She had soft, perfect skin and never wore make-up. Her hair was cut short in a simple, almost tomboy style. She had a delightful smile and a shy, gentle manner. I loved her laugh and found myself teasing and joking just to hear her burst out laughing.

I looked out over the slopes towards Kenwood House. "Why is it always like this? They love me but I don't love them back, I was in love with Josh but he didn't love me the same way. Wouldn't it be so much easier if you could love someone and they loved you with the same intensity?"

"Life's not meant to be easy."

Something in her tone made me glance over to her. She was looking at me with an expression I couldn't read. Her blue-grey gaze unsettled me.

I remembered her boyfriend at Oxford. I had met him briefly once. He had been a tall, good-looking young man with bright blond hair. "Was that what happened, too, with you and Peter? Was it him who loved you or you who loved him?"

She flushed and looked down at the flowers in her still hands. She seemed to be smiling so I went on lightly, teasing. "He was rather dishy, wasn't he? I remember being very impressed. And I was a little jealous, too."

She looked up at me. "Jealous?"

"I can't believe I'm telling you this. I was jealous of you because you didn't have to try. You were just you – no make-up, no high heels, nothing – and there he was, this lovely chap."

She laughed, dismissive. But she seemed pleased.

"What happened with him? You've never talked about him. I'm always pouring my heart out to you about my pathetic love life … but you never give anything away."

"There's nothing to tell. All this love stuff, it's all very silly…" She was flustered.

I had embarrassed her. I stood up. "Shall we carry on walking?"

"Yes, some tea is called for, don't you think?" She scrambled up and hooked her arm into mine.

We strolled towards Kenwood House. She was in a light-weight cotton fisherman's smock, faded with age. It hung baggy and loose over her jeans. Her shoes were like those of a child – in the style of those Clark's school shoes kids used to wear at primary school with the little side buckle and two church windows over the upper foot through which you could see your socks.

I had on skinny jeans and a boyfriend-style slouchy sweatshirt that sometimes slipped a little from one shoulder. A pair of large silver hooped earrings softened the fourteen-year-old-boy-with-Marc-Bolan hair look. I wore high-top trainers – as was the fashion in that decade of aerobics and leg warmers and ONJ breathily telling us all, "Let's get physical..." I loved being out on this summer's day with Lizzie on my arm. She was saying something and laughing, guilelessly bumping against me as we walked. My strides grew longer, as if this country estate and this warm afternoon all belonged to me.

* * *

I imagine her sitting by the window of one of the rooms within the Inner Chamber of her family home. She is at a writing desk, the parchment sheets neatly in front her – blank ones ready for her confident brush strokes, the completed ones laid out to dry. I have not been able to find a portrait of her but I picture Chen Duansheng as having a delicate face with dark shining eyes and intelligent features. Her hair is combed and coiled in the intricate fashion of late 18th century China. She is wearing a luxuriant brocade gown with a high Manchu collar. Her tiny feet peep out beneath its hem. I see her looking down at the pink and white cherry blossom trees in the enclosed courtyard, their soft fragrance wafting in through the open window. Beyond walled enclosure, she can see the terracotta rooftops of Qiantang sloping down the hillside to the glimpse of a Great Canal below.

She recalls the bustle of the city streets seen from the confines of her sedan chair, peddlers and hawkers loudly selling their chickens and pots and pans, grandees striding past, fans in hand. She remembers the smells of horses and fried food and unwashed bodies and fruit and sewage. She sees in her mind the whirl and rush of colours and shapes and bodies, hears the sounds of footsteps and hooves and clattering trade. How she wanted to push aside the curtains of the sedan those times she travelled to pay house calls to her friends and family! To step down into the thronging street and lose herself in the crowd, taking this alley way here, turning along that side street there, pausing in front of the tin pan maker to watch him beat out the pots, stopping at the teahouse over there. But she always stayed where she was.

It would be unseemly for her to be out in the streets, a woman of her class in her beautiful robes and finery, with her delicate little feet, unescorted, walking free. Her little maid would have to be with her at the very least, letting Duansheng steady herself on her strong sturdy arm, bearing both their weights on her big flat feet. They would not get very far in the thronging crowds, slowed by her small steps and wavering gait, the uneven ground and jostling bodies threatening to tumble her at any moment.

A voice calls her name.

It's her cousin, pulling her back into the room behind her. Here in this calm sanctuary, her female cousins and friends are gathered round a table, sewing and working on their embroidery. They are all beautifully dressed, sipping tea, chatting and laughing together, each pair of delicate feet just visible beneath them.

"Have you finished the next section yet?" her cousin asks. The others look up from their work. "Have you? Read us the next bit, please. We want to know what happens to Meng Lijun!"

Chen Duansheng was seventeen when she wrote the verse novel known as *Destiny of the Next Life*. She was born into the gentry class in 1751, two generations before Jane Austen, in the city now known as Hangzhou, the capital of Zhejiang Province in Eastern China. The verse form she wrote in is today known as literary *tanci* and was derived from a street form of oral storytelling, often performed solo by a woman. The street form began to be adopted by literary women in the 15th and 16th century in the middle of the Ming dynasty and had become an established artform by the time that Duansheng was writing in the 1770s. Literary *tanci* was distinguished from highbrow texts written by men by its ordinary, fresh language and its storylines that were written by women to be read out loud or performed for an audience of women. *Destiny of the Next Life* became a 'bestseller' in its time and is now considered a classic of Chinese literature.

Duansheng's heroine Meng Lijun is teenage girl who has achieved the ultimate perfection – her bound feet are only 2.7 inches long. For various political reasons her father is forced to promise her in marriage to an evil scheming man despite her having previously been betrothed to the man she loves. Strong-willed and bold, Meng Lijun runs away disguised as a man. With layers of thick socks over her bound feet, she pulls on men's boots and exchanges her feminine gowns for male robes. She strides about out in a man's world but, like Ivy Ling Po in *Love Eterne*, there is otherwise no other attempt to emulate a man in her voice or facial features. It is as if by simply disguising her female feet – the icon of her womanhood – and pulling on men's boots, she is accepted as a man by the world. Her many adventures lead her to ace the civil service exams and to become prime minister. Under her exceptional government, there is harmony and order in the land. She is adored and desired by both men and women, including the Emperor. She marries a woman and they live together as husband and wife.

I imagine Duansheng picking up her sheafs of parchment and turning away from the window, back into the womb-like haven of the Inner Chamber. She reads out loud to her sisterhood of lotus feet women, her voice at turns lively, ominous, coy, commanding as she builds the drama, bringing to life all the different characters and evoking the emotional highs and lows of Meng Lijun's story.

The women listen, enthralled, down their needlework and become still. Bound here bodily in the Inner Chamber, their minds and hearts stride out into Meng Lijun's world. For a time, they become bold and masculine as she is – they are capable and outspoken, equals of men, making decisions, duelling with words, seeing their fathers kneel before them to respect the office of their premiership, admired and respected for more than their tiny feet, adored for their ability and full selves, loving tenderly those whom they choose, riding and striding in the loud, chaotic, energetic world beyond these enclosing walls.

There is so much longing and wish fulfilment in the story of Meng Lijun. So much that speaks of the hopes and dreams of those silent, obedient women in so many Inner Chambers across China. That swashbuckling energy, that homo-erotic desire and bisexual electricity, the incisive intellect and vigorous wit! And the added sense of thrill and danger in a world where the transgression of cross-dressing was punishable by death. I wonder how many women saw themselves as Meng Lijun – and how many fell in love with her. Did they devour her story because through her, they could vicariously express their own innate power? Or was it because they dreamt of a man who was half-woman or a woman who was half-man to hold them and love them and call them his/ her own?

Duansheng never finished this work that was part narrative performance, part novel. She initially wrote only 64 chapters but years later added several more at the behest of her readers; but she never completed the arc of the story. Some commentators have speculated that she could not bring herself to conclude the narrative because there would have been only two possible endings. The transgressive hero/ heroine would have to die for her crime of crossing the gender divide - or she would have to be somehow forgiven and pardoned by the Emporer in exchange for returning to the fold of normal life as a woman, wife and mother. Duansheng herself died in her forties from what seemed to be consumption, leaving her heroine forever suspended in the midst of her adventures.

Bound Feet Blues continues the tradition of literary *tanci* was a solo performance, often by a woman, during the Ming dynasty

Throughout the narrative of Meng Lijun's adventures, men and women suspect her true gender but they do not confront her. Instead they stay in that in-between territory of knowing and not-knowing, of wanting to find out the truth and at the same time going along with the masquerade. The thrill is here, the frisson, the breathlessness – here lies the uncertainty of incompletion where anything is possible. Despite her feminine features, her soft, beardless face, no-one recognises her as a woman – even her own parents. It is only when her men's boots are pulled from her to reveal the soft, tender womanhood of her feet that the end threatens.

In a tableau in my mind, I see those women of the Inner Chamber sitting as still as dolls in their beautiful embroidered gowns, their tender feet beneath them, as Chen Duansheng performs her story out loud. The scent of the blossom trees weaves its way in through the open window. Perhaps in the distance, they can hear the bustle of the streets beyond the walled courtyard, a faint cry of a street vendor, the clatter of hooves. Here, where their mothers and grandmothers had sat, and where their daughters and grand-daughters will also sit, these women, delicate in body and soles, stay unmoving.

But in their imaginations, riding on Duansheng's words out into the world beyond, they can be as their hearts might long to be. They can be equal to – no, even better than – men. They can be top scholars, they can govern, they can speak out, they can live their lives as they please, they can choose whom to love. It is as if Duansheng has seen into their secret places and spoken for all of their broken dreams and ambitions. And for a little while, they can escape their bodies, be mobile, move, stride, swagger, run, sprint, race.

And then they are back in the heaviness of their flesh and bone, the story over. Duansheng falls silent and puts down the sheaf of papers. There is a burden of stillness in the chamber. She turns back to the desk by the window. The other women look down at their sewing. But there is a reluctance in the air. Not yet.

They glance up at the open window and late afternoon sun pouring down onto the world outside.

Interlude

26 March 2014, Conway Hall, London

The performance was rushing by in a blur light and darkness, faces and dark shapes, gasps and laughter. My own voice rang out across the cavernous hall, sometimes fluid and Oxonian, other times reedy like a child's, now slipping into the sing-song of a Malaysian accent, now hard and angry, now soft and despairing. My body swayed in a slinky walk, stood rigid and bound to one spot, skipped along as a child would.

My mind was racing. Had I forgotten a scene? Did I just swap round several lines in the script? What did I just say? What was coming up next? No time to think. No time to doubt. I had to keep moving onward.

Each moment led the story on through time and place and narrator. I was me aged twenty, then myself as an eight year old, then my mother, then Aunty Diana, then a bound foot mother, then me again…

I fell to my knees on the wooden floor. *How will I endure it?*

We were on the home stretch. Just a few more lines and this would be over. I looked up at the audience from the tiny place where I crouched into myself. There was an electric silence as they watched me.

> *Will I ever dare let anyone see me?*
> The question hung in the air.

"How will I endure it?"

I stood up. I looked at the audience. They looked back at me. There was a long silence. They were waiting for more. I drew my arms to my side, slid my feet together and bowed.

The applause roared in my ears. I felt myself grinning widely. I stood for a moment, absorbing it, trying to process what had happened. Then trotted lightly for the heavy wooden door that led me off the stage. Luke held it open for me and I slipped out into the cold narrow corridor that edged round the central hall.

The applause was continuing, loud and unabated, in the hall.

Luke pulled open the door and scooted me out again.

I stood in the ring of spotlights, taking another bow, catching the gaze of my sister, Angie and a number of other friends. As the house lights came up, a swarm of bodies began to move out of their seats towards me.

They were shaking my hand, hugging me. In the kaleidoscope of faces, I saw friends and people I didn't know. They were beaming and laughing, congratulating me. I heard snatches of phrases – you made me cry, oh my god, you were amazing, you were so funny, I loved that bit where….

Some people hung back and looked at me with what could only be described as awe, as if they were in the presence of a star. I realised they were waiting respectfully to be noticed and invited forward. I caught their eyes and that was the signal. They took turns coming up to me, approaching with that odd mixture of eagerness and reverence that we have for famous people. Each wanted to tell me their experience of the show, explain how it resonated with something in their own lives, share something of themselves with me. I listened to each, trying to make sure that everyone had a chance to speak with me. Hearing all their stories, I marvelled at how my one story from my one life could let so many others bloom, like a single dust of pollen floating into the hearts of so many different flowers.

In the midst of it all, Lucy, a dear friend, gave me a long stemmed rose and as I posed for photos with friends and strangers, the rose in my hand, I felt surreally as if I had been lifted out of my own life into an alternate universe where I was a celebrated and beloved diva. I could hardly process what was happening. In just 45 minutes, my life had changed.

I had done something that I had not thought possible for me to pull off. Dressed in a simple black top and black jeans, without costume changes, without props, without a set, without any formal drama training or direction other than a few hours of voice coaching – without even wearing any shoes! – I had commanded the audience's attention for almost an hour. They had laughed at the right places, been horrified where the story was horrifying, been moved where the scenes were meant to be moving. And they had sat in tense silence after the time was up, waiting to find out what would happen next.

The voices badgered me from all sides.

"You have to finish writing it! I want to know the end…"

"How can you just leave us hanging here? When is the full show going to be on?"

"It's a work in progress," I kept saying. "This is the first draft. I need to finish the script. I don't know about a full production…"

"But you must put on the full show! I can't wait to see what happens next."

Through a gap in the crowd, I caught the eyes of a young Chinese woman. She had a broad smile on her face as she reached in to shake my hand. "It was brilliant." she said, "I'm Annie Kwan – we were in touch by email."

Oh my God. She was one of the producers of the South East Asian Arts Festival. She had contacted me the week before. She had been scouting for storytellers to invite to be part of the Festival and had found my website via Google.

"Annie! I'm so glad you could come…" I began.

Someone else grabbed my hand. They were speaking to me eagerly, edging Annie out of my line of sight. I turned to them, distracted, wanting to be polite.

Annie moved away. I glanced back at her. She was still grinning. She called, "We'll talk soon…"

And she was gone.

* * *

Back at my desk at work the next day, I became again the quiet professional, well-respected in my job, serious, speaking the language of property law and finance, writing complex emails, negotiating technical points on the phone. Here amid the computers and telephones and open plan cubicles that were a familiar part of my everyday life, the scratch night felt as if it had happened to someone else. That person who had cavorted on stage, transforming from sexy twentysomething to cheeky child to severe bound foot mother was surely somebody other than me. That woman who had dared to reveal her soul beneath the bright spotlights – who *was* she?

We had left feedback forms on the chairs for the audience. My sister and friends had gathered them together for me. Now emails from friends were also pouring in. I had to read them several times to absorb all those words that must surely have been written about someone else.

"Mesmerising – not for the faint hearted. Drew us in from the start and left us gasping for breath."

"Terrific… poignant… sexy"

"A riveting bravura performance that brilliantly weaves together personal stories, family history and gender issues with humour, sensitivity and great emotional impact."

"I loved your physicality and performance. The piece was beautifully written – complex, moving, so many layers."

"A powerful message well delivered… It's simply a must see!"

"Spellbinding."

"It was a powerful performance – I had to remind myself to breathe. Truly wonderful! We want more!"

How had this happened? What had changed my previously fairly competent style of Public Speaking Plus to make it something more than a simple live storytelling set?

More to the point, what had happened to me? How had I transformed – as if in an instant - from an introverted writer and serious professional in the City into this dramatic performer who seemed afraid of nothing on stage?

Yes, there was that single experimental moment of arching my body back in ecstasy but that would not have in itself held an audience rapt for a full forty-five minutes. And, yes, there was that sense of purpose and legacy that impelled me onward to tell the stories that my mother and grandmother had told me – but that did not in itself give me the skills and chutzpah to perform the stories with such flair.

I thought back over the last three months since I started working on the script and trying bits out in front of my workshop colleagues. I turned over in my mind the evenings I spent practicing the lines in my open plan kitchen/ dining room at home. What had happened to make *Bound Feet Blues* more than just Storytelling Plus – that is to say, what changed in me that made the story into a theatrical performance?

And then I saw it.

Three weeks previously, just before I showed up at Jessica's for my first voice lesson, I had been discussing the staging of the show with my workshop colleagues. The subtitle of the show is *A Life in Shoes* so how was I going to portray the different shoes in all the different parts of the show? I usually turned up at the class in biker boots or Chelsea boots and every time I got up in front of the group to read what I had written that week, all eyes would be drawn to my feet.

"It's only natural," one of the workshoppers said - an experienced performance poet. "Your story is about shoes so we all automatically look at what shoes you are wearing."

The consensus was that my big, chunky boots were distracting. They tied down the scope of the story to the one pair of shoes even as the narrative whizzed across time and settings.

We talked about having a range of shoes on stage that I could change into.

"But I threw out my stilettos and high heels and girly shoes years ago," I said.

One of the women offered, "You could borrow my shoes. I've got loads of pretty wild heels." She was a burlesque artist.

"They'll be too big. It'll look like I'm wearing borrowed shoes. But thanks, anyway." I sighed, perplexed. "I'm not sure I want to be fussing with changing shoes every few minutes. The shoes are not the point, really. They are a metaphor. It has to be done just right – or it would be better to have nothing at all."

We all exchanged looks. For a moment, no-one spoke.

"Nothing at all." I said slowly.

That night after dinner, I stood in my usual spot in my open plan dining room, facing the kitchen across the half wall, taking in my audience - the toaster, kettle and other kitchen appliances on the counter against the far wall. The script of *Bound Feet Blues* lay

Barefoot, Conway Hall

on the glass dining table in front of me. Till now, I had treated the story as I approached my TEDx talk and stories for storytelling clubs. I would stand more or less in one spot and tell the story, occasionally taking a step to the side to denote the past or a different setting or mood. My voice took on different emotions – lyrical, intense, playful – but there was no real acting. Apart from the arching in ecstasy, my body didn't do very much else.

I took my boots off. Pulled off my socks. I stood barefoot.

The central heating was on high and the room felt toasty. Beneath my bare feet, the wooden floor was warm. It was an odd feeling. I felt free, like a child again. And also uneasy. There was a nakedness about it. A vulnerability. If I felt like this alone in my own home, how would I feel barefoot in a large hall in front of an auditorium of people?

I stayed with the unease. Let it sit there in my chest. Resisted the instinct to fold my arms and curl one foot into the other.

I began to go through the scenes of *Bound Feet Blues*. The sexy walking in the opening moments became sexier. In the scene when I am eight, I suddenly took off half running, half skipping round the dining room – my whole body expressed the gangly movements of a little girl. As the bound foot mother, I stood with most of my weight on one foot, my body twisted sideways, evoking an unstable, feminine shape that was rooted to a single spot. Back as ten year old tomboy me, I raced around with an imaginary rifle shooting at the "audience" and then broke into a Kung Fu kick, howling a Bruce Lee howl. At the climax of the last scene so far, I fall to my knees in despair.

The simple act of taking off my shoes had changed everything. Had changed me.

* * *

I had always thought of myself as a writer and that impelled me eventually to write my two legal thrillers. That had drawn me to gather the stories of my family in numerous handwritten notebooks and to interviewing my Grandpa with a tape recorder that rainy night in 1976. That had led me into fifteen years in a creative wilderness as I tried again and again to write stories in the form of books, all of them languishing unfinished.

Ever since I was a child, I had in my mind what a writer's life would be like. I pictured myself sitting at a desk gazing contemplatively into the distance. Back then, I would imagine a pen in my hand and a sheaf of papers or a notebook. Perhaps it would be evening and there would be a pool of yellow light lighting up my desk and the wise words I would write out feverishly, my pen scratching earnestly on stiff paper. And it was so easy to live the dream – all I had to do was to sit at my desk after school, after all the homework was done, and get out my favourite fountain pen and story exercise book and there I was: a writer.

Later, my dream evolved with technology. My uncle gave me his old portable Olivetti typewriter and I would tap away at the keys, feeling like Hemingway. I graduated to an electric of my own at Oxford, then to an Amstrad in the early '90s and finally a Compaq laptop on which I wrote my two published novels. And with each decade, I loved nothing more than sitting down at my desk in the pool of yellow light – as I am doing in this moment – and creating a whole world with just my words.

As a writer – and for me, writer meant novelist - you can be God. You make the universe your characters live in. You make each man and woman in it. You decide their fate – who lives, who dies, who gets to live happily ever after and who must be punished.

And all the while, you sit alone in your room with nothing and no-one but your imagination to keep you company. You are safe. There is no-one here to judge you or laugh at you. No-one to make you feel worthless and small. The real you, the you who is only little, who has never grown up, who longs to be seen and heard – you can stay hidden away, like the God particle in the midst of all those words. Hiding in plain sight.

But being a writer had also boxed me in.

The conventional wisdom is that there is a 'proper' way to write a 'proper' book. There is a 'proper' way to get published by a 'proper' publisher. This served me well for my two legal thrillers. After realising that my earnest, turgid, unreadable novel *Ancestral Voices* was not an innovative literary novel the likes of which the world had never seen but just simply 'Bad', I deconstructed John Grisham's *The Firm* one rainy week staying with my parents in KL, and decided that I could write one just like that, only set in Malaysia and featuring a dynamic Chinese female lawyer in the lead. That novel became *The Flame Tree*.

Hodder & Stoughton had the vision to take it on but although it was a bestseller in Malaysia, it did less well in the UK because it did not fit into a 'proper' category. There were no novels at that time that took a mainstream white-dominated genre like the legal thriller and populated it with East Asian characters, let alone gave the lead to a Chinese woman. It seemed that the reading public and the media were of the view that Chinese women should only be in novels about three generations of Chinese women and should feature hardship, endurance and, well, bound feet. One of the biggest bookstore chains, I was told, would not stock it because they didn't know which section to put it under – with John Grisham and Patricia Cornwell or with Jung Chang and Amy Tan.

My second novel *Mindgame* did even worse. No-one knew quite what to make of a lesbian thriller with a James Bond ending set in Malaysia and featuring a Chinese heroine and her tomboy lover. I was disappointed and frustrated by the lack of impact these 'improper' works of mine had had. So for my third book, I was determined to write a 'proper' book which would fit into a 'proper' category.

So began my fifteen years in a creative wilderness. I had in my head that I needed to fit my family stories into the conventional narrative format of a family memoir. Would this mean taking a trip to China to track down the Bandit Boy's original village? I wasn't really interested in doing that and besides, we have very little genealogical information that would allow me to track the real boy down. I wasn't interested in recreating in vivid historical detail the life and times of his subsequent life in colonial Malaya – nor the changing eras as the generations that came after him grew up and grew old. Nor was I interested in chronicling the lives of each generation as mini-novellas within the larger frame of a 'three generations' family memoir.

But that would be what I would need to do if I wanted to produce a book that would be taken on by a 'proper' publisher – that is, a book that might turn out to be the Malaysian *Wild Swans* or *Roots*.

So the family project languished despite my resurrecting it several times from different angles but always within the conventions of narrative non-fiction memoir.

It also bothered me that I had this disinterest in the historical and biographical details. How could I call myself a writer if these details that would give life and breadth to my stories just made my brain glaze over? Was my fascination about my family's stories sincere if I didn't care for historical and biographical facts? Maybe I was just a fraud.

I stopped writing for a number of years.

Then, in an attempt to shake things up, I tried my hand at magic realism and wondered about a pseudonym. Perhaps that might free something up inside me. I opted for Alex Yang, a gender non-specific name that retained a Chinese flavour. If I had a go at stories that were as far away from historical and biographical solidity as I could get – and as far away from my identity as well - maybe that might tangentially sling-shot me back to a place where I could approach writing matters close to my heart with fresh vigour. Maybe through fantasy, I could explore those heartfelt matters with greater freedom under the guise of fiction and magic realism and in the not-me persona of Alex Yang.

In the Alex Yang collection of notes and half written stories, one theme emerged. Many of them hinge on a moment of choosing – a pivot point in a character's life which changes everything. He or she arrives at the brink of new possibilities and must decide to step forward or stay standing still. Each story then goes on to explore the life that follows on from that decision. And each story is a love story.

One momentous, life-changing decision about love.

My own.

I had never spoken about it or written about it. Yes, I was 'out' to my friends and family. I had been 'out' for more than twenty years. And to be 'out' you have to talk about being gay so yes, I had spoken a lot about being gay but I had never spoken about the personal struggle that had led me to the pain of that re-birth.

Mindgame has a lesbian theme, to be sure, but there is much bravado and swagger in it, especially with all the pyrotechnics that are required within the thriller genre. It is the same bravado that has camouflaged the tenderness of my experience of coming out and living as a lesbian. It is the *kok-kok* shoes of my literary self, tough and brimming with masculine energy. Out and proud – that's the phrase we all should live by, isn't it? Being lesbian is about being bold and strong and holding your own against all comers.

But of the real experience of falling in love with someone you shouldn't? Of the shame and terror of rejection, of the longing and hope? Of the pain of not being loved in the same way in return? Of revealing all of my naked soul to another human being for the first time?

I had never gone back to those years in my writing – or even in my memory.

And to go back to my coming out story would mean going back to my tomboy qualities and the uber-femme disguise I adopted to hide the *pondan* in me. It would mean going back to my relationship with my family.

I had never before seen *my* own story as being an integral part of the story of my family. I had always going to be in the book of my family but only as the narrator – as the writer who goes in search for her roots and then tells you the story of several generations of a Chinese family. The family book I had wanted to write all my life would be about Them, not Me.

Huh. Maybe I would have to make the book about Me, too.

A book about me felt too solid and enduring and overwhelming. And grandiose. I hadn't been kidnapped by a bandit gang, I hadn't had my feet broken and bound, and I hadn't sat in a rickshaw alone in a deserted road with briefcase full of ransom money. What could I possibly write about me? So I shied away from it.

But once the thought had appeared in my mind, it was like a drop of water that spread its tendrils out to reach into the hidden pool of my life to draw it into the river of my family's life. And when I turned forty-eight, standing in the pouring rain, thinking about my Grandma and her legacy of stories and wondering about what my legacy would be, I became that river of my family's stories and the river became me. The pull of the volume of water

TEDx

from the distant past grabbed me in its wake and hurtled me onwards, demanding release and expulsion from the depths.

Which led me to the storytelling clubs.

Which led me to a TEDx talk.

Which led me to Conway Hall.

There are writers who might sing in a choir or do woodwork or run a marathon. Some might even tell stories live – like Neil Gaiman at The Moth. These other things are their hobbies and they would always still remain A Writer. They would not consider themselves A Singer or A Carpenter or An Athlete or an Oral Storyteller. So it was for me. Live storytelling was just a bit of fun that gave me a break from writing and at best, got my name as a writer out there in front of a fresh audience. I did not consider myself a Performer. I was just telling my story out loud.

And as with 'proper' books, there is a 'proper' way to tell a story or give a talk. You need to be conversational and relaxed. You stand on stage or stroll about a bit. You are careful not to do

Writer/ performer, Conway Hall

too much with your hands though a gesture from time to time for emphasis is good. You are self-deprecating and humorous, emotional but not too emotional.

So in the few weeks leading up to the Conway Hall scratch night, as I practiced the script in my open plan dining room and kitchen to the audience of appliances on the far away counter, I did it the 'proper' way. Apart from arching back to illustrate the metaphor of the stiletto shoe being like a woman in ecstasy, the rest of the time saw me standing in classic TED talk mode – centre stage, hands loosely clasped but ready for a meaningful gesture.

But when I took my boots off, it was like taking off a pair of weights that had up till now sunk me into the floor. They sat like two solid black foot irons in the middle of the room as I skipped and karate-kicked and flew round the empty spaces. The stage area had become a theatre of play.

I was a child again, claiming the long open hallways of my

parents' house in KL as the setting for our re-enacted stories from *The Avengers* and *Star Trek*. Our three beds in the bedroom I shared with my brother and sister, pushed together, became our stage. My parents' dining room table was a cave or a hideout or a tank. The garden was a jungle, a desert island, a wild African savannah. My sister and brother and cousins and I played out the movies and TV shows we loved, each of us taking different characters. I was Bruce Lee and John Steed and Captain Kirk – of course.

So, too, my dining room floor that night became the High Street in Oxford, a mythical China, and the Inner Chamber of a woman with bound feet, my childhood landscape of garden and school and home. I became all the people in the story, just as I had been in our childhood games.

My boots had boxed me in. Kept me safe. Kept me 'proper'.

Without them, I could be as 'improper' as a child.

Without footwear, I was no longer just a writer. Nor even just a Performer. Barefoot as a child - with a child's mind and a child's sense of curiosity and play - I became a creative artist.

* * *

We were having dinner at a hip new restaurant in Forest Hill, all chunky wood and mismatched furniture. It was a year before Conway Hall, on a crisp winter night. I had given up – again – on my books. On Alex Yang, on the family book. On everything creative. I was just trying to enjoy my life – going to the theatre, taking long walks in the country, seeing friends. I was catching up with Carol, a Savile Row tailor, one of the few women in the profession. She had her own label and a client list that encompassed high profile names in sports, music and theatre. She was telling me about her latest project, her blue eyes glowing and her face lit up with excitement.

"I'm creating a sculpture in cloth," she said.

"A sculpture?" I'm intrigued. "Like Michelangelo?"

She nodded, laughing. "Tailoring is all about structure and shapes. It's about working with your hands and creating something that is beyond just utility but has an essence that you can't capture in any other way. When someone comes to me for a bespoke suit, they want something more than clothing. You can pick up clothing anywhere off the peg – it can be M&S or something by the top fashion designers but it's not designed just for you, made just for you. A bespoke suit is about expressing the essence of that person in their clothes – it's an iconic expression of who that person is.

"My client has a shape – is a sculpture, really, in human form. My job as a tailor is to create another sculpture to apply to their shape. Sculptures worn over the body can enhance or conceal depending on what would be the most flattering. This is the essence of tailoring."

She paused. Then went on, "I've always had this idea that I wanted to create something in cloth. A standalone piece. It's like this urge – to express something from inside me. To put into the world an essence that I can't really express in any other way than through cloth and structure. I didn't really understand what this urge was, really, so I never did anything about it. But then one day, I was talking about this to my mentor and she said to me, 'You have this urge because you're an artist.'"

An artist.

Carol suddenly saw herself in a different way. She was not just a tailor. Not just an artisan, making things for others. She was an artist and she could create something that was just for her – and in doing so, could create something that was for all of us.

Being an artist gave Carol permission to spend time with her creative urge and to dare to create something she had never created before. Being an artist allowed her to bring something into the world that had up till then only existed as a spark inside her.

"Seeing myself as an artist gave me this freedom to create outside the order book," she went on. "I want to build a sculpture in wire and cloth. It's going to explore the inner workings of the tailored suit. I want to show what is inside a garment, and express the dignity and devotion that you can't see on the outside."

I sat across the table from her and felt a pang of envy.

Being an artist means that you can experiment - play with shapes and textures and structures, investigate form and substance and style. Break rules, defy what has gone before, and invert convention. Create, make, unmake. You can fail and mess up. You do not have to be right or perfect. There is no 'proper' way to create art, no template. In fact, art demands that you not follow anything 'proper' but rather find your own way. Lead the way. Break through to a new frontier.

I wanted that.

But I also wanted to do things 'properly' as a writer so that my next books would get more traction out in the world of the reading public.

I laughed ruefully to myself. This wanting to write a 'proper' book hadn't got me any closer to achieving my ambition in all these long years. If I envied Carol being an artist in her field, I could still strive to be an artist in the world of writing, couldn't I? Yes, I thought, there was a 'proper' way to be a literary artist as a writer. You had to write a book that would win the Man Booker or Orange/ Costa/ Baileys or Samuel Johnson. In other words, a 'proper' book.

I was a writer and I would keep at it, trying to write this 'proper' book. That was my identity. That was my fate. And maybe, one day, I could call myself an artist, too. Once those who judged these things in the literary world judged me to me worthy of being called a literary artist, then I could claim to be an artist.

It was other people who conferred upon you the status of an artist, I thought. You needed a Masters in Fine Art or an MA in Creative Writing. You needed to write such an astounding book that critics would declare it a work of art. Even as Carol sat before me with her simple statement that she was an artist – without anyone else's say so - I did not feel that *I* could call myself such a thing. I did not have that confidence in my abilities as a writer. All those years of striving for a book within the cultural structure of the publishing world had undermined my idea of myself. I didn't have a Masters in anything. I couldn't even write a 'proper' book so what chance had I of impressing reviewers or ever winning any bookish prize and thus claim the title of literary artist? The envy I felt wasn't just for the role of artist but also for Carol's confidence in her abilities and most of all, her confidence in who she was. As for me, I needed someone out there somewhere to validate me first as an artist before I felt I could create art.

Sitting there in that trendy restaurant, I looked out at the cold South London night. I felt very alone. I did not know how I could ever become an artist.

* * *

Going barefoot was not just about opening out *Bound Feet Blues* from a static storytelling piece into freer movement and use of the stage.

I was seeing the script differently. It had a shape that was more than the words and the arc of the storyline. I had poured it out without thinking too much, scene after scene in sequence, cutting back and forth from my past as a young woman to my childhood to ancient China and back again. Each scene played as an echo or counterpoint to the previous and the succeeding ones. Embedded in each were deeper themes and multi-stranded threads beyond the surface action. Now, I honed and whittled at it, bringing out each thematic phrase, evolving them as the narrative drove onward. Although the piece is written in prose, I felt as if I was moulding it as a poet might with the stylised refrains and mirrored and refracted imagery.

I realised that my physicality and the words needed to work together. I was no longer just a talking head. There was more to this than just reciting words or simply Telling A Story with my mouth. The shape of my body as I stood told the story. A gesture to indicate a three inch stiletto heel can be spine-tingling if I repeated part of the movement later to indicate a three inch Golden Lotus. The taut stillness of the adult women standing in one tiny spot through most of the first scenes could be contrasted with the skipping gait of the child running free all over the stage. As the words and phrases undulated like refrains in a piece of music so too could my physical presence become like a dance to that music.

If I had gone on a playwriting course, I might have produced a different work. It might have been a Three Act play with dialogue given to a range of characters, with each scene properly (ah, that word again) numbered Act One, Scene 1 and so on. Or it might have been a dramatic monologue in the spirit of Alan Bennett or Samuel Beckett. But with my novelist's frame, I had written it like a mini-novel, giving each scene a chapter heading. The whole piece had a single narrator's voice but within it is embedded multiple narratives. I used metaphors and descriptive language as I would in a novel – as in 'the shape of the shoe made my foot arch back like a woman in ecstasy'. It was the only way I knew how to tell a story and nothing new in the world of prose writing. But embodying these metaphors and inner conflicts on stage with nothing but my physicality… that felt fresh and different.

The evening before the Conway Hall performance, I turned up at Jessica's flat for my last voice lesson. In the three weeks since we had started working together, my voice had got stronger and more flexible in its emotional range. I was breathing more efficiently and enunciating more clearly. I was learning to use a fuller scale of notes from darker masculine tones to brighter feminine ones and the sound of the whole ensemble was carrying further. It had been hard work, rather like yoga for the voice. I felt as if I had come to her as a desk bound executive who could hardly touch my vocal toes a few weeks before and now, I was doing spoken equivalent of the Scorpion pose with my legs dangling above my head.

My voice was now more able to express the different colours of emotion and texture that the story needed it to express.

We worked on the last sequence of the script so far. I was on my knees, trying to express 'I bound up my tomboy spirit' miming the binding of an invisible bundle in front of me in a physical echo of the binding of feet.

Jessica stopped me. "What are you binding there? I can't picture it."

"Um…my tomboy spirit?"

"It looks odd…" Her voice trailed off. She thought for a moment. I waited on my knees.

"Try this…" She made a binding motion that circled her torso and head; the binding of the whole self.

I got to my feet and started the section again. This time, instead of sinking to my knees, I dropped to one knee, crouching. As I spoke the words, "I bound up my tomboy spirit…," I mimed binding up my body, as if winding an endless bandage across my left shoulder and under my right arm. A blur of emotion - rage and frustration and desperation - burst out from my core and into my voice. The words spewed out like molten lava from a

"I bind up my tomboy energy", Conway Hall

212

long dormant volcano. That old fury startled me but I let it carry me onward. Those hours raging in the bathroom as a child the tantrums I had not understood, the cold loneliness of the nights beside Andy all drove the manic energy of words and action within that compressed crouching shape.

In the performance the next night, when I dropped to one knee and bound up my body with the same desperate energy, I could feel the electricity in the darkened hall.

I had a new certainty about the piece as a work of art.

Some of the audience feedback asked for multi-media showing bound feet and embroidered slippers or historical photographs of ancient China and Chinese women to evoke that sense of the past. Others suggested props such as the different shoes that are mentioned, costume changes to denote each era or transition of tone and mood.

As a writer, I would have taken these comments to heart if they had related to a book manuscript I might have shown a friend or an editor. I would have immediately worked on how to accommodate what my readers wished. Indeed, I had met with a possible editor for one book project a few years before and she had given me copious notes on how she wanted my proposal changed so that she could sell it to more easily to her editorial and sales team. I had returned home disheartened because what she wanted from me was a completely different book from the one I had proposed. Nonetheless, I then spent almost three months reworking my original outline, changing the structure, adapting my message, making the idea fit into the category that she needed it to be in. But by the end of that long process, the soul of the project had died inside me. Here was my shot at a 'proper' book but when I looked at the reworked outline at the end of those three months, it was no longer my book. It was an exercise in writing by numbers, the publisher's numbers. I felt sick to the stomach and I knew that even if the editor now took the book and slammed down an advance on the table, I did not want to write it.

But now, reading through the audience feedback, I felt a certainty in myself – and in the art I had created – that I had never felt before. I knew very clearly what I wanted for *Bound Feet Blues*. Or rather what I did not want.

In any future production of the piece, it had to be simple and austere. There would be no props – and absolutely no images of shoes or feet – and no costume changes. There would be no scenery or any physical object denoting time and place. I wanted to evoke that sense of being told a story in the way that I had experienced being told stories as a child. The audience were going to have to recreate the stories for themselves in their own imaginations – but in the presence of a shape-shifting narrator.

As you listen to a story, you are right there in the present with your mum or grandma, maybe with your family gathered as well. You are in your kitchen or veranda at home. And yet, the words take you away to another place and another time. China, Victorian London, the docks at Sydney Harbour - you are there also. You hear your grandma's voice but you don't either – it is there but also not there because it's not the words you hear but the feelings and smells and sounds and scenes they evoke.

It is the impact of those stories on us as listeners in the present moment that give the experience of such oral storytelling its meaning. That sense of ourselves in the continuum of time, existing at once in the past and in the present, aware always of the teller and ourselves as audience, knowing we are experiencing a story but also a reality once fully lived and of ourselves as ancestors in the making. The teller offers us a doorway into this magical transformation of time and our senses but it is us as audience who share in the creation of the fullness of it all.

That was why, I suddenly realised, I had never had any interest in recreating the historical details of my family's stories. It was the meaning of the stories that mattered to me and what they told me about living and loving, about what it means to be a woman, a parent, a child, a spouse and a lover. What it means to be me. Or you. It was the grand themes, the elements of myth and family legend in these stores that called to me, not dates or even facts. Each person tells the story that they remember, shaped through what it means to them. And so, there are many versions of any one event, many versions to any one life. In all my bookish attempts at writing the family saga, I had groped towards that understanding only dimly, and longed to tell the version that would hold me within the cradle of my family's sense of ourselves. The version that would place me within a masculine Chinese tradition of scholarliness and respect for the proper order of things. A respect that would finally bring me acceptance despite being just a girl.

But ultimately, I am still just a girl. Who at heart doesn't care for the proper way of doing things. Who is still disobedient.

Which is why all my old attempts at writing a 'proper' family memoir had come to nothing.

I realised that for a long time, I had been ashamed of that failure to conform. That inability to fit my stories into what was expected had left me unable to complete a book. All that time, I had simply been working in the wrong medium. Here, with this odd play that was not a play, mini-novel that was not a novel, storytelling that was not just storytelling, I had created exactly the right medium for what I wanted to express.

I laughed at the irony of it. In all this the exploration of binding and unbinding of self and culture and tradition, I had in the process revealed a new way to unbind myself even further, this time within the context of my creative life.

I had an image in my mind of ancient wandering storytellers from innumerable cultures across the world. I saw them lit by tribal firelight, standing in mead halls and village squares. With nothing but their own bodies and voices, they would bring into the physical world of their audiences gods and demi-gods, heroes and monsters. They would pull out of invisible air heaven and hell, faraway lands and mythical places. They looked into the hearts of the people who had gathered round and told *those* stories hidden there.

Was this what it was to be a creative artist? To create something

To make and unmake myself

outside of genres and rules and yet with stylistic form of its own. To have such belief in the work. To make and unmake myself as part of a timeless tradition. To create beyond boundaries. And to live unbound.

I looked out at my garden through the glass patio doors. It was early evening the day after the scratch night. I was home from work and sorting through the feedback forms at the dining table. It was still light as spring nudged at the edge winter that late March afternoon.

I had not felt such energy for a long time. I had not known such certainty about a creative project before.

It was as if I had stepped into a different space. The anxious, boxed in writer seemed like someone else, fading already from my present. All the things I had worried about in not having a Masters in Creative Anything and not having the validation from a Worthy Someone Out There Somewhere – all of it didn't seem to matter anymore. It didn't matter that the Conway Hall event had been just a small scratch night or that the piece was as yet unfinished. What I had started in a spirit of fun had become something more. Working with Jessica, a creative artist in her own right, had opened up more than just my voice – the energy of collaboration excited me, took me beyond the solitary confines of writerdom. There was so much more creative possibility in my core that was as yet untapped. The scratch night felt like just a beginning. I didn't know where it might lead or where the end lay – I just knew that I had to keep walking this new path that had sprung up unexpectedly like breadcrumbs in a dark wood. I realised I didn't care if this uncertain path led only to a few hundred people ever seeing the piece. I didn't care if no worthy critic or panel of judges ever got to pronounce on its merit. I just knew that I had to complete the work and do whatever it took to present the final version in at least one more performance.

I was no longer just a writer.

For the first time, I could accept it. Celebrate it. Say it out loud.

I was finally what I had longed to become that night in the restaurant with Carol. No-one had conferred it on me. I had not waited for anyone's approval. I had simply and without thinking claimed it the first time I had slipped my boots off here in this room, and I had owned it last night at Conway Hall.

I said to my ever present audience, the faithful kitchen appliances, taking the phrasing from the AA's statement of naming and transformation: "My name is Yang-May and I'm a creative artist."

And there was a shameless freedom to it.

* * *

I met Annie Kwan at a tiny café just outside St Pancras. We sat in a cubby hole on the mezzanine area, the size of a Juliet balcony tucked up high near the ceiling. It was decked out with two old-fashioned wing chairs, a retro standing lamp and a wall lined with a *tromp d'oeil* bookcase of antique books. We might have been in our very own mock gentleman's club.

Annie had emailed me as she had promised after the scratch

night. It was Friday, two days after the performance. Beyond the half-moon windows, black cabs squeaked and travellers with weekend wheelie bags hurried in and out of the entrance to King's Cross station opposite.

I had looked through the South East Asian (SEA) Arts Festival website after she had contacted me. The SEA ArtsFest, as they called themselves, had launched in 2013. I read online:

> "SEA ArtsFest is the first Southeast Asian arts festival in the UK, championing and developing the work of the artists of Southeast Asia and those inspired by Southeast Asia. SEA ArtsFest brings together artists, practitioners, makers and thinkers to increase awareness of SEA Arts and its audience base, and is supported by Arts Council England. The festival features an exciting range of work including film, theatre, music, traditional and heritage arts, outdoor performances, participatory workshops, digital media-based projects, roundtable discussions, and more, taking place across multiple locations in London and other parts of the UK."

Annie was one of their producers and she had found out about me and *Bound Feet Blues* when she had Googled for an East Asian storyteller. Now, she was sitting in the wing chair opposite me and asking about me and the show, my performance experience and my plans for developing the piece into a full theatre production. She was a Singaporean, now living in London, and a multimedia theatre producer in her own right. I warmed to her friendly presence and open, easy smile.

I gave her a big picture version of my roundabout route to creating *Bound Feet Blues*. It felt odd to refer to it as a 'show', which made it seem very grand and as if it should be filled with dancing girls and a cast of at least hundreds. I explained that I thought of it as a story performance rather than a dramatic monologue or play.

"I want to be completely open with you," I said. "I have no formal drama training or theatre experience…"

"Really?" Her eyes were wide. "The way you moved and held

those poses – especially that bound foot mother, so still and for so long. I thought you were professionally trained."

"Well, I had some guidance from my voice coach for some of that."

"Still…" She scrutinized me with curiosity.

"Also, at this point, I haven't finished the script yet but I should be able to do that in the next couple of months."

"Do you have an idea of when you'll finish it? You left us all on the edge of our seats. I want to know how it ends."

"I'm not sure yet how to end it. I just know that this first part opens outdoors and then it gets smaller and smaller until I'm on my knees like going into a V-shaped funnel and the second half opens it all up again. So it will end somewhere outdoors."

"Do you think you can have the show ready by October/November? That's when the Festival will be."

I blinked. Was she really inviting me to take part in the SEA Arts Fest?

I thought she might have been put off by my lack of professional theatre experience and the lack of a finished script. I was confident I could finish the script. That was entirely within my control. But to put on the piece as a full theatrical work in an international arts festival …

"Um… I don't have a director. It's just me. Apart from some input from my voice coach, no-one really directed what you saw the other night.

Again, Annie's eyes widened. "Really?"

"Jessica helped me with voice work and gave me ideas for some of the sequences like the body-binding bit - but I kind of just, well, let the rest of it happen…"

She took that in, nodding.

I went on, "The lighting and everything was all put on by the workshop as part of the scratch night."

"Yes, I could see it was just general lighting."

"I have no technical team. I don't have a producer. And I don't know anything about getting it into a theatre venue…" My voice trailed off.

"We'll be interested to see whatever you have by then. If you manage to pull a full production together that would be fantastic, but six months is probably not enough time for that. Even if it's a still work in progress or you offer us a rehearsed reading, we can programme it into the Festival."

Now it was my turn to look astonished. "Really?"

She laughed. "It's an interesting and unusual piece. It needs to be seen and we're keen to help new South East Asian artists."

I stared at her. I could hardly believe it. She was offering me an incredible opportunity. I had tried to dissuade her with all the reasons I was not competent to do this and yet, here she was, still inviting me to be part of this huge event.

This was a once in a lifetime chance and instinctively, I knew I wanted use it as a catalyst to develop the piece into something greater than I had so far imagined. I wanted to take it as far as it could go in the timeframe of six months. To see how close I could get to a full production of the full script in theatrical form so that I could premiere it at the Festival.

As an umbrella body, the Festival would not be able give me any funding or provide a venue or production team but they could offer advice and letters of support. I had no idea how I was going to pull together all the elements needed for a full production of a theatre show – a director, a producer, lighting, sound, a venue, marketing, funding and more.

Was my ambition in danger of out-vaulting my capabilities? Maybe. But I had to try.

Yet, I knew that even if all I aimed to do was to repeat a similar work-in-progress scratch night at a Conway Hall type venue, it was going to be a huge undertaking. To drive myself to achieve much more than that was almost beyond what my brain could conceive. And even if I could rustle up a production team – how was I going to pay for it all. I had no idea how you applied for Arts Council funding. And besides, would they even look at an application from a non-theatre professional like me? I was aware that the hire of the main auditorium at Conway Hall ran to £3,000 or more for one night – we had only had the use of it for free because the scratch night had been part of the workshop offering. On top of the venue cost, there would be everyone's fees and who knew what else.

Could Annie hear me hyperventilating?

She pressed me, "We'd like to include *Bound Feet Blues* in the SEA ArtsFest programme. Do you think you'll have something ready for us by then?"

Whatever my doubts, whatever I didn't have in place at this moment - there could only be one answer.

I said, "Yes."

Bound Feet Blues, show flyer

Bound Feet

BOUND FEET BLUES – THE STORY

Chosen

My great grandmother was born into a good family China in the late 1800s. She was the eldest daughter, and after her came two more girls. Three girls.

Her father was a physician but he became an opium addict and smoked away their fortune.

For a family left with nothing, having too many girls was a disaster. Because for each girl to marry, you have to pay a dowry to each husband's family.

I imagine her mother looking at her 3 daughter, thinking about their future.

The eldest, Ah Mooi, is four, pretty with delicate features. The second is sturdy and plain. The youngest is still a baby.

If all her daughters have small feet, they could marry well and escape this hard life.

There will never be enough money for 3 dowries.

So she must choose. If she cannot save all her daughters then at least she can try to save one of them.

She chooses Ah Mooi, the one who is pretty and delicate. It is Eldest Sister whose feet she binds. Ah Mooi, who would become my great grandmother.

[Ah Mooi]:

> On the day of my wedding, there is great cause for celebration. I marry a man whose family is better off than my own, with land and servants and a good income. My Mama made this happen – she chose my feet over my sisters' feet. And my whole family, also, all of them working and saving, saving, saving all their money for one dowry.

Runaway

It should have been a happily ever after for Ah Mooi after her wedding. She has married into a good family. She would be provided for and her children would never go hungry. But she cannot give her husband a child.

Then the family she marries into falls on hard times.

Ah Mooi is no use any more as a wife or a mother. She's just another mouth to feed. She is worthless. So they put her to work.

[As Ah Mooi's mother-in-law:]

> Go till the fields. Clean up that mess. Fetch water.

And every step is an agony.

But she is resourceful – so she crawls. She harvests the big heavy pumpkins on her knees, she carries water on her knees. She lives her life on her knees.

[Ah Mooi]:

> This is not the life I was meant to have. My Mama promised me – if I was obedient, if I endured, I would have a good life, a good husband. And it has all come to nothing.
>
> I cannot endure this. I will not endure this.

I have a cousin who owns a goldsmiths shop in Malaya. [Reading a letter] "Come," she says, "work in our shop. Life is good here. No-one cares about bound feet. This is the new frontier."

A new frontier. Like that Gold Mountain in the America where so many people have gone to find a better life. "Malaya is overflowing with the riches of tin and rubber." But I have heard it's a wild, dangerous place – it's hot and humid, it's a jungle and busy with so many people, it's a place of ruffians and loose women.

She imagines for the first time a place without shame. A place where women walk, and run, where they please.

I picture her crawling out of the fields and taking her first step onto the road. How long does it take her to walk from her husband's village to the coast, to board a junk to Malaya? How many days, how many nights? How many tiny baby steps does it take to make such a long, long journey?

That pain, that journey she can endure.

And this is her power.

This cry to the universe, I am not worthless, my hopes matter, my heart matters. I matter.

THE STORIES BEHIND THE STORY

In the few weeks after I met Annie Kwan, I set to work feverishly on the second half of the script. I gave myself the deadline of the end of April, just over a month. Because without a completed script, I may as well have had nothing.

I would come straight home from work every evening and shut myself in my study. After a quick break for dinner with Angie, I would disappear again late into the night. I dug out the piles of notebooks from my twenties when I had spoken to numerous relatives in Malaysia for their stories. I had written up the interviews in long hand, the black ink marching hurriedly across the lined pages as my hand tried to keep up with the movies playing in my mind. Many of them were from the summer of

Editing the finished script spread out on my dining table

1990, when I had spent six months at home with my parents after being made redundant in that bleak financial crisis that ended the exuberance of the eighties. Now, more than twenty years later, it felt odd sitting in my study in London, leafing through those pages again.

I remembered back to those hot mornings in Malaysia, looking out at my parents' lush, tropical garden with a notebook in front of me. I hadn't thought about that time for two decades and now, I was back there in my mind. I could see the desk in front of me, feel the sticky heat of Asia. Next to the notebook on the desk were sheaves of paper scribbled illegibly with notes I had taken during the interviews with my elderly relations. My mother had come with me to meet these relatives and sometimes, acted as translator for many of these elders spoke only Chinese.

As I wrote up these interviews there by the window all those years ago, listening to the cacophony of tropical birds in the trees, I wondered how I would eventually transform them into a book. Or if I ever would, because many of the stories were intimate and private.

It surprised me back then that so many of these elderly women were willing to share with me some of their most private stories, sometimes as tears poured down their cheeks at that memory from seventy or eighty years ago. They knew I wanted to collect them in a book to tell the family story and they saw me writing it all down. These stories involved others in the family as well as the storyteller herself and offered to me the pain and fear and darkness that we all share as human beings but which we rarely talk about in families.

Now looking back from my own middle age, I understood those women's impulse. It was as if they needed to tell those hidden stories – even more than the stories that showed them and the family in the best light. There was a sense of a confessional in some of them and testimony in all them. It was as if in having their stories witnessed, they were allowing their inner most selves to be finally seen.

I realised now that in each of those interview sessions I had been witness to an unbinding. It was as if they had all been women with bound feet, who had slowly, trustingly, unravelled their reams of bandages to reveal to me the tender nakedness within. And I knew in that moment, that as the family member entrusted with their stories, I could not share the ones that were most intimate for my own glory or gain – even though they were the stories that would make the most sensational impact.

Now sitting at my desk late at night in London, I knew I needed to bear witness for these women and yet remain always still that guardian. I would have to find a way to tell these stories without breaking that deeply held value in my heart.

I found my notes about Ah Mooi – or how I usually think of her, Great-grandmother No. 1. Her story written in my notes had been told to me by Great-grandmother No. 4 – the fourth wife of Great-grandfather Lim. There are very few personal details about Ah Mooi's life in China and some twists and turns before she runs away to Malaya. In the broad brush strokes of the story, told to me second hand after seventy or more years, the detail of the pumpkins stood out. I saw a small, serious young woman struggling with the weight of those pumpkins, her tiny feet hardly able to support her. I thought of my research into women with bound feet and how the fashion trickled down from the wealthy elite to the poorest classes, like Princess Kate's long, brunette mane and Top Shop dress creating clones out of young women across the UK today. I remembered reading about peasant women who did their daily work on their knees because they could move faster and be more effective that way.

From my reading of my notes, in the first version of the script that I worked on after Conway Hall, I gave Ah Mooi a rural, peasant background – and especially in order to contrast the high born bound foot mother of the early sections. I wanted to underscore the mother's choice – that in that culture, the binding of a girl's feet was felt as an act of compassion and hope and that it was an honour for Ah Mooi to have been chosen above her sisters.

I spoke to my cousin Pey on Skype and she told me her version of Ah Mooi's story. "No, she was from a high born family. Her father was a physician. But you know, at that time, it was the Opium Wars and many families were ruined by opium. He smoked away all their money. So that's why they ended up poor."

We compared the rest of our versions. The details that matched were clear. Only Ah Mooi as the eldest had had bound feet. She had been married to a man whose family had treated her badly and so she had run away.

There was one significant detail that did not match. Pey said that Ah Mooi had had a son but he may or may not have died. She said, "There's a version in our family that the son died and around that time, Ah Mooi's husband's family also fell on hard times. They blamed her for bringing bad luck to them. That's why they bullied her."

"But if the boy didn't die?"

"Maybe they blamed her anyway for the lost fortune. After all, she came from a family that had suffered that same sort of fate."

"How could she abandon her own child?" I wondered out loud. Then remembered my other research about families and the role of the daughter-in-law. I answered my own question. "That child would have belonged to them, not her, especially if it was a boy. She was the outsider, and married in from a family tainted by bad luck. They would probably have kept them apart or something like that if they despised her so much ..."

Still, it was a harsh thing for a mother to abandon a child.

I mulled on this. It was a huge act of courage and defiance for a woman of her time to break the marriage contract, to disobey her husband and his family and to run away. Even though she was being taken in by her cousin, she would be tainted by shame. And perhaps she carried that sense of bad luck inside her despite her defiance. Perhaps she thought that he would be better off with his family for what future could he have with her, the runaway wife? Perhaps she sensed that if she left without him, they would not bother to come after her – after all, she had no value to them. But if she took the son who belonged to them, they would hunt her down, reclaim him and no doubt punish her even more harshly.

We would never know the definitive story.

I felt I should reflect at least the social circumstances of Ah Mooi's family more accurately. I re-worked the script to the version we now have here. And in some ways, it makes more sense. As daughter of betrayed privilege, who had been promised so much in what she could expect from life, her defiance resonates more stridently. Perhaps her mother had hoped that the bound feet would have given her daughter back the splendour that the family had lost. And so finding herself treated like a servant or worse, her furious indignation would have been so much more potent than that of a peasant girl used to accepting her lot.

I have kept the script simplified on the question of her ability to bear children. It makes for a strong, clear motive for her being bullied harshly. And what we do know for certain is that she was never able to give Great-grandfather Lim a child.

Which brings us to a question that can be troubling for a modern Western audience - if she couldn't have any children with my Great-grandfather, how could I say Ah Mooi is my great-grandmother?

Great-grandfather Lim had four wives. Not sequentially but concurrently. In Chinese tradition, that used to be the norm. They were all of them his wives and so by Chinese logic mothers of his children, grandmothers and great-grandmothers jointly. So Ah Mooi is rightfully my Great-grandmother by heritage if not by biology.

Grandpa was the eldest of the fifteen children that Great-grandfather Lim fathered between the three wives, with Ah Mooi as the matriarch of them all. Great-grandfather Lim was prolific into his old age even as his elder children started families of their own. So the generations in the family bleed across each other like the loosely coloured imprints of ornate *batik* cloth.

My cousin Pey (who uses a shortened form of her full Chinese name) is a few years younger than me but technically she belongs to my mother's generation. Her mother is the same age as my mother but she is Grandpa's sister and daughter of Great-grandfather Lim, which makes her my mother's aunt. So Pey is my mother's first cousin - and therefore my first cousin once removed, I think.

Confused?

Well, the Chinese have a system to help us work out the generational layers. So stay with me.

You may have noticed that Chinese names generally have three bits to them. Our names tell you who we are in order of importance. Family is the overarching, most defining part of our identity. So the family name comes first. Hence, I am really Ooi Yang May.

The next most important element is the generation you were born into. Yang is my generational name. My sister and brother also have Yang as the first part of their double barrel personal names. My mother's generational name is Meng and all her siblings are Meng, too – as well as all her cousins. Her father, Grandpa, had the generational name of Swee, as did all his siblings. So Pey's mother is a Swee generation and that tells everyone that in relation to my mother, she is her aunt.

Finally, last in order of importance, is the individual. So the 'me' bit of my identity is May. My sister and brother have their own individual identity names as well, each coming at the end of the three word sequence. My mother and her cousins each are Meng plus their individual names, too.

Living in the West, my siblings and I have all adapted to local custom and now put our family names at the back. For me, that solves the problem of being filed under 'May' in people's address books and having to untangle all manner of confusion whenever I have to deal with officialdom. I also hyphenate my personal name to stop being called just 'Yang'. My cousin simplified her name to Pey and now takes her English husband's surname, those words clearly reflecting her fusion identity.

For the Chinese there is a power in words, and in particular in a name. Huge importance is placed on the passing on of a family name – which can only be done through the males. Through the continued existence of that name, symbolically the existence of a family endures. The name is even more important than descent through biology – so in Chinese tradition, families without sons have adopted male children in order to bear the name of the family on into the future. And, of course, through the lynchpin role of the eldest male in any generation to keep open the channels of communication with the dead from generations before.

For us girls, the family name – like the proverbial buck – stops with us. So in ancient tradition, females born into a family were thought of as visitors just passing through until they were married off to bear the children of another family. Their names were rarely recorded on the ancestral tablets of their birth family. It is as if their lives left no footprints.

But family is family. Despite strict Confucian theory, beyond the formal traditions we love those we know regardless of the teachings and there is an instinct to look after your own. So Ah Mooi was able to escape because of her extended birth family network

The family name links you to a network beyond your single family unit of mum, dad and their kids. Because there's dad's brother too, all having that same family name. And Granddad (dad's dad), his brothers, and so on back through the male line. So as an Ooi, by Chinese tradition, I am related to all the other Oois spreading out all over China, Malaysia and the world via those pathways made by eager Ooi sperm. The Ooi clan.

The Chinese formalised this sense of clan into an entity somewhat like a corporation. This was especially significant during the tumultuous years of the second half of the 19th century when China saw much upheaval and social change. Many Chinese migrated during those decades, heading to the west coast of America, especially San Francisco, to escape famine and poverty working on the railroads and servicing the gold rush with their laundry and other businesses. Others like the Bandit Boy and Ah Mooi escaped to *Nanyang*, the Lands Beneath the Wind – Malaya and the Indonesian islands. The clans became international networks, bridging the home country and the new. Their overseas headquarters became the bedrock of the Chinese diaspora, offering help and refuge for new migrants of the same names in these lands of hope and opportunity. Each clan often had a *kongsi*, which worked like a community hub centred around the clan temple and into which members paid financial dues. New arrivals would be given help on the understanding that they would contribute their dues later when they had found work. Members would help each other in business or family matters, much like the guilds, associations and networks of the West.

So Fong Cheong Mooi – Mooi of the Cheong generation of three girls and born into the Fong clan, through her cousin who may or may not have been a direct cousin but nonetheless a Fong blood relative, arrived in Malaya on her tiny bound feet. And it was here that destiny brought her into the life of the young hospital orderly who would become my Great-grandfather.

* * *

I don't know how Ah Mooi actually 'ran away'. It is a simple phrase that can mean so much. A friend of mine told me that she once tried to run away from home when she was eight but did not get any further than the next suburban train station because it was getting dark and she started thinking about dinner. I don't think she actually ran, puffing and panting, from the doorstep to the train station with her little backpack. The phrase is used in Monty Python's Holy Grail movie to comic effect when the knights are terrified by a cave-dwelling monster that turns out to be a white rabbit. More darkly, we speak of wives 'running away' from unhappy marriages and abusive husbands.

That is how the story of Ah Mooi was passed down through the generations in my family. At each telling of the story, details of her life before Malaya might have changed but it always came down to this. "She ran away."

Did she really walk and crawl her way to the port? Perhaps in reality her blood family came for her. Perhaps she found a means of transport - donkey cart or carriage or some other vehicle? A proper historical biographer or memoirist might try and find out, research the likely options available to her. In a 'proper' memoir of my family history, I would have needed to do that.

But this is not a 'proper' memoir.

She ran away.

For me, the power of that sentence has a mythic quality when we see it enacted in the defiant body of woman with bound feet.

The opportunity to run away begins as a shift in mindset. If you do not think you have a choice, you will not dare to let in the idea that there is an alternative to the way life is and always has been. Running away begins as a separation, a rending apart of your individual self from the collective whole. A valuing of your Mooi essence above your Cheong place within the continuum of generations and beyond the vast, immoveable eternity that is the meeting place of the Fong clan and the clan of your husband.

It is this creation of the self out of the depths of pain and despair that fascinates me in this story of my great-grandmother.

And so her physical journey of escape, for me, is an epic rendition of her psychological and emotional escape. More than that, through the breaking away from a millennia of collective expectation, in each tiny painful step, there is a becoming and a reaching towards the modern female self.

In truth, to me, it does not matter that she is not my literal, biological great-grandmother. She is me. And she is all of us.

* * *

The stories we tell stake a claim. They say to our listeners in that moment, this is who I am. Our stories show them that we are kind, funny, foolish, hard done by, sad, lost, triumphant, decent, heroic. We are also creating ourselves to ourselves in the telling. As we speak the words, we hear them and relive the re-created event in narrative. Yes, look at me there in that story, I *am* kind and foolish and all these other things. And as our listener laughs or cries or holds their breath along with the narrative, their attention remakes us even more so into that image that the story has offered up to them.

Beyond that moment, our stories tell the world: I was here. As our listeners drift away back to their own lives, the memory of us remains with them. When you put down this book – or when you come out of the theatre after watching *Bound Feet Blues* – you will know that I existed. So, too, as you share your life in stories and anecdotes with friends and strangers at dinner parties or down the pub or chatting idly on a Monday morning at work, you are staking your claim in the world. You are this kind of person – who loves the theatre or works on the garden at the weekends or has had yet another disastrous date or skids down mountains on a rugged bike – and you were here on this earth for this brief moment of a lifetime.

We know the story of how Ah Mooi came to be in Malaya because she told us. She had the temerity to say to the world: *I* was here. In a culture of obedient, submissive women, to tell your story takes a healthy sense of ego. I don't know who she told this story to – perhaps to her husband, perhaps to the children who were hers by tradition, no doubt to the other wives. The broad sweep of it has always been known in the family and only the details waver in the different versions. And it is this specific story – the origin story – that survives most vividly for us because this was her defining moment.

The stories that we remember – whether our own or others' stories – are the ones that have the most meaning for us. Ah Mooi's story has been passed down through the family because for each of us, we take from it a meaning that resonates. The prime significance for the family as a whole, is I think its role as an origin story. Like the story of the Bandit Boy, which told us of our heroic masculine roots, this story of Ah Mooi, tells us of our strong, female lineage. For me, it is above all else, her self-creation out of the clods of earth.

These stories of family and heritage in this book and in the theatre piece come from my mother's side of the family, the Lims. Perhaps it is always the way in many families that the stories come down via the mothers, those chit-chatting garrulous women folk who may never disturb the quiet maleness of the altar of the ancestor. For sure, there are stories on the Ooi side of my family but they are fragmented, piecemeal and do not go back beyond the personal recollections of Grandmother Ooi. The Oois are more circumspect, my father and his brothers making a quartet of quiet men and my Aunty Diana and Aunty Leng too young to have known much about the past generations. Or perhaps it is just that there is a particular storytelling streak that runs down through the Lims.

A young Chinese woman told me recently that it is rare for Chinese families in Malaysia and Singapore to know their family stories in the same intimate way that my family stories have been passed down through the generations. The younger generation do not think to ask about the past and the older prefer the comfort of silence. As she spoke, I remembered that summer of 1990 when I was trying to collect stories from the past and how a number of elderly folk would say, "*Haiya,* why for you want to hear stories for the old days? So much suffering in the past. What for you want to talk about it?"

Perhaps the Lim men were unusually wordy. From the Bandit Boy who told his epic story of devastation and courage to Great-grandfather Lim's tender love story of tending to the lady with bound feet to Grandpa's public orations that played their part in the making of Malaysia, these were men who loved to tell and listen to stories. And there was Grandma, who brought her love of storytelling into the Lims, passing it on in all singing technicolour to my mother – and along with Grandma, too, came the 'making life into parables' skill of at least two generations of Presbyterian preachers.

So it is the Lims who have staked their claim in my imagination and my sense of who I might be. And it is Ah Mooi who has demanded to take centre stage despite her barrenness and her crippled feet.

Perhaps I have always felt drawn to her story because she was the eldest daughter. Just like me. Perhaps it is that she never had any children of her own. Just like me. Perhaps in her serious, bespectacled face, gazing out earnestly from that old black and white photo, I see my own.

In Chinese tradition, if a family had to choose only one daughter whose feet to bind, it was most often the eldest girl's. In the way that the eldest son has his special role as the intermediary between the ancestors and future generations, the eldest daughter

It would have been my feet that would have been bound if I had been born in an earlier time

has a place of honour. Under Confucian rules, age confers respect and status. So elder daughters must be married first before younger ones so as not to lose face and eldest daughters especially have the privilege of being the one to achieve the best marriage of all the girls.

And so, it would have been my feet that would have been bound if I had been born in an earlier time. My sister, younger by three years, might have escaped if there had been good reason not to bind her feet. But not me.

As little girls, did Ah Mooi's sisters, Ah Ngan and Ah Yong, envy their elder sister's tiny feet. Did they feel ashamed of their own big, ugly feet? Or did they feel lucky to be able to skip and dance in the courtyard and run rowdily up the stairs with that untamed energy that all children have? At her wedding to the landed gentleman, did they try to hide their large feet beneath their gowns and feel the embarrassment that modern girls might feel if they turned up at their sister's wedding in trainers beneath their bridesmaids dresses? Or did they feel a relief at their vigorous spinsterhood?

There are different versions of what happened to Ah Ngan, the sturdy and plain second sister. One story goes that she was offered to a businessman in marriage – there were men back then who were prepared to marry women with natural feet in the way that there are men today who would be happy with tomboyish or plain women. But she refused, breaking a bowl as a traditional symbolic gesture of her defiance. I like this version, along with the rest of the family, which gives us an image of two feisty and disobedient Fong sisters.

But there is another version that breaks my heart. According to my notes from 1990, she was pawned by her father to another family to work for them as their servant. With her big feet and sturdy build, she would have made a good workhorse. Was this how they had paid the dowry for Ah Mooi? Or did the money he made from this transaction go still further to feed his opium habit?

I see the two sisters in their alien fields, far from home, one on broken stumps falling to her knees, the other trudging silently over the clods of earth on thick, flat feet.

Others in the family tell one version because that is the version told to them. And there is the second version because that is the version told to me. Which is the true version? I don't know. None of us will ever know.

Whichever one is true or not, Ah Ngan's story is as much a part of my story – all these stories – as Ah Mooi's. What we do know for certain is that, unlike her older sister, Ah Ngan ultimately did become a mother and grandmother and great-grandmother in her own right. While Ah Mooi's barrenness leaves nothing of her for us but her story, Ah Ngan's fertility means that she will be forever remembered in our DNA, and silence will not annihilate all that she has been.

Yes. Our DNA. Because Ah Ngan is my true biological great-grandmother.

* * *

I think of Ah Mooi in the hot, tropical climate of Malaya with all its vibrant colours and thick, lush vegetation. She may have started out with her cousin in the goldsmith's shop but we know that at some point, she was earning her living as a seamstress. I see her focusing intently on embroidery or a garment, her eyes and hands working together in swift harmony. I think of her as a quiet woman – perhaps it is that earnest stillness of that photograph that makes me imagine that she is not a lively extrovert. I sense a contentment in this tableau – a room of her own, her needles and thread, nothing more needed than her skill.

How did that steamy climate affect her feet? For hundreds of years in China, women would have to take great care of their feet to prevent infection and skin problems under the thick layers of bandages – and that would have been in much cooler air temperatures. With the heavy damp heat of the tropics, would she have had to unwind the bandages more often and wash and powder her feet more fastidiously?

What was it like for her adjusting to this new culture, the jostling of races and religions, the Wild West frontier feel of a tin mining town like Taiping? I see her tottering carefully along the bustling street, a small woman on small feet, walking without a chaperone, making her own way in the world. Did she laugh more, chatter more, and in the looser structures of a foreign land, did she find affinity with other women friends?

Lying in that hospital bed with an eye infection, it must have seemed to her that she had arrived in a fairy tale. Her father and her husband had been men who had judged poorly and loved poorly. Because of her father, first her mother and her own family had suffered the desperation of having little money. Then she herself had endured the harshness that poverty made of her husband's family. It seemed all her life she had known only hardship. Till now in this wild, chaotic land. And beyond all she could possibly take in, here was this young hospital orderly coming to her bedside every day, being so solicitous, so kind, "nursing her back to health" as the family story goes. Was it any wonder she fell in love and married this prince of a man? But she could not give him any children. And she knew that he wanted a family.

It was common for a man to take a number of wives – especially if he was a man of substance. Great-grandfather Lim earned enough as a hospital orderly to be a man of substance in his community. He still loved Ah Mooi, that was certain, so he was not going discard her for the simple fact of infertility. He would just find a second wife who could bear him children.

I can see Ah Mooi thinking this over. Her life here was good. She had a house to live in and a husband who loved her. He did not make her do harsh physical work. He earned enough to give them a good life. I see her thinking about her sister, Ah Ngan, indentured for years to a family who would never release her if their loan was not repaid. And heart ached for her little sturdy sister.

In this version of the story, Ah Mooi took her husband back to China and he redeemed her sister from servitude. And Ah Ngan became his second wife. What does it take to give your sister to your husband like this? What love for her. And for him.

Would I do such a thing for my sister?

I cannot imagine it.

But perhaps if we both lived in a world of desperation and suffering and powerlessness…I picture Ah Mooi weighing up the situation. Her sister was somewhere beyond the many oceans, scrubbing, cooking, cleaning, working in the fields – a once well-born girl, her own blood, enduring what she herself had refused to endure. While she, Ah Mooi, lived this good life – soon to be shared with another woman, a stranger, someone else who would enjoy all this abundance. Why should not that woman be her own sister for whom her heart hurt each time she thought of her?

In the other version of the story, Ah Ngan is simply at home, unmarried, not doing very much. It's the less painful version. The version where she is safe and keeps her dignity.

But without the desperation, what Ah Mooi did does not make sense. Or perhaps it does not make sense only in the context of my modern sensibility. Perhaps it was a logical and reasonable option in the context of a woman in that period to do such a thing without there being a heart-breaking reason.

Whichever version you pick, we find Ah Ngan arriving in Malaya as Great-grandfather Lim's second wife. She became the mother of Grandpa, the eldest son. As was the tradition in Confucian hierarchy, she 'gave' this most precious child in name to Wife No. 1, her elder sister, so that as the first wife, Ah Mooi did not lose face for having failed to bear a child into the Lim family in her own right. So Grandpa was beloved of two mothers – with that double love and the mark of greatness on his forehead, how could he not have had the life that he did have?

As if they had a sense of what lay ahead for him, the family feared the jealous gods whom we all know take for themselves those things which we most cherish. In a culture brought up on hardship and the uncertainties of failed harvests, opium addiction, bandits marauding through the countryside, for the Chinese our gods rarely love and protect us without getting something out of it. More likely, these powerful unseen beings destroy on a whim, or out of mischief and malice, or simply grab whatever they want from you like thugs. So we make offerings at their altars to appease them like we might pay protection money to appease the *triads* – oranges symbolizing gold, food for their voracious hunger, spiritual paper money. We are also cunning and hide from their greedy eyes whatever we hold most precious.

So the family gave Grandpa the pet name, *Babi*, which means Pig. The gods would not want a dirty, ugly pig. And so they kept him safe.

This unease about the power of these pagan gods is so strong that it cannot be dispelled by the Christian baptisms that were intended to wash away such stuff and nonsense. Great-grandfather Reverend Quek - Grandma's father - had the arrogance to challenge the gods as a young, fervent Presbyterian. He named his two eldest sons with perfect, heavenly names. They were beloved and precious to the whole family. But the Christian god could not protect them. They died before their twenties, snatched by the jealous, covetous Chinese gods.

Which is why, when my mother asked Reverend Quek's advice about naming her eldest child, he told her to name me Yang-May – which means Reflection of Beauty. I am only a reflection – *yang* - of beauty – *may* - and not perfect, glorious beauty itself.

Our Chinese gods are like us mortals, imperfect, messy, a tangle of goodness and unpredictable appetites – the only difference being their interactions play out on an eternal, cosmic scale. In my mind, they are somewhat like Great-grandfather Lim. In the old sepia photographs, he is a big, dominating figure. He was an Elder in the Baptist Church and yet had four wives according to

Chinese tradition. He was kind and caring with Ah Mooi but his capacity for love was huge and gathered in to his home more and more women.

There's a story that before Ah Mooi, he had had another woman. We know her as the 'Malay mistress'. She was never a wife, only ever a mistress. Her name is lost to us as is any trace of who she was. We only know that she was a *bomoh* – a healer, a witch, a shaman – and she had taught him shamanic magic, which he passed on down into the family. We don't know what happened to her and how it is he came to be alone at the time he met Ah Mooi.

Beyond Ah Mooi and Ah Ngan, he needed more. He took a third wife, Wong Hee, who in her turn had also experienced domestic servitude before he found her. But he was still restless, remembering a young, pretty girl.

The story goes that while he was in China all those years before to broker the arrangement that made Ah Ngan his second wife, he had met that young pretty girl in the Fong family household. He had not been able to forget her and when she came to visit Malaya some years later, his desire for her was still as strong and wanted her to be his wife.

She was the youngest Fong sister, Ah Yong, the one who had been a baby when Ah Mooi's feet were bound.

Did the two older sisters object? Could they object? Or did they view their lives as the lives of mortals in the hands of a godlike figure that had saved them both? Or perhaps they were happy for their baby sister that she, too, would have the same good life that they had been granted.

By rights, Ah Yong should have become Wife No. 4 but he wanted her to be No. 3, closer to her sisters in the hierarchy. So Wong Hee became my Great-grandmother No. 4.

Wong Hee was the last remaining elder from that generation for many years after her husband and co-wives died and she became the keeper of the old traditions and stories. It was her that I spoke to at length in that summer of 1990 when I was gathering the family stories from so many sources. I remember her laughter and tears as she relived the past, her wistfulness for all that had gone and her gratitude for the life she had had. By the time she died only a few years ago, she was the matriarch to children, grandchildren, great-grandchildren and great-great-grandchildren – her own and those of the three Fong sisters, actual and in name - who had spread all across the globe.

I think about these women – three sisters and the outsider – all of them living with their children and their one husband in a single house. Each mother had one room and with her were all her children. Each wife had a night allocated to her for visits with her husband. What tensions were there? What rivalries? And what pleasures and contentment?

This was all that they could aspire to, these women whose education was limited to the domestic world. Even for those who had all the advantages of wealth and a good living, like Chen Duansheng, the Jane Austen of her time, all they knew was calligraphy, poetry, music, the running of a household and the art of foot-binding. All the safety, comfort and luxuries they enjoyed depended on the beneficence of their fathers or husbands, or the goodwill of relatives. Beyond marriage and the clan was the world of trade and commerce. To earn your own living – to be independent - you have to have something of value to sell whether it is goods or services. For the women of that earlier generation, all they had to offer was their bodies.

Women who could not find the protection of a husband could only offer their domestic skills. They were servants or seamstresses, with very little earning power. Or prostitutes. In the new frontier of Malaya, women were freer to be traders or artisans but that needed capital for tools and goods and a boldness for barter and trade. The career path of a cross-dressing heroine like Meng Lijun could only be imagined in the fantasies of housebound women and never lived by them. There were no women lawyers or doctors or public officials. No women earning their own living with their intellect. No women with personal economic power. So even as Ah Mooi could escape from the harsh servitude of her first loveless marriage, she could only ever have hoped for a good life through the power of another man, with all that his contradictions entailed.

I think about these women – these four wives and mothers. No doubt, they were grateful for how their lives turned out with the love and respect that they found with Great-grandfather Lim, his children and within their community. But did each of them ever dream of more? Of having one man who devoted all of himself to her and her alone? Of having money of her own? Of making choices based on her own whims and desires and wishes? How much more might they have been had they lived in a later time? What richness of choice might have been open to them, what economic independence? Who might they have become in their own right?

* * *

I imagined England long before I stepped into its cool embrace. In the sticky humidity of my childhood, listening to my mother tells stories of her *pak tor* days with my father in Cambridge and London, England took root in my mind. It was strange thinking of a place where outside could get as cold as an air-conditioned room – and even be coated with ice and snow like the freezer compartment where I would dig out the ice-cream from amid the clatter of frozen meat. She told us about peasoupers and how scary it was trying to find her way home through the thick smog after going to the cinema one night. She remembered fondly picnics by the river where you didn't have to worry about snakes in the long grass or fire ants dropping down from the tree above or mosquitoes humming for blood.

I read the *Famous Five* books, the *Secret Seven* and *Mallory Towers* series. There were the Ladybird books and *Look and Learn* magazine. I loved *The Avengers*, *The Saint* and *The Champions*. With my lawyer father, we all huddled round the black-and-white TV to watch *Crown Court*. England was a place where people wore jackets and coats without sweating. London in the swinging

'60s with its streets edged with black iron railings and teeming with hipsters in mop tops and Chelsea boots was the city I wanted to be in. The English were erudite, clever, brilliant with words and had a haughty, understated *sang-froid* that was fascinating to me.

England was also the land of Shakespeare and Dickens, the Brontes and the Bloomsbury set. It pulsated with the heart beats of writers and great literature. My super cool Uncle Hugh in London sent me an Everyman's Classic hardback of Wilkie Collins's *The Woman in White* and I devoured over two days, the misty meeting

My first English dress with a pair of Clarks

of the narrator Hartright and the eponymous ghostly woman on Hampstead Heath forever steeped into my imagination. The Oxford English Dictionary felt like a secret book of magic to me – for in it lived the richness and power of the English language. I spent hot, languid afternoons reading the dictionary, learning new words and phrases, exploring their origins and trying to work them into my stories. I loved the complexities of English spelling and grammar, and the multitudinous explosion of its vocabulary. Mastering it was a joyous challenge like learning sword-fighting. You need precision and speed and flow as well as flair and courage and power to use language well. You need to know when to thrust and when to hold back, when to use flourish and when to be sparing, when to cut and when to parry. You need to know your tools – foil, sabre, epée, broadsword, rapier, adverb, past pluperfect, third conditional, subjunctive – and use them as if by second nature. In the heat of Malaysia, the dictionary and these great books of literature connected my thirsty soul to England, a land that seemed almost mythical in my imagination.

In my child's heart, England was my new frontier. It was the place where I would become a writer. A place where I could fully become me.

It seemed so impossible there in my bedroom, looking out at a practical, bustling Malaysia. It was a world of doctors and engineers and lawyers and business people carving out a modern city at the muddy meeting place of two steaming rivers, for which Kuala (intersection) Lumpur (mud) is named. There was no place for daydreamers and idlers. In this precarious foothold in the jungle, you had to find a way to make a living, to find security for you and your family, or slip down into the oozing depths. My family, over generations of hard work and sacrifice, had built something to be proud of - solidity in reputation and income as well as in bricks and mortar. Everyone was a high-achiever, straight A students, top of their university classes, well known and respected professionals.

And here I was a rebellious, sullen child in my odd tomboy

outfits. I was the eldest grand-daughter to one of the founding fathers of the nation - I should have been like JFK's daughter, Caroline Kennedy, well turned out, polite and appropriately dressed. In a family known for their academic prowess, I was bringing home report cards and exam scores that made me simply average with Bs and Cs and comments about careless mistakes and not paying attention in class.

"This writing stories is all fine for fun, but you got to get a real job," they would say. "You can't expect your dad to support you all your life. You got to work hard at your studies, not just reading story books all the time."

But I could not imagine becoming a doctor. Blood and gore frightened me. The technical names of biological parts in text books and anatomy posters seemed like gobbledygook. Maths and Physics felt like the piling high of concrete blocks only to unstack them all again. Law was all about rules and making people bend and shape themselves to fit inside the cages that those rules built.

I felt useless. The only thing I loved was English. And it was the only thing I excelled at. A grades - always A grades in English and Creative Writing. But what was the use of A grades in such pointless subjects?

When I got into Oxford, it surprised my extended family. And I was there to read English, not Medicine or Law or Engineering.

"All that money that your dad is spending on your education and you will just end up an English teacher. Cannot earn money like that-lah."

After Oxford, the thought of going back to Malaysia made me sick to the stomach. I had been away from home for ten years by then.

Boarding school had given me the social confidence and cut-glass voice of the England that had run the Empire. Oxford had polished away any remaining awkwardness into a persona that radiated feminine sensuality. The brittleness of my public school tones were softened into a mellifluous *sang-froid*. I found there my glittering set of friends and I had done all the things that one should do at Oxford from the punting to the balls to the self-consciously theatrical White Evening.

I was on my way to becoming me, wasn't I? How could I go back now to a place where I had last lived as a child of twelve, uncertain and trapped inside an awkward, loathed body?

In KL, my father was - and is - a well-known lawyer. My late Grandpa's status was still shining bright in many memories. If I went back to make a life in Malaysia, I would always be Mr Ooi's daughter and Dr Lim's grand-daughter.

So I decided to stay on in England.

In my twenties in London, I lived in a flat in Pimlico - one of those white Regency blocks with black iron railings at street level just like I had seen on TV all those years ago. After two years at law school in Chancery Lane and two years as an articled clerk - trainee solicitor - at a law firm in Westminster, I was at the centre of a high-brow, high-achieving group of friends and I was doing all the things one should do as a part of the English professional classes - opera, theatre, museums, art galleries, weekends with friends in the country, trips to European cities.

I had achieved everything that had seemed so impossible once when I had dreamed of England as a child. And yet, I had not become a writer. Nor had I become me at all.

As a newly minted solicitor, I had my own office looking out over the skyline of the City and my own secretary, Diane, a blonde ex-sergeant in the military who commuted in every morning from Essex. After my articles, I had had 11 job offers from some of the best firms in London. I had chosen this 'bluechip' firm, one of the top five in the country, a glossy multinational full of glass and steel and power. I was earning more than some of the young men in my social group who were starting out as junior accountants and that was surprisingly pleasing.

My desk was by the window, looking into the long, blue room. I had a fancy multi-buttoned phone and an official-looking desktop dictating machine. In the days before computers, I worked from a large diary and A4 notepads amid the beige file wallets. I wore

A-line skirts and smart tops with a small knotted scarf, giving off a European air. I had a range of navy and black loafers and pumps, depending on my outfit, ditching heels in favour of shoes that I could move quickly in but which retained a feminine elegance.

I had proven my family wrong. I had made it into one of the top law firms in the world as a Chinese woman in a foreign country. I was comfortable and accepted within English society. I was not the useless daughter who would be living off my parents indefinitely as some in my extended family feared I would become. And I was going to surprise them even more and prove them forever wrong.

My supervising partner was still in his forties and making a million pounds a year. Not only was I now making a good salary, I would work my way up the corporate ladder to partnership. I was going to have it all - a great job, a great flat, a handsome and wealthy boyfriend (soon to be husband of course), a great set of friends. And somewhere in the mix, I was going to be a bestselling author, too.

My extended family was right. Money gave you the power to make your own life. With money, you can make your own choices. And I wanted more than anything, to be free to make my own choices.

I had made it to a new frontier and yet, I carried the old world with me.

I looked around at my friends and colleagues, at London at the height of the '80s. I saw the confidence of all these people in big shouldered suits, the strutting way they moved, their exuberant energy. This was a new frontier - this world of financial speculation, hot trades and rising stocks. Many of these bankers and lawyers and stockbrokers and accountants had nothing but a good education and their brains. They were all making something of themselves and there was a pride in that. I wanted that certainty and boldness. There was a tribal vigour in the way they all bonded around success and prestige. And I wanted that absoluteness of belonging.

With my outward confidence and a look and voice that gave me prestige, I passed as one of these Bright Young Things. I

Bright Young Things

had been doing this for years now, ever since Oxford, and I had become a master craftsman at it all. But it seemed that the more I worked at it and the longer I spent as Her, the China Doll, the more pronounced the fracture grew between myself and my disguise. The gung-ho confidence of these other yuppies seemed to flow from inside them out into the world and I wanted that unshakeable oneness.

Sometimes, after a night out, I would come home to my empty flat in Pimlico and stand for a moment in the living room with the lights off. The curtains would still be open. The room had 12 foot high ceilings and French windows that stretched up to the all the way from the floor. The orange street lights through the translucent net curtains gave the cavernous room an eerie glow. I would find myself sitting down in an armchair the semi-darkness, my jacket still on.

It felt like the end of a performance. Everyone in the theatre was gone. It was just me here in the darkened wings in full stage make-up and half out of my costume. The script had run out. There was only a blank page. There was nothing left for me to do but wait. To start over the next day when the show would begin again.

Out there in the day time, my mind felt under assault. There were leases and contracts, development agreements and tax issues, documents upon documents filled with words. The tangle of statutes and rules and legal concepts fought for my attention. Huge consequences hung on minutiae. I spent hours on the phone arguing over the meaning of the phrase 'material defect'. Arbitrary deadlines dotted my diary like land mines with millions of pounds at risk if they were not met. I counted out my life in six minute chunks, each bite worth £35, each cumulative hour £210. Time was literally money and the law owned mine.

I was seeing Andy but Mark was hovering on the edges. There were parties and drinks and dinner with a wide circle of lively and witty friends. I flirted and teased, laughed and joked. I talked about the latest plays and operas, planned city breaks, discussed books and what was going on in the news.

These days and evenings spent acting out my life of success were exhausting. Often, my back would go into spasm and it was agonizing to sit or stand for too long. My acne was flaring up in angry red spots that screamed to be stared at. There was a tension in my chest and it felt like a struggle to speak, my lips and tongue caught in a scrambling stammer. I hid it all with furious determination, switching impossible words with easier synonyms, taking paracetamol for the pain, coating my face with acne cream and desperate make-up.

Sitting there in the dark, off-stage at last, there was something comforting about those moments. I liked the quiet. It reminded me of the quiet of those solitary moments in the bathroom long ago where my mother would leave me to cool off in the midst of one of my tantrums. They gave me the space to remember myself. I longed to stay there in the eerie half-light, unmoving in the armchair. But I knew I could not.

I had staked my claim in my new frontier. It had to be a success. I needed it to be a success.

I wanted to offer this gift to my parents and my family. I am not a failure any more. You chose me to groom for success, despite my disobedience and tantrums. You chose all of us, my brother and sister and me. You saved whatever money you had and you gave me everything I needed to make this life here in England. My dream came true because of you. All that I have become - this attractive woman, this high-powered lawyer, this successful professional - I could create of myself because I was here in this new country far from home. I could escape because of you.

I needed this new life, this new me, here in England to be a success - as a gift for them. And a vindication for me. And I would stand up, flick on the lights and get ready for the next day.

* * *

I see the Bandit Boy, a grown man now, sitting on the steps of his atap house late in the evening, the coconut fronds forming the roof rustling in the light breeze. He has settled the indenture that brought him to Malaya, two years' service of labour to pay off the debt of the sea passage. Ten years on from that he has made enough to buy this small piece of land in the forest outside Taiping and built this wooden house on stilts as is the local custom, the height keeping the interior cool. Out there in the dark is his market garden, teeming with ladies fingers and marrows and cabbages to sell in the frontier tin-mining town a few miles away. He has done well enough to own a bullock cart, the old neutered bull snorting every so often in the night like a snoring grandfather.

He thinks about his mother. How she would beam with pride sometimes when she looked up from the washing line and saw him coming home from the fields. He remembers his father and his younger brothers and sisters, clustered round the table in the kitchen, hunched over their chopsticks and bowls, the dim lamplight casting their faces in a yellow glow. He cannot bear to think of the night of the bandit raid so he clears his throat and rolls another cigarette. He is rich enough to enjoy these small luxuries.

Inside the house behind him, he hears his wife stir in their bed. His two sons sleep close by her - he cannot hear them but he knows they are there. All this that he has achieved he has done for them. And also for the ghosts in his heart. He survived and they did not. He bound himself to the men that destroyed his home and his village. Sometimes he used to imagine that maybe his mother escaped or that his family somehow survived. If he could run away from the bandit gang and find his way home, maybe they would be there waiting for him. But he never went back for them. He stayed with these men, too afraid to run, too grateful that they had not killed him, too loyal for the small decencies they showed him. He did things with these men and for them that he would never speak of. He survived. And when he could escape, he never went back.

He had made a good life here. There were so many opportunities here where the old hierarchies did not hold such power. Where with hard work and your wits, you could rise above the hand to mouth existence of the old country. Bad harvests and famine were memories from distant lands, war and turmoil were stories from other lives lived faraway. He would not be here if the bandits had not come that night. He would still be in that old village, working in the fields with his father, without education bound forever within his peasant class and accepting whatever fate brought them through weather and harvests, no more than a single tiny entity amid the desperate millions of China.

This good life he had made was for his family long gone. They would not have given up their lives for nothing. Their line would still continue. The values they held would still endure. This was for them, this hard work and success, this rootedness to the earth. A foreign earth that was now where he belonged. He would prove to them he was a good man. He was the man they had brought him up to be - a farmer, a family man, the eldest son who would make good for the sake of the ancestors and whose children would justify the exchange in fortune he had made with his dead family.

I think about Ah Mooi, too, sitting sometimes in the dark of her room just before the time for dinner. The children from the many mothers are spread out across the house, studying, playing. The other wives are in the kitchen or in their rooms or with the children or their husband. Here alone in the darkness, with the sounds and smells of all that is good in her life, she cannot help the pang of shame that will never let go of her heart.

She was not as strong as her mother wanted her to be. She did not endure her first marriage as she should have done, like a good wife and an honourable daughter would have done. She was willful although her mother taught her to be obedient. She blamed her mother for a promise no mother could possibly have been able to keep, no matter how much she might have wanted it for her daughter: that Ah Mooi would have a good life. She railed to her cousin when she should have kept silent. The pitiful complaints tugged at the hearts of her kin who broke protocol to help her. She defied the traditions of the old ways. She ran away despite knowing the shame that such behaviour would bring to her parents and family.

The smell of the warm night wafts in through the open window. Ah Mooi thinks of her mother in China, bound at home on her tiny feet and shackled in duty to her opium-addled husband, doing what she can to eke out a living with her sewing. She and her sisters send money home when they can and that eases her heartache a little.

She remembers making that trip home those many years ago, her new husband beside her. She could not save her mother but at least, she could save one of her sisters. And as it has turned out, she saved both of them because of this big-hearted man with his big appetite for love.

Perhaps that is why she offered Ah Ngan to her husband, whichever version of Ah Ngan's story you prefer. Even without any dire circumstances of a sister in bondage, perhaps Ah Mooi's sense of shame for her transgression impelled her to give first one sister and then the other the good life they could never have as big-footed spinster daughters of an opium addict in China. She did what she felt was right by her family in spite of how she may have felt for her own pride and dignity. She did what was right for her husband. That is what you do as a daughter, a sister and a wife.

Sitting there in the dark in my flat in Pimlico, the ambition and hopes of generations throbbed like pulsing heart inside me. The story of the Chinese diaspora is the story of wanderers who walked out of the fields away from poverty and famine and wretchedness to find better lives for their families beyond an empty horizon. They could bring with them nothing but their minds and bodies. In the precariousness of their new lives, scorned as aliens wherever they landed, they worked on silently and endured. My family had endured for four generations in Malaysia and now, in the fifth, I was moving on again. Back home, I had everything - and I could have even more if I went back. I would be able to walk into any law firm there, there would be a line of eligible young men from KL's elite, we would soon own a huge house with a pool and a host of servants. I would be somebody there just like members of my family had been for the last two generations. There was no poverty or famine or wretchedness waiting for me back home.

And yet, I needed to leave.

We are all haunted by an ancestral past.

For those of us who do not question all that has gone before, we pass it all on for millennia as the bound foot mothers passed on their love and cruelty. We pass on the bondage of tradition and culture, values of love or hate, acts of honour or selfishness, alcoholism, activism, depression, service to others, abuse, compassion. Our family and clan and heritage entangle us so deeply that our choices seem to be our own.

For those of us who struggle to break away, the past remains with us nonetheless, fragmented and reshaped but still with a hold that seems impossible to sever. We can see its looming shadow, try to pull out from its reach but like a slip-knot noose, the more we battle against it, the more its stranglehold tightens on us even as we think we are escaping.

For all us, whether we question or struggle, the winding sheet of the past always tightens as we tie another knot in it or as we thrash to break free. The only true freedom - as I was yet to learn - comes from turning towards our pasts with an acceptance that will allow the ties to slacken: and it is in that moment of loosening that we will find that we were free all along.

* * *

I wanted to be in love with Andy. He was certainly in love with me. I liked the way he drank me in with his bright blue eyes. I liked his big, barrel-chested frame hovering protectively over me. He had soft dark hair in a Hugh Grant cut and wore glasses despite his sporty Rugby playing looks, giving him that charming mix of sensitivity and hunkiness. He was charming and polite and made the perfect escort to any social function.

One evening, we stood on the balcony of my flat in Pimlico. He had walked me home after the theatre. It was a warm night and I was wearing a soft white man's shirt, over a turquoise skirt. I stood in a low pair of Italian pumps but balancing my feet close together as if I was in higher heels. The shirt was too big for me and slid lightly off one shoulder.

Andy stood behind me, standing close but not touching. He leaned in to kiss my bare shoulder. I felt his arms slide around my waist and I let myself fall into his all-consuming embrace.

Across the street, I noticed the man walking his dog turn and walk the dog back again, trying not to look like he was staring up at us. I couldn't help smiling and tried not to look as if I had noticed him. I leaned my head back into Andy's broad chest and reached up a hand to his cheek. I knew we looked like a beautiful couple.

I wondered how many people were watching from behind those shaded windows across the street. Or at the building across the junction. The man with the dog had given up pretending not to watch, making his third or maybe fourth pass, eyes riveted. A couple strolled by, holding hands – they smiled and then looked at each other, foreheads touching, drawing together into a cuddle. Other passers-by looked up, necks craning as they carried on walking.

I turned and draped my arms around his neck, reaching up with my mouth to find his. He drew me tight against him as we kissed. For a big, athletic man, his kisses were gentle and sensuous.

He lifted me up. I laughed, and cupped his face in my hands. Looking down at Andy, feeling his arms holding me aloft, I thought: *I could be happy with him, couldn't I?* I leaned down and kissed him. We hung there in this perfect iconic tableau for what seemed a long time, just kissing.

He took me home to visit his parents in Bath. They lived in a tall townhouse on a wide avenue of Regency houses. Stepping into its solid, tasteful interior, I felt as if I had walked into a film set. The rooms had the timeless elegance of those English houses you see in *Upstairs, Downstairs* or any Merchant-Ivory movie, with white bookcases and heavy sofas and wingchairs mixed in with Wedgewood and mahogany. But it had the lived in feel of a close knit family. Oil paintings and family photos jostled for place on the walls. Green wellies and Barbour jackets spilled out of the coat room. A newspaper folded to the crossword page lay on the

Oriental rug on the floor. The old black Labrador came to sniff at me and wandered back to its place by the fire.

His father had once been a partner in one of the major management consultancies and now headed his own firm serving the West Country. Like Andy, he was a big broad man, but with a commanding gravitas that made his son seem like a small, eager teddy bear beside him. His mother had something of Katherine Hepburn mixed with Shirley MacLaine about her - a combination of grandeur and mischievousness that gave the house, and the family, its vitality. She radiated wit and intelligence, dancing in her conversation from art to musical theatre to literature and the local cultural scene. I sensed them assessing me curiously while we talked about *Les Miserables,* the theatrical phenomenon of that time, and adaptations of novels into plays and whether the books or shows were ever comparable. They were erudite, witty, at ease with themselves.

In his mother's company, Andy was amusing, enthusiastic, confident - a young man who knew where he was going. His sister Frances was home that weekend, too, a down to earth vet who had a seriousness that made her seem older than Andy. I wondered if she had arranged her visit to coincide with ours so she could see this new girl of Andy's for herself. She seemed more at ease with quiet, sharing warm low exchanges with her father - and at times, I sensed them both metaphorically rolling their eyes at Andy.

Seeing him with his father, I felt my heart soften even more for Andy. His father had been captain of his rugby team but Andy was just one of many in his team. Andy was in his second year at one of the big national banks but he kept failing his banking exams. In his father's company, everything he said seemed foolish. The more he tried, the more he seemed like an uncertain but eager-to-please panda trying to ingratiate himself to a big black grizzly.

We took a drive with his mother out to the countryside surrounding Bath. He wanted to show me this county that he loved. He pointed out his school and the hills where they ran the paper chase. I widened my eyes, "A paper chase? You mean, like in *The Railway Children?*"

"Yes."

"Any young girls waving their knickerbockers at you?" I teased, thinking of Jenny Agutter and her bloomers, flagging down the train near the end of the film.

"Aah, if only, if only…" Andy sighed like a forlorn Romeo. His mother laughed.

She liked me. That was a good sign. I was that dusky maiden again - that outsider who had come into the life of another English son. Was I their kind of person? Would I fit in? Would I make him happy, work well within the dynamic of their family, be someone they could take to social functions. I could talk about theatre and literature - tick. I could reference the beloved classics of an English childhood - tick. I was mischievous but not too much - tick.

We turned down a winding lane through a thicket of trees. It meandered deeper into a dappled forest.

"Where are we going?"

Andy beamed. "You'll see."

We came to a tiny Norman church. It was like something you would find in a fairy tale. We got out of the car and strolled in the churchyard. Some of the headstones were ancient. The overhanging trees and song birds gave this sacred knoll a magical feel. As I took all in, appreciating the beauty and its special secrecy, I sensed them noticing my responses.

We went inside. The whitewashed walls were bumpy with the weight of centuries. Rainbow sunlight streamed in through the stained glass windows. "It's beautiful," I said.

Andy said, "This is where I want to get married. My parents got married here and this is where I will, too."

Was he asking me? For a moment, I was thrown.

No, no. He was he showing me his dream, the tender part of his heart. Here, with his mother, his sense of history and family, he was showing me what could be if I could love him as he would like me to.

"It would be a fairy tale wedding," I said softly.

That evening, watching this family at dinner together, I envied their self-possession and contentment. On Andy's father's side, the family had been in this area going back to before Jane Austen's time. Although his father had worked in London and travelled internationally as a management consultant, he had ultimately been drawn back to Bath. This rootedness gave them a solidity that placed them in the continuum of English history and a belonging that was so much a part of who they were that they did not even notice it. They knew so many families and businesses in the area, and spoke of them in tones that wove in decades of friendship and knowledge. They talked with each other as they talked with the world outside without changing, even as my family and I, in contrast, would change between a Malaysian voice and an English one. Their conversation took in the practical and banal as well as the philosophical and highbrow, treating ideas and values and morality as part of living and working and making money. They included me with warmth beyond cordiality and it felt as if, for an evening at least, that I belonged within this rooted, solid fabric of an England that encompassed a thousand years of history and innumerable generations of one family in one place, confident in themselves and in the world.

The next week, back in London, back in the office, I felt a sense of collapse. I had not made any friends with the lawyers at work - their tall, black-suited cliques were like an impenetrable cabal. I did not stay at the office as late as they did, could not break into their sharp, in-the-know sense of humour as I fought to hide my incapacitating stammer. I was having difficulty negotiating leases for harsh-voiced clients and every time the phone rang, my stomach churned in knots.

The million-pound partner called me into his office. My billable hours were down. I had made several mistakes. He sat me down and said, "You need to focus. You can't just leave by 6pm - or even 8pm. The others are here through to one in the morning. You need to show us you are willing to do what it takes."

That was my life he was talking about, these evenings that I laughed with friends, cuddled with Andy, tried to write, watched theatre and opera. I felt tears welling and fought them back. I nodded.

"I hired you because I have a great respect for your people. You people work hard and don't make trouble. Your people are like worker ants. You have what it takes to become a partner. I don't want to see you throw it all away just because you don't put the hours in. Don't let your people down."

My people.

He might as well have said Hong Chong, Ching Chong.

I felt the urge to laugh despite my sense of humiliation. But I didn't. Nor did I let my tears show. I apologised, promised to do better, asked for a second chance. Did what I had to do to keep my high flying job, to save myself from the shame of being a failure.

My family was right after all. I didn't work hard enough. I wanted the prestige and the income from a great job but I wasn't prepared to do it what it took. I was lazy and disobedient. I thought of everything that my family had achieved. My father had made a name for himself from no more than his skill as a lawyer - a skill given to him through his Cambridge education that his family had saved hard to give him. Grandpa Lim had built up a GP practice with nothing but his knowledge of medicine and had contributed to the making of a nation with his dedication and service. Each generation had worked hard to give the next one greater opportunities, more choices and better lives. And here I was squandering it all away with friends and parties and looking for love and hoping still that I could be a writer. I was spoilt and entitled.

My back went into an agonizing spasm. In my lunch hours, I shut the door to my office and lay on the floor behind my desk, pulling my knees to my chest to relieve the tension.

I wasn't very good at being Chinese. What was wrong with me that I didn't want to go home to Malaysia and live within my own community, close to my parents and enjoying all that life there had to offer? I didn't go home to visit very often as a filial daughter should. I didn't celebrate Chinese New Year. I hardly spoke Chinese and what few words I knew I could hardly string together into coherent sentences. I still cooked Malaysian food for my friends and still took pride in my Eastern difference but they felt like surface accessories to my life, part of a performance that was becoming increasingly insincere.

I was having difficulties speaking. My breath was tight in my chest. My voice seemed to shrink into itself. Words hid in my throat. Sentences tangled into each other, punctuated with second-guessing and doubt.

My disguise was crumbling. The acne looked hideous even with thick make-up. I would stand in front of my vast wardrobe of girly clothes, trying to choose something to wear and I would feel a wrenching in my gut. Looking at myself in the mirror as I dressed to go out, I saw a clown. I felt naked in my little shoes, the slightest heel making me wobble. I would take a few steps in them in the bedroom and feel self-loathing creep up my spine like icicles. Frozen there in front of the glass, I had become uncertain and fearful - like Caroline our housemate all those years ago in Oxford, caught between having boiled potatoes or not, incoherent, indecisive. Seeing her unravel before our eyes that evening had terrified me - I had not understood it back then but now, here she was. Here I was. She had been me.

I was meant to see Andy that week to go the opera. We were going to meet outside the Coliseum. As I dressed, I felt sick. My back was killing me. In those days before mobile phones, you either made it to your date or you stood them up without a word. I called his flat and left a message, my breath tight in my chest. I called the Coliseum box office and incoherently, with little breath in me, tried to get them to look for him for me - they took a message but they were busy with box-officey business and in their tone, I knew it was not their problem to help me. I could have gone. I was dressed; I could have hopped on the No. 24 bus and been there in half an hour. I could have explained and we could have got some money back on our tickets. No doubt, he would have been happy to have spent the evening giving me a back rub.

But I stood him up.

I didn't want to see him. Or for him to see me. I didn't have the energy to play Her for him. I couldn't be charming or feline or flirtatious. I didn't want him to look after me and all that that would mean. Giving over to him my power and defences and strength. Letting him see beneath the disguise. He had not understood the other times when I had tried to talk to him about work and my inexplicable sense of darkness - both of us inarticulate and inept with these things, communicating only with sex that made him feel closer to me and me more shut off from him.

I was failing at everything. I belonged nowhere - not as a lawyer, not in my family, not within my heritage, not as a woman, not in the orderly civility of Englishness.

The promise had been unspoken. If you're a good girl, if you study hard, if you dress nicely and behave like a woman should, if you're feminine and desirable and fit in with everybody else, you will be happy. It doesn't matter if you stay where you've always been or if you head off to make your way in a new country. You'll be loved, you'll get married to a good man, you will become a mother and grandmother, a matriarch. This is the promise that our culture makes with us. Do all the right things and you will belong. You will have a good life.

I had kept my side of the bargain, even despite my own dreams of becoming a writer. And even in spite of the lurking desire that I bound up tightly day after day. And the promise had delivered. I had everything outwardly that denoted a good life and I was on the threshold of a something even greater with Andy, a man who could give me all that I longed for - with him, I would belong here in England and I would belong at last within the continuum of my family's history as much as within his.

But inside, I felt like I was in bondage, on my knees amid the barren furrows of a dead harvest.

Hiking Boots

BOUND FEET BLUES – THE STORY

The Canyon

I'm twenty-six. I'm in Australia. I'm wearing my first pair of hiking boots. They are heavy duty grey leather with blood red laces. Struth, mate, I'm Crocodile Dundee!

I'm visiting my best friend Susan. She is a rising star at a multi-national and she's on secondment in Sydney. We hire a car and drive into the Outback. We're going to Ayers Rock as it then was, Alice Springs, the Olgas and Kings Canyon

After these few months apart, it feels good to be laughing and talking with her again.

I tell Susan about Andy. He is hunky and sporty and a great kisser. There's also Mark who's not so good with the kissing but he's sensitive, an intellectual type. They are both waiting for me back in London - which one should I choose? She teases me, you and all your men – do you even like any of them?

We drive for days through the red desert. There is only us in this vast landscape. We camp beneath the upside down stars. We watch the sun rise over Ayers Rock turning it into living fire.

Here, beyond the gaze of others, we let slip our disguises. Our voices turn soft, speaking only to each other. Our eyes become gentle, looking only at each other. I tell her about Bruce Lee and John Steed. And she tells me shyly about a secret agent caught behind enemy lines. I see the girl she used to be – turning cartwheels in the sand, laughing without shame, warm and affectionate without embarrassment.

And sometimes when our eyes meet, I feel as if she sees the girl in me.

We spend a long hot day hiking through Kings Canyon. My boots are stiff - I haven't worn them in enough. I have blisters and my toe nails feel sliced through. Every step is an agony. But I plod on, down the steep trails into the gorge and back up again. My feet feel torn and raw.

But I don't care. Because I'm with her.

Night

That night, I'm sitting on a bench at our campsite near the rim of the canyon. There's a single candle on the picnic table next to me. We've just had our evening meal. Susan comes back from the washing up block. She has short hair and strong shoulders. She seems so at ease here in the outdoors. I'm sitting sideways on the bench, hugging one knee. My feet are bare and free. She comes up behind me and sits down, straddling the bench.

She takes me in her arms.

I can feel the warmth of her body against my back. I cross my arms over hers as she holds me. I can feel her cheek against mine. I can hardly breathe. My throat is dry. My heart feels like it will explode.

And it feels like the most natural thing in the world. Everything else disappears. My life in London. Andy. Mark. The world beyond this moment. There is only her.

We sit there and talk. The sky above is bright with stars. We talk about the places we have been. We plan the route back to Sydney. We talk about everything but this one thing right here, right now.

In the darkness, this moment seems to last forever. And it

is over just like that.

We put out the candle, and crawl into our little tent, into our separate sleeping bags. We do not speak. Susan seems to sleep through the night. We do not touch. Bound up in the tight bag, I lie awake and stare into the darkness.

The next morning, she is cold and abrupt. She does not look at me.

I want to tell her how I feel. But every time I move close to her, she moves away.

And I'm back in the school canteen: *You don't go near that pondan. People like that, they should lock them up in the mental hospital.*

Before we leave, we stop by the Canyon for one last time.

They say this part of the Canyon could be a mile deep, maybe more. It's a strange thing to stand right at its very edge. If we miss our footing, fell, how long would it take to reach the canyon floor?

Susan stands a few feet from me but it might as well be a hundred miles.

She heads back to the car.

It doesn't matter if what happened last night was no more than the gesture of a friend, soon to be forgotten. It doesn't matter if she can never love me.

All I know is – I feel alive, and I can never put on that disguise again.

I look down at the abyss and I see infinity.

And it seems to me that in that moment I step off - into air.

The Garden

I'm awake in my old bedroom, the one I've had since I was four. It's 1990 and it's the recession. I'm twenty-seven and I've just lost my high flying law job. I am home in my parents' house in Malaysia. It is dawn and I can't sleep.

I get up in my pyjamas and go and look for my mother. She is outside in the garden, hanging up the laundry. She is in her long night dress and the sun is just coming up over the palm trees.

[Mum:]

Hello, my noi – my daughter – you're up.

[Me at twenty-seven:]

Yah, jet lag.

I had a dream. I dreamt I was in a dangerous place, like on a rocky ledge and if I took a wrong step, I could fall. Then I came to a cross roads and I had to choose. Which way should I go? And then I realized you were with me in the dream and everything would be OK.

[Mum:]

It's just a dream, darling. Of course, everything will be OK.

[Me:]

Mum, I'm gay.

And then I'm rambling, talking, it's all disconnected, words coming out of my mouth. Maybe the words will hold back the next moment because I don't know what she's going to say.

She puts down my father's shirt and holds me in her arms.

[Mum:]

Are you sure, darling?

And I can see her thinking about all those lovely young men I've brought home over the years to show her.

I nod and we start to talk. We walk arm in arm, taking turn after turn round the garden. The sun is brighter now behind the palm trees.

[Mum:]

Did I do something wrong? Is it my fault? Did I do something to make you this way?

[Me:]

No, no, mum, it's not your fault. It's just who I am. I've always been like this.

We take another turn round the garden. We are both wearing flip flops. My feet feel free as if I am a child again.

[Me:]

I tried so hard. I wanted to get married. I wanted to give you grandchildren. I wanted to have the life that everyone – the whole family – expected me to have. And now, I'm letting you down.

[Mum:]

You can never let me down. You are my noi and I will always love you. All I want is for you to be happy. I just worry that your life will be more difficult because you are gay.

[Me:]

But it is already difficult because I was trying not to be.

And suddenly, we are both laughing. We walk on beneath the gaze of the arching sky. It's a beautiful morning.

THE STORIES BEHIND THE STORY

I didn't want to have these feelings for Susan. Or for Lizzie. Or any woman. It was meant to be a phase, these crushes I had had on ONJ and other teeny bopper icons. They were meant to go away once I grew up. Miraculously, when I turned eighteen and became an adult, just like in fairy tales, the ugly duckling would become a swan. Miraculously, these ugly feelings would become normal feelings of love for a man. Miraculously, I would become the woman I was expected to be - a feminine woman who could love men and wanted to put on make-up and wear pretty dresses, always demure and obedient and girlish.

And if not miraculously, then eventually. Once I got to know some lovely young men. It would be easy and without so much hard work and drive. They would turn my head as I turned theirs. My heart would beat fast and I would feel breathless. Like in the books I read and movies I watched. Like my friends who slipped so naturally into their relationships with their boyfriends. These girls wore their emotions so easily and whose paths from dating to coupledom to marriage flowed so effortlessly.

I wanted that. I had wanted that with Josh, with Rhys. I wanted that with Andy, with Mark. But it was Lizzie - and Susan - each in their own way, who created a space for me to become me.

After I stood Andy up, things cooled between us. We still saw each other but kept the distance of friends rather than lovers. I knew I had hurt him but I could do no more than apologise and tell him about the spasm in my back that had laid me on the floor in my bedroom for an hour. I talked about the stress of my job, he said he had to focus on his next banking exam. He still looked at me with those devouring blue eyes but there was a caution in them now, a holding back.

And it felt like a relief.

I hung out more with Lizzie. We had known each other since Oxford and being with her was easy. I could relax in my slouchy sweatshirts and skinny jeans, kicking of my shoes and sprawling on giant cushions on the floor of her room in her shared house in Kilburn or lounge against the wall on the bed. We would go for a walk on a Saturday through Green Park and St James's and end up at my flat in the late afternoon, sitting barefoot on the floor on my living room. As the darkness of evening fell, we would light candles rather than break the twilight with the bright spotlights in the ceiling.

I told Lizzie about my love of writing as a child. How I had dreamed of having a book published and seeing my name on the cover of my books in a bookshop. I felt embarrassed. It seemed so childish. Grandiose even. "I've been trying to write a novel in my spare time…"

I expected her to laugh. But her eyes widened in excitement. "That's wonderful. Can I read it? I'd love to read it! Please."

"Really?" Was she just being polite?

If I showed her what I had written, squeezing in a few pages here and there late at night and at weekends, incomplete, unpolished, no more than fragments really - would she look up awkwardly from the manuscript with pity and condescension, thinking: did this poor girl really hope to become published writer with nonsense like this?

She persisted, her blue-grey eyes fond and sincere.

I gave her a chapter I had been working on somewhere in the middle of the book. It was an existential thriller set across time with the battle for good and evil played out in different incarnations of timeless immortals (I feel embarrassed even now describing it!). I flicked on the side lamp in the living room as she sat up on the sofa and eagerly opened the ring binder.

I couldn't sit there and watch her read. I paced anxiously for a few moments and then retreated to my bedroom, leaving the door ajar. I wandered around straightening the duvet, re-arranging the items on the side table, folding and re-folding the clothes hanging over the chair.

I heard her turning the pages. Flick. Long pause as she read.

Flick. And then, flick. Flick. Flick. Flick, flick, flick. She was reading faster and faster.

"No!" she cried out.

I rushed out into the living room.

"No! You can't leave it there!" She moved the last page back and forth. Gestured to the empty folder that came after it. "I want to know what happens next!"

I beamed. "So, you liked it?"

I sat down beside her. She was excited as a little girl would be, shifting in her seat, flushed. "Of course! I loved it! You are so cruel, building up the tension like that and making us wonder who is after her - and then, stopping right when she turns around…"

She threw her arms around me. I slipped mine around her and we hung there, laughing. Did we stay a moment too long? Soften and lean in to each other when we should have pulled away? I pushed away the lurking thought - hope? - and got up to make us some more tea.

Lizzie became my ideal reader - the person in a writer's mind whom she is writing for. I found myself staying up later than I should on week nights - despite my brain tiredness from work, despite a pile of bills and admin that needed my attention - and writing more extracts that one day, I promised myself, I would be piece together like patchwork to make a novel called *A Game with the Devil*. I treasured weekends - two whole days to myself when I could scribble away, my pencil scratching across pad after pad of A4 lined paper. Or I would be at my Amstrad, typing up the illegible scrawl into neat, printed sheets.

She took my work seriously, as if it was great literature, treating the pages as she would treat the works of Goethe and Rilke that she used to read at Oxford for her degree. She went through what I wrote carefully, interpreting the themes and analysing the characters.

I had been so afraid of showing my writing to anyone. I had been so afraid of really, truly trying. Of making my dream real. All those years of wanting to be a writer and not writing, of feeling directionless and without purpose. The terror had been palpable. What if I spent months and years of my time on writing a book and when I sent it out there, people just laughed at it. What if I did my very best, laboured my utmost to create the most excellent literary work that I could possibly achieve as a writer and the world rejected it. What if I poured onto paper my thoughts and feelings and everything that I was and everyone would see this sad, pathetic, furious, unlovable, desperately lonely perverted loser.

And now, with the way that Lizzie held my manuscript and the way she looked at me as she talked about how my writing had affected her… I felt suddenly as if it might really be possible for me to become a real writer. One who could finish a novel and send it out there and get it published, a writer whose books - real, solid books with my name on the cover - could actually be in real bookshops and read by real readers.

But I never finished that manuscript. When you write for just one reader, what happens with them also happens with your book.

We didn't always talk about writing. Sometimes, we talked about my love life.

"I'm giving up on men," I would say, "It's too hard."

And we would both laugh.

It was a litany that some of my friends and I sometimes played out. We single girls would get together in wine bars and give vent to that semi-mock semi-true moaning that made up our girl talk. We would sigh: "Where are all the good men" and "Men, eh? Who needs 'em." And we all knew that in a little while, we would be out there trying our luck again.

But Lizzie never seemed to care about dating. She would listen to my stories, making all the right noises, but when I asked her about her love life, she would bat away my questions with a dismissive wave.

"You ask a lot of questions, don't you," she said once.

"I'm sorry, I don't mean to. It's just…" I took in her half-smile, half-exasperated expression. Our eyes met and I lost my thread.

Something about her distance suddenly irked me. It was as if she was holding the power in this friendship by hearing my confessionals, reading my writings, encouraging me to talk about what I cared most deeply about - but in her turn revealing nothing of her emotional life. I found my thread and grabbed it with full force. "You're a good listener. But why don't you ever give anything away? It's me... You can tell me anything. I tell you everything about Andy and whoever..."

She looked away.

"I don't even know if you've had a boyfriend since Peter. Why don't you want to talk to me?" I peered at her in the half-light. "Have you never been in love?"

She seemed flustered suddenly, blinking back... tears? I tilted my head but it was difficult to see in the candlelight. She jerked away, waving her hand at me.

I said, "Are you okay? Why...?"

"Why! Why!" she burst out. "You're always asking Why. Why this, why that! Like those two year olds - why, why, why..."

I felt sheepish. I hadn't thought she would be so upset. I reached out and touched her arm. "I'm sorry..."

She seemed about to pull away but didn't. I could feel her relaxing. As if giving in to my touch.

Then she shook herself off, blowing out a tense laugh. She looked at me with glittering eyes. The intensity made my heart stop.

She reached out and with light fingers, stroked my hair. Her voice was a whisper. "You're impossible."

I wanted to lean into her touch. To feel those soft caresses forever. But I didn't move.

She's just one of those touchy-feely girls, I thought. She doesn't love you *that way*. If I showed anything, any emotion, she would freak out, pull away. There would horror, disgust - her face twisted with disbelief and contempt. It would be as if I were sitting here in men's clothes and men's shoes, my hair Brylcreemed back, a pathetic woman trying to be a man. A needy wannabe writer longing for approval and mistaking it for love. I could not bear the humiliation.

I didn't love her *that way* either, I told myself. No, not at all. I thought of Andy and Josh and all those other boyfriends. That was love, being with them. Not this… this fantasy, this loneliness, this pitifulness.

Not this.

I couldn't remember when our friendship had somehow become so intense. What had seemed so easy - a safe haven from my difficulties with Andy and the whole drama of dating, a place where I could at last share with someone my creative aspirations - had become fraught with emotional exchanges like this.

We would be laughing and talking breezily and then, it was as if we had taken a turn down a dark, narrow alleyway. Something I said would upset Lizzie and she would be angry with me. Or she would rile me with her sudden evasiveness, her drawing me towards her and then pushing me away. She would become tearful all of a sudden and refuse to talk to me. All I wanted was to be with her, to sink into that giggling, teasing warm affection that we had for each other. Being with her was like luxuriating in a steaming, hot bubble bath and I knew that she loved hanging out with me, too. But I didn't know what had happened to change it all.

After fraught exchanges like these, Lizzie would now disappear for weeks, sometimes months. I wouldn't hear from her and when I would call and leave a message with her housemates, she would not get back to me for days. Was she angry with me? Was she afraid of me? I would go back over everything I had said and done - no, there was nothing in any of it that could have horrified her, made her fearful of me, I had made so sure of it. She was my friend and I was treating her just like a friend.

Wasn't I?

* * *

With Andy no longer always by my side, Mark started to drop by and invite me out. He was skinny and bookish, with messy brown hair and deep, dark eyes - more Woody Allen than Hugh Grant. He was well read in English and ecclesiastical history and the classical works of Homer and Virgil. He wrote poetry and spoke as easily about *Piers Plowman* and *Beowulf* as about Seamus Heaney and Ted Hughes. Sitting in the pub, with a cigarette smoking in his expressive, long hands, he might have been one of those great intellectuals of the Parisian Left Bank, Gitanes curling white smoke against black polo necks. We talked about writing and he encouraged me to try my hand at poetry. I showed him my poems and he showed me his.

I was determined that I would fall in love with Mark. He would make me forget the confusion of being with Lizzie. She wasn't the only person whom I could talk to about writing and my hopes of publishing a book one day. I could bond with a man about such things. It just had to be the right man. Maybe the problem with a man like Andy had been that despite his interest in arts and culture in general, his lack of interest in literature in particular had created an issue between us that I had not acknowledged. Maybe if I just gave a sensitive, literary man like Mark a chance, I might start to feel about him how I felt when I talked about writing with Lizzie. Maybe if I stopped being so shallow about men, valuing only the ones with dashing good looks, dazzling CVs and social charm, I might be able to relate to them at that deeper, more meaningful level that I longed for.

Mark and I spent a spring day walking in a bluebell wood. I wore high-top trainers with skin-tight black leggings and a loose boyfriend-style sweatshirt. It was an idyllic setting, with a shallow sea of blue and lavender rippling at our ankles and their dewy, delicate fragrance suffusing the air. The trees formed a canopy of variegated jade, the leaves rustling in the warm breeze. He laid down his Barbour for us to sit on and recited a poem to me amid the blue perfume.

It should have been perfect. But when he kissed me, I felt sick.

* * *

Susan was a new friend. I had met her at a party where I had gone on my own. I didn't know anyone among the crowd of lawyers and architects and accountants. After doing the rounds of light banter with a hint of flirtatiousness thrown in for the men, I started to flag. I looked great, I knew, in a floaty skirt and patent leather Italian slip-ons. My arms jangled with bracelets and bright hoops flashed from my ears. Taking that in along with my big hair and caramel colouring, someone asked if I was Brazilian. I laughed gaily. But I was off my game, my stammer getting more and more in the way these days, a new *ennui* mingling with the anxious knot that seemed to churn without respite in my gut. I was wondering about going home when I saw her sitting quietly in an upright chair beside me.

We started chatting and found we had some friends in common. She was an accountant in one of the top four multi-national firms. She didn't seem to mind if no-one at the party spoke to her but was happy to engage when someone did. She was dressed simply in a classic style with low navy loafers. Her gaze didn't wander off in search of more interesting company in the way that many of us scan the room at drinks parties. I ended up pulling up a chair alongside her and staying for several hours in a long, rambling conversation that took in the latest contenders for the Booker, how we would both love to visit Italy, our relationships with our families, and how much she loved walking in the countryside.

"I've never been walking in the countryside," I said.

She was incredulous. "Really?"

So we went walking in the countryside.

The landscape of Wessex had spread its canopy in my mind through the novels of Thomas Hardy. I had trudged alongside Tess of the D'Urbervilles down the slow, winding paths between

It was everything I had imagined and more

her home and that of the dastardly Alec and walked each step that Jude the Obscure had taken on his way to Oxford. I had followed Henchard into Casterbridge that fateful day of the country fair with his wife and babe-in-arms. And now, that rich and ancient landscape opened out all around us as we made our way through a rutted country lane into a vista of fields and copses and dark silhouetted hills.

It was everything that I had imagined and so much more. In the early summer warmth, the wheat fields were soft with billowing apple-green fuzz alongside fields blazing with yellow rape. Skylarks hovered high above trilling unseen against a sky of infinite blue. Hedgerows buzzed and hummed with crickets and tiny sparrows. The smell of earth and animals and wildflowers hung heavy in the heat. We took a wrong turn off a track and laboured for a while along the edge of a ploughed field before heading back, stumbling unevenly on the large clods of soil hard like rubble beneath our boots.

Something inside of me let go, here in this bright, magical landscape.

In Malaysia, the outside is a tamed jungle, held at bay with concrete and vigilant maintenance. In our garden at home, we would have to be careful not to play near the empty land next door with its long grass and overgrown shrubs in case of cobras and pythons lurking underfoot. Beyond the towns and cities, few people went for country walks in the thick, sticky heat. There were wild monkeys and civet cats, scorpions and iguanas, leeches and fire ants, mosquitoes and other biting bugs. A wrong step away from a defined path could lead you so deep into the forest that you would never be found.

But here, with the thatched farms dotted about the patchwork fields - and yes, it thrilled me to see for myself that the English countryside was indeed made up of 'patchwork fields', just like the cliché of that phrase - and the languid cows eyeing us blandly as we passed, this place, this moment here with Susan felt safe and peaceful and calm. The tension strangling my voice and tongue eased away. The twisting in my gut untangled. Everything seemed fluid and fluent as we talked and laughed beneath the embracing sky.

Sometimes we walked along in companionable silence, pausing to watch clouds of butterflies dust off from the long grass, speaking only to point out a white chalk figure on a distant hillside or a little skipping lamb. I had never had a friendship like this that had such an intimate feel of warmth and ease.

I would go round to her flat in Beckenham for supper on a Friday night and end up hanging out with her over the next couple of days, going for walks in the local parklands, lounging with the papers in the living room, chatting over cups of tea. Some Saturday afternoons, I would work on a short story or fiddle with a play I was experimenting with, sitting in an armchair while she read on the sofa.

I loved her good nature and kindness, her laugh and the fondness with which we teased each other. I loved the way she looked at me sometimes from under her lashes, a shy smile playing on her lips. She had a strong, independent manner about her but as our friendship grew closer, she seemed to slip off her armour. Her face softened into the openness of a young girl. It was as if she let me see who she could be, unprotected against the judgement of others, open to the gaze of another, giving of herself. Her voice, which exuded capability to the world outside, became tender and intimate when we were alone together.

How do you fall in love with someone? Across a crowded room, a rugby field or a river washing clothes? Or sometimes, imperceptibly, unexpectedly. Without ever wanting to. And even against your conscious will.

But once it happens there is no going back.

In the short time of our friendship, it was as if I glimpsed at a way of being I had not imagined possible before. I loved my thick, sturdy hiking boots that gave me the feel of adventure whenever I pulled them on. I loved who I could be when I was with her - funny, warm, affectionate, unmasked. I loved the relaxed togetherness that we had fallen into.

She had the ground floor flat in one of those sixties modern blocks a mile's walk from the station, down a long avenue of trees. There was a small yard at the back by the kitchen where there was a rose bush and clematis making its way round the window. She had a few basins of herbs but otherwise had done little with it. She talked of having a wisteria covered cottage in the country with a beautiful garden. I wondered: what would that be like - to live in a little house with a lovely garden with someone like her? That picture had never been my dream but - I cocked my head - it might be.

I sensed she did not feel the same way about me. Yes, there was deep warmth of friendship there but love...? Not that love that would take us from friends into a private, intimate space that would endure for a lifetime and beyond. So I tried to ignore how I felt - suppress it, crush it down hard. And yet, in the way that we were when we were alone together - in the caress of her voice and the tenderness of her manner - it was sometimes easy to forget that what I felt was not also in her heart. Alone together for three weeks in Australia, it felt as if we had stepped into a landscape where time stood still and where there was almost no language, no words, nothing to define and hold down what we had that was our friendship or love or everything in between. In the breathlessness and vertigo of being with her there by the canyon, I gave in to all my forbidden, ugly, queer, *pondan* feelings - whatever might become of me or of our friendship because of them.

Hiking the canyon

Back in Sydney, the world encroached again and our lives took hold. On the morning she took me to the airport, she finished packing up my rucksack, tying the straps tightly. We went out for an early breakfast, both of us quiet. We never spoke of what happened and I guessed that over the years, she forgot about it.

But for me, in all the confusion of emotions and inner denial and turmoil that I had struggled with over a lifetime, in my fragmented relationships with Josh and Andy and all those other men, in all the uncertain desire with Lizzie, in my unsustainable uber-femme persona, that moment beneath the stars was the moment I allowed myself to feel the softly beating heart that I had bound up all those years ago and I would always remember the darkness of the night and her.

* * *

Back in London, Lizzie came by to return some books. I had not seen her in months. She was subdued and tense. We had an argument. I don't know how it started but it was something to do with the tone of my note asking for my books back.

"But I hadn't heard from you for ages. I didn't know if you were angry with me," I cried. "So I just kept it short!"

She started to cry again.

My frustration faded. I put my arms round her. It hurt so much to see her like this. "What's going on, Lizzie? Please tell me. I can't bear this…"

She looked up at me. Her blue-grey eyes melted me inside. Her face was naked with emotion.

She said with a hoarse intensity I had never heard in her voice before, "I love you."

They were words I had never expected to hear from another woman. And words that I had longed always in my heart to hear.

Yet, all that I could think of was how much I had hurt her - in all my dim-witted stupidity for all these past months as she had wept in front of me, I had not allowed myself to think that she had been weeping because of me. I felt a twisting in my gut of self-loathing for my talk of men and my determination to be anything other than a woman she could truly love, for my fear of my own desire for her and for the betrayal of her with the intimacy of my feelings for Susan. Seeing her here, this delightful, charming, loving and sensitive woman in a tangle of distress because she loved me.

I was afraid and disbelieving and uncertain. How could someone as gentle and warm as she really love me?

"I love you, too" I said - lightly, as a friend might.

She had bared her soul to me and I had betrayed her again.

"You've spoilt it now," she cried. She had offered me the gift of who she was, trusting as a child. And I had thrown it back in her face. She pulled away from me.

I had spoilt it all. And perhaps I had always been spoiling it all between her and me. Because of the desire I felt for her and the terror that depth of feeling unleashed.

That fearful longing had lurked inside me for so long, prowling and hungry and all-consuming, it had taken everything of my drive and will-power to hold it at bay. And her tender touch and soft whispers, her tentative caresses and the equal longing in her eyes had stirred the demon, bringing it to writhing, raging life. In the back of my mind, unspoken, unacknowledged, I had known her feelings for me and I had pushed them away. And I had denied my own feelings for her even as I let myself relax into her touch and loving gaze.

Her words came in a rush. "I don't want to love you. You make me feel this way. I don't want to feel like this. I noticed you in Oxford. I'd never known anyone like you before. I never thought we could ever be friends, someone so beautiful as you. And now, you made me love you with your candles and spending all this time with me and being so interested in everything about me... How could I tell you, with all the men in your life, how could I show you I loved you, and you always asking me questions, being so concerned when I started to cry. I don't want to cry, I don't want to feel this way…"

"I'm sorry…" The words seemed so pathetically inadequate.

She poured on, unable to stop. "And it's so easy for you to forget about me. Why didn't you come to my Halloween party? I waited for you all night…"

"I didn't know… The invitation just came in the post with no note. I thought it was your housemates' party. I thought you didn't want to see me - that last time we talked on the phone, you were cold and distant with me, like you were angry with me…"

"…And that time you came to dinner, you talked to everyone at the table and ignored me…"

"I thought *you* were ignoring me, you just sat there in silence all night…" My head was spinning. She had walked me to the tube station after dinner and we had just eased into a warm conversation when she had started to cry. She had stood with tears streaming down her cheeks, refusing to speak, as we waited on the platform. *Do you want me to stay?* I had asked as the train pulled in but she had said nothing and I had got on. Perhaps I shouldn't have, perhaps things might have been different if I had stayed that night.

What had become of her and of me? How had that fondness and electric delight of being together turned into this agony? We looked at each other as if across a vast distance.

"Can we find some way…?" I started. But there were no words that could heal this. "Maybe you should go."

She nodded and we stood up. I opened my arms to hug her as we always did on parting. I expected her to pull away but she didn't.

We held each other carefully, lightly. And we stayed there. She began to caress my back and run her fingers down my arms. She held her cheek against mine. "You're so beautiful," she murmured.

I could feel my body responding to her touch. I wanted to lean into her, to trace my fingers on her back, to stroke her hair as she was stroking mine. I wanted to give in to this desire, this physical longing, to kiss her lips and throat and trace my tongue down into her warm cleavage. But this was not the way it should begin. Not like this. Not with this anger and blame and self-loathing.

I could have led her into the bedroom then. But I saw it all playing out that night and the next morning, all in an instant in my mind. We could have given in, explored each other's burning bodies, and devoured each other with the longing of all those years. But in the morning, we would have hated each other, blamed each other, and hidden ourselves with shame. And even if we were to have stayed somehow bound together in weeks and months to come, it would all have been secretive and hidden from our friends, all of whom we had known since Oxford, all of whom would have seen something strange and intense in us. This was not how I wanted love to be.

And so, standing at the door, longing for her caresses to never end, longing to stay in her embrace just a moment longer, I stepped back and disentangled her arms from around me.

I said again those feeble words, "I'm sorry."

* * *

Many of the great love stories are about finding The One. In *Pride and Prejudice*, Elizabeth meets The One right at the very beginning but it takes many unsuitable suitors and much misunderstanding before she and Mr Darcy finally get it together. I wondered about putting a Spoiler Alert notice just before that last reveal as to who The One is in that novel - but even if you have never read the book, Jane Austen sets him up as The One from the first page that proclaims 'the young man of large fortune from the North of England' as the prize of all the local gals to the very fact that he and Elizabeth rub each other the wrong way on first meeting.

In *When Harry Met Sally*, the spoiler is in the title and we know that somehow by the end of this rom com, the unlikely pair of Harry and Sally will discover that they are each other's The One. In particular, the set up at the start of the movie of elderly couples talking about how they met and fell in love taps into and reinforces the cultural trope that there is such a thing as The One that we are all destined, some day, somewhere, somehow - some enchanted evening - to meet.

In the telling of this story - my story - of looking for love, according to the convention of those love stories The One should be Lizzie, shouldn't it? She was there at the beginning in Oxford, just a mention at first and then noticed for her natural simplicity in contrast to my over-performed femininity, slowly growing in significance and presence. In all my unhappiness with the men I was trying to date, my easy friendship with her suggests the potential for something more meaningful, if only I would stop and pay attention to the lurking emotions I was trying to keep bound down. And perhaps the role of Susan is there to teach me something about what might be possible for me and Lizzie if we only both allowed ourselves to truly love.

Here at this point in the story, this is where everything seems lost (known in plot development terms as 'the reversal'). About two thirds of the way through *Pride & Prejudice*, Elizabeth Bennett rejects Mr Darcy's proposal, accusing him of being unjust and ungenerous towards Wickham and calling him arrogant, conceited and selfish. In *When Harry Met Sally*, the reversal happens when the two leads end up in bed together - which seems to be the climax we are all waiting for - but it destroys their friendship. Oh no, we cry as readers and audience in each case, how are they going to get it together now?

It's that well-known story structure of boy meets girl, boy loses girl, boy gets girl. So by all expectations, we are now at the girl loses girl stage and should be moving into the girl gets girl again Third Act.

The thing is, the Third Act in a girl meets girl or boy meets boy genre is much more precarious. These days there are more gay men and lesbians being featured in TV dramas as if they are normal people - notably in *Brothers and Sisters* and *Grey's Anatomy* - but in terms of Hollywood, I have yet to come across a great movie romance in those genres which doesn't go something like: girl meets girl, girl loses girl, the gay one dies. For the girls, there's the black-and-white classic *Children's Hour* which ends with a tortured and self-loathing Shirley MacLaine (the gay one) hanging herself, unable to bear her wretched love for (the straight one) Audrey Hepburn. For the boys, there's the more recent *Brokeback Mountain* where Jake Gyllenhall (the gay one) ends up being beaten to death in a bar to be mourned broodingly by Heath Ledger (the straight one).

Back then in the late '80s, for Lizzie and me, lesbians were outcasts of nature in the cultural unconscious - and even now, outside of the cosmopolitan, liberal consciousness of cities like London, New York and Paris, we still are. Gay men might be our witty friends so long as they stayed camp and funny and a-sexual or sexual only in a tittering Benny Hill sort of way. But lesbians - even now the word can send a shudder down the collective spines of those with more traditional worldviews - lesbians are ugly, butch women like Radclyffe Hall who seduced innocent, unwordly young straight girls. Lesbians are short, stocky, ugly women like Rosa Klebb in the James Bond movie *From Russia With Love* - in contrast to the tall, beautiful blonde straight Bond Girl Tatiana Romanova - who could kill you with hidden daggers in her mannish lace-up shoes. Lesbians are ugly, man-hating feminists who don't wear make-up or shave their legs or - *eeew* upon collective *eeew* - under their arms and who let themselves put on weight. If lesbians are beautiful and attractive like Susannah York and Glenda Jackson in Jean Genet's *The Maids* - or in recent mainstream films directed by straight men featuring two women allegedly in love - then they are strange and twisted in mind and unsympathetic in character. Or if there is a story about a lesbian couple like *The Kids Are All Right* or A. S Byatt's *Possession*, then a man has to come in to the picture and show one of them the error of her ways, literally setting her straight.

Lesbians are to be laughed at, feared, loathed, pitied, and corrected. They are wicked, controlling or at best, misguided. They do not know how to love properly without a man. And any way you slice it, according to the accepted wisdom of traditionalists, lesbians would never ever find true love and all would die sad, unloved and alone.

For Lizzie and me back then, those cultural stories bound us up in silence and fear. For a woman - to be ugly and mannish, to be known as a man-hater, a ball-buster, a dyke: it is one of the worst things in the world. The shame and derision is unbearable. Even if we've never experienced it, that vitriol hovers on the edge of our knowing. It is out there in the papers and the media and in the casual contempt and ridicule as people chat and laugh over a drink. It's in their eyes and the way they look you up and down. The way their lips twitch in a smirk or in disgust, no matter how quickly they hide it. It's in the way they turn away or in their kindly condescension and patronising tone.

It's in the fury of religion and the harshness of workplaces, the controlling power of parents and the overriding pride of families. It's in name calling and condemnation, in not getting the job, in being shunned, in being thrown out of bars and supermarkets and taxis. It's in happy slapping and casual attacks, in rape and assault and murder.

In those stories where the gay one dies, we learn the punishment for our ugly, monstrous queerness - it is a death, whether an actual dying of the body or symbolic death from society and family and God.

Lizzie and I were so afraid of becoming those monstrous beings that that fear created monsters out of us.

It took a year or more before Lizzie and I could see each other again without pain and distrust, before we could touch again that tenderness and delight we once had for each other.

As I reflect on that time so long ago, and think about those stories and tropes in our collective unconscious that continue now as ever in the UK and throughout the world, these beliefs and constructs that have been so damaging - not just for me and

Lizzie but also for others whose dreams of The One do not fit the norm, I long for one thing: Wouldn't it be nice, for a change, to see great love stories where the gay one goes off in the end with another lovely gay one to live happily ever after?

The One

In *Bound Feet Blues*, on stage, I have ten minutes, if that, to recreate a moment in my life that has the most visual and emotional impact to tell you about my coming out. So I chose that image of the canyon and Susan with all its metaphorical power. And yet, here in the book, it is Lizzie who plays a central role, not Susan.

I hope you don't feel cheated.

It's about the right story for the right medium. In the same way that the stories of my family, passed down to me by word of mouth from my mum and the other women in my family had to be told out loud and embodied in my physical presence in front of a live audience, the story of my coming out, in contrast, can only be more fully told in a multiple layers in the meandering and leisurely form that a book offers.

In stories, we simplify, create a single narrative out of the multiple strands that make up a life. In the convention of the novel or memoir or movie, we prune away the irrelevant and shape an arc that cuts through the mess of reality like a trunk road to a known destination. We take our readers and audience on a journey. We are their tour guide, pointing out this important edifice, that significant structure, retelling the story of a particular historical event but not others.

But real life is of course much more chaotic than that. Major characters fade away. Minor characters suddenly play an unexpected critical role. New people turn up out of nowhere and knock the narrative sideways. We are not always the hero we would like to be. Sometimes, without knowing it, without meaning to be, we end up the villains or the fools.

So this is why this chapter is not just about Susan. Or even just about Lizzie.

It is clear from the script that heads this chapter, and from the performance for those of you that have seen the stage version of the story, Susan was not The One.

For me, all those years ago, being with Susan opened my imagination to the possibility that love is not about how we look or our sexual desirability or fitting into a role structured by society. Love cannot be condensed down to one thing, like one tiniest most perfect foot fitting into a glass slipper that makes a helpless Cinderella of us all. Love is not about the best marriage you can make or the most prestigious husband or the finest house. Love comes at you unexpectedly despite your will-power and focus and drive and makes a mess of your best laid plans. Love is not about the continuum of family, of heritage and inheritance, of past or future. It is not about generations or traditions, gender or culture. It is about character and heart and who we truly are beneath our disguises and armour. You love who you love, regardless of everything else that might be in the way.

There were moments, beyond the gaze of others, as we passed lazy weekends alone together in her flat and walked together in the timeless outdoors, when the cocoon of that privacy wrapped me in a hope that she might become The One. But I knew the hopelessness of it all. Within each encounter, even as that intimacy drew us close, like the cloak of that dark night beneath the stars, she would step away. Out there in the crowded world, with all our friends, with everyone around us, in the busyness of our real lives, she kept a distance between us again, her voice losing its tenderness, her expression cool. I would never be more than friend for her. It was so simple - and so devastating.

Susan came back from Australia and we tried to pick up our friendship but everything was different now. We were awkard together and the reserve and politeness in her manner towards me was evident.

Lizzie wrote to say that she was moving to Geneva. She had got a job at one of the universities there teaching Business Studies. We exchanged letters and sometimes spoke on the phone, cautiously, tentatively. Over the months, we relaxed and a warmth began to return. Then in the spring of 1990, about eighteen months after our last meeting in my flat, she invited me to visit her for the weekend.

In this period, I had decided I was going to be a nun - or, at least, celibate. I was not going to go out with any man and certainly, not any woman. It was all too confusing and painful. This love nonsense was making me unhappy and ill. If The One was meant to be in my life, he knew where to find me - I wasn't going out looking for him anymore. I was just going to be a good friend to all these people in my life: Andy, Mark, Lizzie, Susan. That was it. A single life with plenty of good friends had its virtues, didn't it? So I set off for Geneva with strong resolve.

At Gatwick, I saw a fluffy toy bunny that had the classic shape of irresistible cuteness, with a round tummy, chubby little cheeks and a straw hat decked in flowers. I thought of Lizzie's collection of stuffed teddies and child-like figurines that scattered her room. On the spur of a moment, I bought the bunny.

And that was my undoing.

Lizzie adored the little bunny, cradling it in her arms like a baby. She was laughing and flirtatious, making me take my turn holding the toy. "You'd make a beautiful mother!" she teased.

She christened the bunny Francesca and it went everywhere with us that weekend. It peeked out of her backpack as we walked around Geneva so it could see the sights, too. "Not 'it,'" Lizzie would correct me, "'She.'"

Francesca sat in the back of the car as Lizzie drove us out of town for a picnic. The old tensions and recriminations were gone. We were back to being two good chums having a fun weekend.

Except for the make-believe game that we were playing with Francesca. Lizzie said that the bunny was ours, that we would look after her together. I played along, uncertainly. What was Lizzie doing? We bombed along in the car singing loudly to Abba on the radio, playing at happy families and what might be and despite myself, I surrendered again to her bubbly charm.

We went for a walk through a pine forest. It led out into a meadow full of buttercups. We were in jeans and old T-shirts. I was wearing my high-top trainers and loved the confident bounce they gave to my step. Lizzie carried the picnic blanket and the backpack full of food. I carried Francesca. We were the only people for miles around.

Sitting on the red and white checked blanket, sharing bread and salami and cheese, we talked for the first time about what happened, our feelings and uncertainties, our families and our sense of belonging and not belonging. We talked openly, without fear or blame, hearing each other and seeing each other for who we were. We snapped some photos of each other cuddling up to the bunny, laughing at the absurdity of it.

Lizzie lay back on the blanket so close to me I could feel the warmth of her body. She looked up at me with her soft blue-grey eyes. It was a moment of acknowledgement for all that had happened between us.

I leaned down and kissed her.

Her lips were warm and gentle. She kissed me back tentatively. Tenderly.

Was this what had terrified me all these years? This moment that seemed so natural. So simple.

As I pulled gently away, I was struck by the thought: I'm just me, not a monster, not a freak, just me.

She reached up and ran her fingers through my hair in that old familiar caress. I could see it in her eyes that something had changed. She said my name over and over. With regret and fondness and sadness.

She sat up and said, "I don't want to be gay."

There was her family, her parents, her life here, our friends. She wanted to be normal, just like everyone else.

I didn't try to persuade her or change her mind. I wasn't really surprised. We sat side by side, not touching. I listened to her talk and I watched the struggle playing out on her face as if from a distance. Even as I felt the hurt of her rejection, there was also an odd sense of certainty and confidence. I had taken that step in my heart at the rim of King's Canyon to let go and to allow myself to love - now, here in the meadow, it was as if I was spreading my wings and catching a current of warm air. I glanced up at the sound of a skylark warbling somewhere in the infinite blue above.

Looking back at that bright morning, I have sense of that day as the culmination of the seven years of friendship that had gone before. That meadow was the place where all the heart-soreness and inexpressible love and fear had been leading us towards. The struggle and denial and fear were over. She finally made her choice and I made mine.

That kiss was at once an acceptance and a goodbye.

* * *

I was made redundant from my big, corporate job the week after I came back from Geneva. Walking slowly of the partner's office, I felt humiliated and ashamed. They had picked me because I was still not working long enough hours. I was still not embraced by the tall, black-suited cliques. I was not making it as the successful lawyer I had been determined to be. I was letting myself be distracted by the drama of all those intense friendships and trying to be a writer - spending all my energy on these things that didn't matter in the hard-nosed world of law and making a good living.

And the Presbyterian part of me experienced it a punishment. My dark, filthy secret had been found out by an all-seeing, all-powerful, all-judging God. I deserved to lose my job - for letting my heart get in the way of hard work, for dispersing my focus with that old childish hope of being a writer, for giving in to the lustful lesbian feelings inside me.

But kissing Lizzie had not felt wrong. It had not felt evil or sinful or lustful. It had felt completely right, the most natural thing in the world. What had been tortuous and painful and awful had been all those years of fear and denial and suppressing my feelings for her, and for Susan. And going back long before that was the turmoil and confusion of my teens and childhood that had only been expressible in fury and tantrums and rage. Here and now, in this place, despite the end of my friendship with Lizzie and the distance between Susan and me and the loss of the career that I had worked so hard to maintain - despite losing everything, I felt powerful in a way I had never felt before.

Losing everything was a freedom.

I booked a flight back to Malaysia. I would give myself three months. I would research my roots and give myself a chance to be a writer. Then I would come back and see where the next phase in my life would take me.

I threw a party to celebrate my redundancy and invited everyone I knew.

An old friend from law college, Karen, arrived late with her flat mate whom I had met a few times before, Shane, who was a counsellor at a women's charity. Shane had always seemed serious and earnest at the gatherings I had seen her at before, sitting back into herself, quiet and private. Today, there was something different about her. Perhaps she had changed her hair - it was shorter than it had been, thick with dark curls above and sleek in the back. She looked striking all in black, her dark eyes bright against the creamy paleness of her skin. In her slim jeans and crew neck top, she had something of a beautiful boy about her with her swimmer's shoulders and thick lashes. Tonight, she seemed to be stepping more forward into the room, with a bright energy that I could almost touch. I was aware of her watching me throughout the evening across the crowded room and when I caught her smiling gaze, it took my breath away.

As the night wound down, we found ourselves in the kitchen. We caught up on what she had been doing since we'd last met a year or so before. I talked about the relief of losing my law job and my hopes for finally becoming a writer. She wanted to write a book, too. Her eyes glittered as she spoke. She wanted to tell the stories of the refugee women she worked with.

"They need a voice and I want to somehow help them be heard," she said intently. Among the lawyers that surrounded me all day in my work, I never saw such passion. In my own life, there was nothing I was focused on that had such purpose.

Her quiet energy was inspiring. I wanted to know her more, to spend more time in the mix of soft-spoken intelligence and warm charm.

She saw me taking her in and blushed. "I'm getting too intense, aren't I?" But a smile spread across her face

I shrugged. "I like intense…"

We both laughed. Shifted where we stood, shaking off the tension. Neither of us wanted to break the spell.

We took turns tossing out some casual chit chat until something caught. We eased into the unremarkable conversation, keeping the flow light and easy. And soon were talking about the things that mattered to us - our families, books we loved, our childhood in foreign countries, the beauty of nature. As we discovered each other in this dancing exchange, our eyes said it all. I couldn't stop looking at her, or her me, her dark gaze making my head spin. We were both smiling, at once coy and bold, flirtatious and shy.

My other guests came to say goodbye and I hugged and kissed them, promised to write from Malaysia, thanked them for their good luck wishes. There was just Shane and me in the kitchen and Karen and a handful of other friends in the living room.

"I'm not seeing anyone at the moment," she said hesitantly.

"Me neither." I had on a stupid smile that was making my cheeks ache.

"I've always had relationships with men," she went on, looking away. "But I've been wondering what it might be like to go out with a woman…"

"Me too." God, could I sound any more inane with my two word responses?

Her dark gaze came back to me, her shy smile creasing dimples into her cheeks.

We stood stupidly like this for a long moment, uncertain what to do next.

Karen appeared tentatively at the door. She was grinning widely at us. She said apologetically, "If we're going to catch the last tube… or, I can go, you know…"

Shane and I spoke over each other.

"Oh, gosh, is that how late is…"

"No, no, I'll come with you…"

"Yes, you'd both better hurry…"

It had been too intense, too sudden, for both of us. We needed to think, re-group, take a breath.

Shane turned to me. "When are you leaving for Malaysia?"

"Thursday."

It was Sunday night. We had three days.

We met for a drink the next evening at a basement bar in Covent Garden, both Shane and Karen coming from work. Shane and I had insisted that Karen join us and she gamely obliged. Her presence diffused the intensity, created breathing space for us in the way that a chaperone back in the old days would disperse the sexual tension of a courting couple. At a corner table, they had beers while I sipped an orange juice as the top hits of the '80s bounced out over the speakers. Karen stayed quiet, letting us play out our hesitant 'getting to know you' ritual with the pleased satisfaction of a match-maker and mother hen.

Shane was a vegetarian and talked about the principle of not eating meat or using leather goods.

"What about shoes?" I asked.

She was wearing vegetarian shoes.

I was intrigued and ducked my head under the table to check out her feet. The black canvas lace-ups she had on were smart enough to pass as work shoes.

"Who knew…" I laughed.

Over the speakers, Kaoma came on, the undulating, hip

winding and thrusting Latin rhythms of the Lambada ululating through the bar. "I love this song!" I cried, swaying to the beat in my chair.

Shane watched me with her smiley eyes. "They say that the best way to dance the Lambada is to imagine you have a pencil between your bum and you're drawing a figure of 8 with it against the wall."

A picture of her bum flashed in my mind and I flushed. In my embarrassment, I knocked over my glass and the juice fanned out all over the table.

We jumped up to avoid being drenched, grabbed paper napkins to soak up the juice. And bopped in our places to the Latin beat, watching each other over the checked table cloth. I clenched my buttocks and wiggled my hips, a phantom pencil drawing squiggles in the air behind me. Even now, whenever I hear the Lambada, this moment in the bar comes to mind.

We ended up back at their flat, lounging in the living room while Karen cooked up some pasta for dinner. Shane's two cats tumbled around us, brushing up against me curiously. The three of us watched *Thirtysomething* sitting on the floor as we ate, the domestic and relationship complexities of these tanned, beautiful people not making much sense as we laughed and talked over them. Afterwards, Karen made a big show of being tired and went off to her room.

Shane and I carried on chatting for a few minutes, and then fell silent. I was leaning against the sofa beside her. We looked at each other.

She put her arm around me and drew me towards her. We kissed for the first time, softly exploring each other, taking our time. I moved closer, turning, straddling her legs as she tilted her head back and held me, my hands cupping her face. Her lips and cheeks were so smooth, so unlike the grating stubble of men, her kisses careful and tender.

She led me to her room, to the soft, downy futon, flicking on the side light. We undressed each other in the warm glow, our gaze intense and curious. We left the light on, appreciating every aspect of each other as if we had never seen the female body before. Each touch felt like a new wonder, each soft, smooth curve a fascination.

Afterwards, we lay in each other's arms as if suspended in time and space. Shane reached over and switched off the light. In the semi-darkness, I could smell her muskiness and hear her breathing. Entwined into her smooth, warm body, I hardly slept, taking in these new surroundings, this woman in my arms, this me I had finally set free.

* * *

On our last night together, Shane gave me a tape. It was k.d. lang's latest album, *Absolute Torch and Twang*. On the cover, a handsome young man - no, it was a woman, in denim and a sheepskin jacket - looked intensely out into the distance, a Stetson in her hand and the bright blue prairie sky behind her. I had never heard of k.d. lang.

Shane grinned. "You've got a lot of learning ahead of you about lesbian culture. Everyone loves k.d. And Patsy Cline. And country and western generally. Anything to do with an achey, breakey heart…"

"Oh my god, I love soppy country and western," I threw back my head, laughing. "Ever since Olivia Newton-John! That was a dead giveaway back then, wasn't it?"

This afternoon, here in my suburban house in South London, I found that old cassette again. It was at the back of a cupboard full of out-dated gadgets and gear that I had packed away over a decade ago. The cassette was intact and the brown metallic strip seemed to be still taut and smooth. I dug around and came across an old Sony Walkman but no headset. More scrabbling turned up some AA batteries. I pulled off the earphones from my iPod and plugged it into the dusty jack. The cassette slipped into the Walkman with that distinctive click-clack that I hadn't heard in years. I put the earbuds in and pressed 'Play'.

The haunting keen of k.d. lang's liquid voice poured into my senses, whirling with steel string guitars and sluicing fiddles. And I was back on that flight to KL twenty-five years ago.

I had played the tape on an endless loop on that long haul flight, on another Walkman, headset hooped on my head. The rich layered country sounds swirled with heartache and hope and the endurance of outsiders - a lonely soul stepping the Wallflower Waltz, a brash Big Boned Girl shaking her thing. This lush music seemed to fill the cabin, float past the synthetic seat covers, glide down the long beige tube, swamp the other passengers where they sat. It filled all of me and it seemed impossible that only I could hear it. This music that belonged only to me made my heart soar and swoop like the swallows in the rain that I had chased as a child, barefoot and half-naked. Bathed in this music that was mine alone I felt strangely powerful, the keeper of a secret that no-one else could see or hear or touch or smell.

I had taken this flight so many times before ever since I had first arrived in London, at the age of twelve. That first trip, I had come with my mother, to start school in England for the first time. I was excited and scared and anxious, dependent on my mother to take charge, show me what to do, explain how the whole process of an international journey worked. Then when I took the return trip that first Christmas holiday, I had to do it by myself - and all those times after that, back and forth, like a spindle across the web of the earth. With each parting and westward going, I had to bind my childish self a little tighter, saying goodbye to my mother, being bolder and braver each time, putting on the layers of my English self. With each coming home, eastwards to the sunrise, I was more grown-up and polished, that veneer of strength and self-sufficiency hardening like layers of lacquer over the months and years. By the time I had finished Oxford, with each returning I was woven into intricate armour, so subtle you could not see it intertwined within the pretty clothes and big hair and charming manner.

And now, I sat here in this window seat, the hum of the engine beneath me, in the cocoon of this secret music and I was undone. The disguise had unravelled - not outwardly but on the inside. I still looked the same on the outside but in my nakedness within, I felt again like the child I used to be. I felt again that cheekiness I had lost, that sense of fun and mischief. That tomboy energy. There was a fragility, too, that was unsettling but also unexpectedly joyous. I had forgotten who she was, this tomboy girl who loved to run in the rain and do karate kicks and tell you all about the music and books and movies she loved without taking a breath. This girl who used to allow herself to cry and be scared and make mistakes, who did not protect herself against anyone and who was always the one to love first. This secret that I held in my heart took the shape and face and smile of Shane that I only I could see, and undulated in the swooning sounds of k.d. lang that only I could hear. But its power lay in the silent stillness where I could sit and be with me again.

* * *

I had always been close to my mother. As a child, I would cuddle up to her as she did the crossword and help her with the puzzle of words. I would tell her about what happened at school every day and rave to her about the latest storybook I was reading. We would talk about TV shows and films together. I would show her my stories in my little exercise books and listen carefully to her feedback, resolving to do better the next time. From school in England, I gave her her beloved blow-by-blow accounts of my weeks, writing in Royal Blue Quink ink on hundreds of blue aerogrammes over the many years away.

Any major decision I had to make, I made with her. At Oxford and later in my twenties, I would tell her about my men and she would see me through various break-ups and new boyfriends.

We talked about clothes and make-up and dishy movie stars, romantic stories, the great novels of English literature that we both loved, family and gossip and scandals, struggles and heartaches and doing the right thing, sex and love and contraception. We would laugh and cry together and as with any mother/ daughter relationship, argue too. She loved listening to stories about my holidays and friends and social events, about silly things and hard things and all the little details of my life. I got good at telling stories to her about my life, making her laugh, surprising her, keeping her in suspense.

Round the dinner table with my parents and my brother and sister, sometimes one of them would tease me, "You're just like Mum. How come you can talk so much?"

"I dunno," I would shrug. "It's in the genes, lah. What to do?"

My brother and sister were more like my father, quiet and self-contained. In my turn, I would tease them, becoming my mother in voice and manner, "Tell, tell, tell, lah - your turn to tell about what you been doing? I want blow by blow..."

And they would groan and roll their eyes.

"See? You're both just like Dad!"

And they would say with mock defeat, in an Eeyore tone, "Yah, it's in the genes. What to do?"

I would tell her about everything, everything except the lurking feelings flitting just out of my line of vision. There was nothing to say about them anyway because they did not exist. They were just shadows and dreams, fleeting thoughts, hopes that could never become reality. So why talk about them? Why even name them? And now that they had become real, now that there was Shane, what was I going to do?

That first night back in Malaysia, the synthetic smell of the long flight still clinging to my clothes and hair, I stepped into the airy house that was home, the warm night air swirling gently beneath the ceiling fan, the cicadas humming in the dark garden and I did not know what to do. I showered in the old tiled bathroom where I had spent so many long childhood hours alone and put on a faded T-shirt and a pair of pyjama trousers as I had always done, from the chest of drawers in my old room. I went out into the long house made up of interconnected halls, moving from the wooden floors of the bedroom to the cool red tiles of the hallway, barefoot as I always was at home. I sat down at the dining table with my parents who were also now showered and in their pyjamas and the maid served dinner.

Everything was the same as it had always been. And everything was different.

If Shane had been a man, I would have told my parents about her there at dinner. But she wasn't. I wanted to share her with them as I had shared with them the men in my life. I had brought home these men, or stories of these men, like report cards from school or trophies I had won. I would tell them about his achievements or his CV or his family background, all the lovely and charming things he had done for me, or how he had made me feel special. But with Shane, none of that seemed important. I wanted to tell them how she made me feel - how on the number 38 bus home to my flat that first morning, the colours of the world seemed more vivid, the sounds around me brighter, how I felt breathless and vibrant and full of energy. How my acne seemed to have cleared up as if by magic, and how I could speak with an ease and fluency I had not had for years. I wanted to share me with them.

But I didn't want to hurt them. After all the difficulties of my tomboy childhood and the tantrums of my teens, after feeling like a failure and a disappointment and a lazy, disobedient girl who would never amount to anything, I had finally become someone that the family - and my parents - could be proud of. My parents had never made me feel like a failure but the echoes and internalised expectations of my culture and clan and heritage, the high achieving family names on both sides, that unacknowledged awareness of always being the outsider, had shamed me into believing that I had shamed them.

My father had worked hard to give me the best education in the world and I had just lost my job. He and my mother had been kind when I had called to tell them the terrible news. *It's not you, they said, it's the economic climate, come home, take some time out, relax, spend time with us, things will get better and you'll find another job. You're a clever girl, you'll get another job, you'll see.* But I knew they were worried for me. And I didn't want them to worry.

And if, on top of that failure, I told them about Shane, about me, the real me. About whom their eldest daughter really was. A lesbian. A dyke. A *pondan*.

So I kept quiet over dinner and chatted with them as I had always done. We didn't talk about my job or my plans for the future. There was only the next three months - the friends and family in KL I was going to meet up with, all the Malaysian food I missed and wanted to eat, how I was going to fit in swimming and trips to Taiping and maybe jaunts to Penang and Singapore to see people there. I said I wanted to research our family history and collect stories about the past. The idea grabbed their imaginations and we were soon making a list of relatives and elderly friends I could talk to. It was fun and light and I could see that my parents were happy to have me home again for such a long stretch and with a project they could both chip in with. Why break the mood?

But it felt wrong. More wrong than sleeping with another woman. More wrong than being gay. It was the secrecy and deceit I could not bear. How could I lie to my mother about this most beautiful and most precious thing in my life?

At first, when I woke up that next morning with the dream, I didn't understand it. But when I narrated it to myself in the dark air-conditioned room, it all made sense.

I was at a cross roads. Mum was there. And I felt safe. I knew which way to go.

And I knew the right thing to do. So I told her, out there in our garden as the sun rose over the palm trees.

Later that morning, as we sipped fresh jasmine tea at the breakfast table, the doors to the veranda opening onto the lawn outside, I could hear my father moving about in their bedroom. I said, "Mum, please can you tell Dad?"

She smiled, "Of course, darling."

I don't know when she spoke to him but a few days later, while he was at work, a basket of flowers arrived for me. There was a note with it. In his almost illegible lawyer's scrawl, it said simply, "Love, Dad."

My sister came over from London for a few weeks holiday and Mum told her when we were spending a few days in Penang. She hugged me and said in that rude but loving tone that siblings have, *"Haiya,* no big deal, lah". My mother told my brother on their weekly call from his home in Worcestershire and I took the phone afterwards. He said, "We all still love you, stupe."

I had stood for so long on the edge of two worlds. I thought of that night in Oxford, the White Evening, poised precariously high up on those ceremonial gates, tomboy and seductress, masculine and feminine, thinking I had to choose between them. I thought of that moment standing on the precipice with Susan, hovering between the safety of denial and the terror of surrender. And of that evening in my flat with Lizzie as we stood in an embrace at my door, caught between desire and letting her go.

And here I was, on the other side.

I thought of Shane, and catching her smiley eyes across a crowded room.

I was different. And yet, I was the same as I had always been.

It had seemed almost impossible as a child to find my place in my family. All I knew back then was that I was not as I should be. I felt that there was something wrong with me. I needed to be fixed so that I could be like everyone else and like how everyone else expected me to be. And I had tried so hard to fix me.

My parents never treated me harshly, never abused me, never showed contempt or derision of *pondans*. They were firm and strict when they needed to be but taught me through love and by example and my mother and I had always talked about everything. And yet, I had felt such shame for this queer part of me, such an inability to articulate it, or even let it appear as a conscious thought in my mind. Where had that come from?

The disgust and horror is in the fabric of our culture. In the theatre version of this story, I portray a scene in the canteen with my school friends ridiculing the butch woman. But in reality, there was no single incident or moment where the shame of being a *pondan* crushed me. It was all around me - and it still is in most of the world. The visceral anxiety about humanity's homosexual nature is enacted in laws and religious edicts and is played out in contempt, derision, brutality, rape and murder. And even if we never encounter violence or venom or hatred in any direct way, it's in small remarks, a sneer, a disapproving tone of voice. It's in casual jokes and the way that children pick up what the adults around them say. It's in the stories we read or see in the movies and on TV. It's in pity and condescension. We are made to know it even if we don't consciously know it: it is a terrible and shameful thing to be gay.

But in those few months in the protective cocoon of my parents, that unforgiving world seemed like a faraway place.

I had not had this space since those long summer holidays back when I was a student. I would wake every morning with nothing but an abundance of time, reading or writing or just hanging out with my mother and sister. The house sat in half an acre of garden, with views on all sides of palm trees, bougainvillea, orchids and jasmine. In prime position was the flame tree, planted by my mother when I was six or seven and only now beginning to bloom in its full, abundant lusciousness. When we were not out seeing friends and relations, I would loaf around at home barefoot, in T-shirts and shorts. I felt as if I was becoming a child again and rebirthing into the woman that I should have been all along.

For now, I let myself revel in this idyll, this new place I was creating for myself within my family. After my sister headed back to London, I watched Hong Kong soap operas in the afternoon and managed to learn more Cantonese then I had ever been able to speak before. I would go swimming at the sports club where my siblings and I used to swim as kids. There would be time enough to go out into the unforgiving world once more, beyond this momentary Eden, when the nakedness of who I was would have to be clothed again - not in the disguises I used to wear but in clothes that would be my own.

It was strange to be here in this bright tropical landscape so soon after being with Shane, my body remembering still the coolness of her flat, the pale light of London, the smell and touch of her. I felt as if I had stepped through a disjuncture in time and space. Was it a memory of what had already happened? Or a hope of what could happen? Did she exist at all or was she just a creation of my imagination?

In those few months, the reality of her arrived in her thick letters wrapped in air mail envelopes, the clear black inked sentences striding across the pages. I would write back on leaf upon leaf of fragile air freight paper. We spoke on the phone every few days. We tried as best we could from a distance to tend to this thing between us, born too early and with only three days of nurturing. But the infancy of love needs more than words - words in black ink, words crackling through the telephone, words from thousands of miles away. It needs the touch of swaddled warmth, the resting of a head to hear the beat of the other's heart, the reflection of the other's gaze that at once creates and affirms our self. Even as we reached out with our hopeful words, we both knew it was fading away like a fragile bundle in the loneliness of an incubator, despite the oxygen tubes and monitoring electrodes and warm, incandescent lights.

One of the family stories I dug deeper into that summer was the story of the Malay mistress, the woman that Great-grandfather had loved before he met Ah Mooi, the one who was said to have been a *bomoh* - a witch or shaman. We do not know if she was actually Malay, the people who are related to the Indonesians, or whether she was a Peranakan Chinese, one of the many generations of ethnic Chinese who had settled in Malaya hundreds of years before and who had adapted to the Malay customs and lifestyle.

The Peranakan women wore the *sarong kebaya*, a close fitting lacy tunic and shapely *batik* sarong, honoured internationally now in the uniforms of the Singapore Airlines 'Singapore Girl' and Malaysian Airlines female cabin crew. Whatever her actual ethnicity, the woman we know as Great-grandfather's first great love was always known to us in the family as the Malay mistress.

I had always been curious why she was the mistress and never a wife. If he had taken her as his wife, we would have known her as a Great-grandmother. But despite being the first love, she had never been given that honour. 'Mistress' suggests something clandestine, forbidden and above all, sexual. Mistresses are temptresses, transgressive, wild, beyond the scope of marriage, husband-stealers, home-breakers, sometimes powerful sexual vamps, sometimes sad lonely creatures who will never get the man. It is mistresses who become *pontianaks*, never wives.

We never did know why she didn't become his wife. We never even knew her name. In one version of the story, she is the *bomoh* who teaches Great-grandfather the secret art of spiritualist healing. In the official version that Grandpa tells into my tape recorder for posterity that evening in 1976, she is simply a Malay woman his grandfather lived with - but the shamanic skills are taught to him by his Malay *bomoh* friends. At that time, in the prime of his life in the early 1900s, before he met Ah Mooi, Great-grandfather Lim became a master *bomoh* through these influences, using the ancient folk practice to heal those in need, despite his modern training as a hospital orderly and despite his involvement in the local Baptist church where he was to become one of the Elders. In his later life, he taught these shamanic skills to others in the family and I remember seeing at different times, when I was very young, one of my great-uncles and also Great-grandmother No. 4 going into trances and communicating with unseen spirits and ancestors from the other world.

From the moment I learnt of her, in my childish imagination, the mysterious Malay woman lured me into her story. In my version, growing and thickening like the vines in an unwatched jungle, she has become the one great love that Great-grandfather lost and the one great love who stayed with him forever. I see her always in twilight or in the night, emerging from the primeval jungle for a brief moment in time only to dissolve back into the impenetrable foliage again. In my mind, she is beautiful beyond this world, with long black tresses and an easy sexuality as she glides in her flowing sarong through these few years in his life. She is not yet the *pontianak* but a woman who stands on the threshold of the spirit world, mediating between the unseen and the real. He is a young man, his masculine energy angular and virile, drawn into the vortex of her allure and mystical power.

He wants to own her, possess her, and marry her. And for a while, she, too, is in thrall to his vigour and youth and all-consuming passion. She shares with him the secrets of generations of shamans, she teaches him their ancient wisdom, shows him the performance of healing trances and the enactment of spirit journeys into the minds and dreams of the soul-sickened. It is the bond that ties them together and the more he learns, the more he longs for her to be his forever. But the spirit of the jungle cannot be tamed and after a while, she begins to prowl his house like the tiger spirit she has taught him to rear beneath it.

Many shamans have a spirit familiar, a helper from the unseen world with magical powers, sometimes known as djinn - translated into Western culture as *genie*. Great-grandfather's *djinn* takes the form of a tiger that he learns to nurture and control, and which he feeds with offerings, growing in power as his shamanic skills grows. Perhaps he senses that the Malay woman longs to return to the jungle, that despite all that he can give her, his love, his heart, his life, it is not enough for a creature who needs to belong in the wild. Perhaps he tries to control her, offering her all that he has within his power. Perhaps he tries to use all that she has taught him - the *djinn*, the spells, and the magic that once was - to keep her enchanted. But she leaves him - in sadness, in anger and defiance, or for the simple need to be unfettered?

During my few months in Malaysia, we sat round one evening after dinner with some of the family, talking about the old stories I had been collecting. The ceiling fan buzzed overhead and we sipped jasmine tea as we talked, the light from the hanging Malacca-work lamps casting the airy hall in a warm glow. Outside, the cicadas and frogs filled the dark with their noise. A *tok-tok* bird punctuated the night with its eponymous rhythm. We talked about the Malay woman and our speculation spanned out to the Peranakan and their women, who were known as *Nyonyas*.

"Hey," my mother said suddenly, "I've got a *sarong kebaya* that used to belong to Grandma. I think she used to wear it sometimes - oh, long ago in her young days - to be more Malayan. You know, to be more like the local Chinese rather than always like Chinese-Chinese with her *cheongsams*." She looked me up and down. "I'm sure it will fit you. Come, come…"

In my parents' bedroom, we opened one of the two carved camphor chests. The spicy smell of the wood filled the air. My mother looked carefully through the layers of in-built trays and drawers and found the lacy white top and colourful sarong. I stripped out of my T-shirt and shorts and she helped me dress in the embroidered tunic and tie the sarong around my waist.

I emerged into the hall to the *oohs* and *aahs* of the family there. I tried to place my feet gracefully, to sway with mystique but it was hard to do barefoot without the feminine shape of high heels. I saw myself in the ornate Chinese mirror on one wall. My big hair looked out of place and my gaze was too direct, too modern. I turned and twirled for everyone to examine the lace work. I felt a deep connection suddenly to this house that used to my home, to this warm night, this thick verdant country beyond, to Grandma who used to wear this tunic and sarong, to the ancestors who seemed to be out there in the dark watching and listening to us speak of them. And to Shane, too, wishing that she could see this part of my life, wishing we had had more time.

In the story in my mind, I imagine the Malay woman deep in the forest, in her own *atap* house on stilts, secluded and distant from the *kampungs* - villages - that might be some hours walk away. The light here is perpetual jade and emerald twilight and her home is decked in amulets and palm fronds, birds of paradise and rare orchids found only deep in the jungle. In this place between worlds, this is where she is happiest, where she belongs even as she keeps Great-grandfather in her heart. And it is here that she screams alone in childbirth, bearing her lover's son or perhaps daughter, conceived before their parting and his final unknown offering to her. In this half-seen version of the story in my dreams, she and the child die, returning to the world of unseen beings, where living energy and mystical spirit become one with all things.

Spirits from the other world can take many forms at will. Folklore tells of demons coming into our world as civet cats to maul the sick into convulsions. Some spirits lurk as floating logs in still water to drag the unwary into the depths. I imagine the Malay woman rebirthed as a *pontianak* from the gore of her undelivered and undeliverable child. But she does not seek vengeance on her lover for it is she who abandoned him, she who broke free. Perhaps this half-embodied state gives her at last a freedom beyond all she had ever dreamed of - half ghost half woman, part demon part lover, of this world and not, mother and mistress but never a wife. In his grieving for her, does he conjure her in spells, reaching out into the dark void beyond what we can see and touch? Does she come to him, her sarong flowing over her unseen feet, her black tresses falling over her face - but just beyond his grasp, not close enough for a shaft to be plunged into the nape of her neck, not close enough to fall into his power?

Perhaps she shifts and shimmers and is gone, no more a woman, slipping away into the freedom of the jungle and the night, boundless beyond past or present or future, journeying to the other world and back. And when she next returns to the living world of Great-grandfather and his family, does she choose instead to slip into the guise of the tiger spirit beneath the house? When he next conjures his familiar, does her lover whom she once abandoned see her in those luminous eyes? Does she prowl free now in death between this world and the other as she had once longed to do in life - yet still return at times to share her magical power with him, to watch over him, to remain always part of his family?

Does he long for her throughout his long life in this world of the flesh, seeking out those qualities that enthralled him in the many women he came to love? Is he always looking for her in their eyes and in the lines he traces on their bodies with his hands and mouth and tongue? Does he hear her in the spells and incantations that he teaches to his wives? Or see her in the trances and performances that possess them as they, too, work the art of the *bomoh* and walk the passageway between both worlds?

That evening with my family, wearing a *sarong kebaya* like one the Malay mistress might have worn, I moved about on the tiled floor in my bare feet playfully swaying in a stylised feminine gait. The older generation talked in mellow, wistful tones of the family long past, with so much unknown and unknowable. I shared what I had learnt from the interviews with other family members and asked questions of those in the loose circle around me.

Out of the corner of my eye, there was a movement, a fluttering by the windows. The others saw it too. We glanced about, trying to catch the shadow that was dancing too swiftly in the air.

There, it had landed on a wall.

It was a giant moth, its wings open like two dark, mottled hands resting in splayed prayer against the whitewash. It was brown like the bark of forest trees, two large black eyes gazing out at us from the lower quadrants of its wings as if from an unseen world behind the wall.

I moved towards it to shoo it away back out into the night. It lifted off, flitting above our heads as if to anoint us with the dust of its wings, then settled on another wall, its eyes large and unblinking.

My family and I looked at each other, our glances flowing

round the circle in a fluttering ripple and our unease floated out of us in semi-laughter.

"Hey, why you think it's come, ha?"

"Only a moth-lah…"

"But just when we're talking about *bomoh* things and going into trances and communicating with the ancestors …"

"Well, if it's a family spirit, then it must be a good spirit, right?"

"Yah, so not spooky-lah. It's a good sign."

"I can't believe we're having this conversation. A moth is a moth."

"Yah, but where got fun?"

And that was the heart of it. Where got fun, indeed, if we live always in a literal-minded world, if we search only for the truth in the facts as lawyers would do in a court case or the measurements of scientists and the data of researchers. In one of the worlds we live in, it was just a moth and its appearance a coincidence as it was drawn to the bright house from the darkness of the night. In the other world we inhabit, it was a spirit from our ancestral past that had come to watch over us or to be part of the family gathering. The dark shapes on its wings were markings grown out of millions of years of evolution - or the watchful eyes of a shapeshifting spirit woman. In our world constructed by a myriad of stories, both versions are true. And there may be versions yet to be told that would also be true.

In the healing rituals of a shamanic culture, the *bomoh* would bring together the family and community of her soul-sickened patient in a special ceremonial gathering. In our modern day healing rituals, our version of soul sickness tells of depression or chronic illness or stress or eating disorders and we would seek medical prescriptions or the counsel of psychologists or scientific research. The shaman heals a different version of that story. I see them all sitting cross-legged on the wooden floor of a long house, the verdant jungle beyond loud with birds and cicadas and monkeys. With the patient at the heart of the circle, the *bomoh* starts to chant and dance, traveling deeper and deeper into a trance. Perhaps the patient, too, becomes mesmerised, as he follows the shaman into an inner landscape that is at once manifest in the physical present of the long house hall. There, in the unseen world that is also seen in the minds of their audience, the *bomoh* and patient enact a psychodrama and a journey from sickness to healing. Spirit familiars come to give aid, malevolent spirits are battled and cast out, ancestors walk again, the souls of those watching arise and take part. Through the witnessing of the patient's pain by his community and the enactment of what might have been unspoken, unacknowledged, unrecognised within the web of the relationships present in that hall, it is not just one individual whose soul returns to him but also those of the each person gathered there. That the healing journey takes place in the presence of others, and with the participation of their hearts, is the core of shamanic healing. The fragmentation of the self and the community and also their shared heritage, their past and present and future, their ancestors and those yet to be born, their spiritual forebears and adopted kin are woven together again through the shared trance state of the re-enacted drama.

That evening in the circle of my family, close as always with my mother, at ease with my father and dressed as a *bomoh* once beloved of my great-grandfather - in the presence of a moth that might or might not have been a shapeshifting fae and that watched us with eyes that were not eyes - at once a tomboy and a woman, lover and tiger spirit, an outsider and yet accepted within, I found at last the place where I belonged not just in my family but in the world.

Biker Boots

THE STORY BEHIND THE STORIES

Coming out is a rite of passage.

In the world of debutantes and high society, it is an ancient tradition going back generations. When a young woman comes of age, she is invited to a coming out ball to introduce her to society - and in the aristocratic classes in Britain, to present her to the monarch. It is her "debut" into the world as an adult - or, rather, as a fertile virgin of a marriageable age. This custom continues to this day among the elite not just in Britain but also, surprisingly, in the ideally classless societies of Australia and the United States.

The coming out ball is the moment when high society gathers to view the future of their dynasties. Debutantes customarily wear white ball *gowns*, sometimes with long white Cinderella gloves and sometimes with tiaras or both. If you Google images of 'debutante ball coming out', you will see that the styles of the ball dresses have changed little since Victorian times and often the young women are indistinguishable from each other in their demure, beautiful uniforms. The eligible young bachelors gather round them in white tie and tails and suddenly, we are back in the world of Jane Austen and Downton Abbey and fairy tale princesses.

For a young woman in that society, to come out is to emerge from childhood to womanhood, to put herself on public display as a potential wife and mother. There at the ball, she is gazed upon, looked at, compared to her peers. She must be graceful and charming, glide round the dance floor and float through the night in her pretty white gown, impress the older generation and enchant the young blades.

She is there to be chosen. To be the one who is a class above all those other girls, to find the best and richest husband.

Coming out is a rite of passage.

How do you come out to your friends and family?

For me, I know how lucky I have been to have still been loved and accepted after I came out to my mother and my family. I do not feel brave - simply grateful and appreciative of the people in my life. For many others, coming out means rejection by those closest to them. Coming out means facing violence, abuse, shaming, correction 'therapy' and homelessness. And yet, we come out and we keep coming out, in whichever society we may live around the world, despite the sanctions of our religions and punishments of our cultures. We cannot help it. We have been part of families and tribes and clans and nations for generations. We have always been here and we have always been on the margins of the norm, our love unseen, and our roles unacknowledged. And yet, regardless of whom others want us to be or how our cultures want to shape us, we have to live in our own truth. Coming out is staking a claim for who we are and who we can be. Coming out is a terrifying - and courageous - act of selfhood.

It is saying to the universe, I am here and I matter.

In the idyll of my few months at home with my parents, I didn't need to think beyond the safe haven of my immediate family. But there was the extended family and my friends and acquaintances. And once I found work again, my colleagues and bosses there also. All these people I needed to come out too. Or not.

When I arrived back to London in the autumn, I wasn't sure what to do. Who could I tell? Who shouldn't I tell? If only, I thought ruefully, it could have been as simple as sending out an embossed invitation on gilt-edge card: *Yang-May Ooi requests the pleasure of your company at her coming out ball. All in favour, RSVP. Those not in favour, please don't come.* But there was no etiquette for this sort of thing. I was in unchartered waters and I would have to make it up as I went along.

Over the next few weeks, I caught up with my close friends individually. It felt easier - and safer - to tell each of them one-to-one. The formula that seemed to work the best went something like this:

"I've met someone…"

My friend's face would brighten. They were happy for me.

And then before they could say anything, "… It's a woman. It's been a bit complicated because I've been away. But she's lovely and we're trying to see if it can work…"

All the hard lifting would be done by the personal pronoun as I carried on chatting as if the 'her' element of this new person in my life was not a huge, enormous deal for me. It almost didn't matter what I said, my monologue gave them time to process the news. I could see the momentary surprise - and then they would recover and recompose their expression. They would listen, nod, smile, taking their cue from me - this was cool, this was fine, the most natural thing in the world.

With my closest friends, they would sometimes see my anxiety under the nonchalance, sense my fear of their rejection. In her flat, Pippa got up from the sofa and came round to give me a hug. "Oh, petal, we still love you!"

Jane was going through her divorce when I met up with her that year. As we sipped coffee in Soho and shared this fragile moment in our lives, our friendship became closer than it had ever been.

At that time, I was afraid of using the G word. Or worse, the L word. Gay. Lesbian. They stamped a label on my forehead. An ugly label. A shameful one. Like *pondan*. And I wasn't ready yet to be that thing, that alien creature set apart from my friends and from the 'normal' world that I had known and lived in all my life.

In the script of *Bound Feet Blues*, I come out to my mother by saying *I'm gay*. But that is not what I actually said. I shuffled and perambulated around the topic, I umm-ed and aah-ed, hesitated, circled around it and eventually, managed a clumsy and stumbling version of "I've met someone…" But for the pacing and drama on stage, for simplicity and clarity, for not having to explain the whole complex story of Susan and Lizzie and Shane - I made the creative choice to streamline it all into that bold statement. I'm gay.

Back in my twenties, all those years ago, it felt so new and strange to be this thing. Gay. It felt even stranger - and scarier - to be this other thing. Lesbian. The word seemed so heavy - pregnant? - with derision and contempt and titillation in the world out there. I was still so afraid of being clumped together with ugly, vicious monsters like the brogue-wearing Rosa Klebb or buxom bimbos with too much make-up fondling each other's porno-sized breasts. I didn't want to be like those Greenham Common, dungaree-wearing, protest-marching, asexual women with shaven heads I had seen in college on the edges of the punting and picnicking Oxford experience. I didn't want to be the tragically beautiful lesbian of high drama, wailing in self-loathing and hanging herself for unrequited love of 'normal' women who would always go back to real love with a real man.

I was me. And I just happened to love women.

Some friends said, "Yes, you love the person. It's not about gender. It's not about gay or straight."

And that felt comforting.

I met Susan at the South Bank and it was still warm enough to sit at a cafe table outside. We looked out at the river and tried to make conversation. She had been busy at work. There was the possibility of a permanent posting to the Sydney office.

I said, "I've met someone. Her name is Shane. She's …"

"I knew it!"

The energy in her voice startled me. I searched back in my memory. We hadn't seen each other since my redundancy party. We had exchanged a few letters while I was away but I had not said anything revealing in them. "How… how did you know?"

"I saw how you two were together at your party…" And she stopped.

I did not know what to say. Shane and I had not touched at the party. We had only looked, smiled. Talked.

I felt suddenly I wanted to say I was sorry. But there was nothing to say sorry for. Susan and I were just friends.

And so we both sat there in silence.

John was one of my avowedly Christian friends. He came round for tea one afternoon. I hadn't been going to tell him - or any of my more overtly religious friends. They would judge me and reject me and it would be painful and awful, I thought. But as we sat and chatted, I realised that this friendship with John - with my other Evangelical friends - would be a sham if I could not share with them this most true part of my life. I told myself that I was judging him before I had given him the chance - maybe his friendship towards me would over-ride any judgmental reaction he might have. After all, his group of friends from church were big on God's love and having love in your heart and loving your neighbour as yourself. Maybe it would be all right.

So I told him.

And he said I would burn in hell.

He said it in the most concerned tone. He loved the sinner (me), he said, not the sin (the gay thing). He didn't want me to burn in hell. He wanted me to be happy in the bosom of the Lord and to do that I would have to walk in the path of righteousness. He quoted scripture and said we could pray together so that I could be healed.

I was upset. But not because I believed that I would burn in hell. I was upset because it hurts when someone, a friend especially, condemns this most precious and most beautiful treasure in your life as an evil, dirty sin. It hurts when someone thinks that a lifetime of struggle and despair could be so easily fixed as with a prayer. And that I would give up this hard won battle for my own heart simply for another's approval - and the approval of a God he felt that only he spoke for. I was upset because I had believed all of these things in the past and they had made me ill and unhappy and had destroyed my friendship with Lizzie. Listening to John, I was upset because I saw the hurt I had done to myself for all these years, saw the harshness with which I had treated myself in the name of a love that I thought would keep me safe.

I let him go on. I did not try to argue with him or persuade him otherwise. I watched him as if from the far side of huge chasm. It struck me that he truly believed in what he was saying and that he really was worried for my soul. But looking at him from this place of freedom, it seemed to me that hell had been the place where I had come from. Hell had played itself out in my stammer and acne and back pain, in my inexpressible rage as a teenager, in the anguish of my confused feelings for Lizzie and in my soul destroying disguise as a successful, over-achieving uber-femme. And now, here in this new way of being, I felt a strange certainty.

He was wrong.

"I think you should go," I said at last.

"I've upset you," he said, "I'm sorry." And he meant it.

In that period, although there were good friends who remained, there were many other friends like John whom I lost. The distancing and discomfort were sometimes overt in those first few minutes, growing over time. There were encounters where I knew that friendship was over even before we said our goodbyes and parted. In other cases, it would peter out over the next few months as they rang at the last minute to cancel or would not commit to a time for a get together or would not return my calls.

Things with Shane ended a few weeks after I got back. It had become unsustainable over the months and the distance, already fading away while I was in KL. But we had not wanted to do it over the phone, leaving it merely uncertain during our last difficult call. We had not had time to know each other, to build a history together. We were ciphers, voices over the wire and words on a page. There was no time to kick back and lounge together, to share a laugh, a story from our past, a silly thing we saw on our way to work that day. And an old boyfriend had come back into her life. He had been here. I had been there.

Without Shane, my safe little formula did not work.

"I met someone. It was a woman. But it's over now…"

It begged the question: so you had a fling with a woman but now are you back to men? Was it just the person I had loved, not the gender? Without Shane, was I gay? If I went back to men, was I straight?

Or maybe, I was bi. That felt oddly thrilling and glamourous. It opened up the possibility of having it all, of truly loving the person and not the gender, of exploration and adventure, of being free.

But I remembered the sense of aliveness when I was with Susan, the teasing lingering of touch and gaze with Lizzie, the breathlessness of being with Shane. I had never felt the same way with the men I had gone out with, pleasurable as those relationships had been. I thought about the way those men had looked at me with desire and love and how powerful that had made me feel, how beautiful. And yet, when these women had looked at me, the world and everything in it had simply fallen away.

I walked back into my empty flat after Shane and I saw each other for the last time at a coffee shop near Victoria. Lizzie was in Geneva and I would never see her again. In time to come, Susan and I would only meet at mutual friends' parties and when she left for Sydney, she did not tell me. I had lost a number of friends whom I had trusted. If these good friends could just me so harshly, how many more others out there would more easily hate me if they could see that I was a lesbian? Life out there felt suddenly cold and unsafe.

I had been unemployed now for coming up to six months. Back home at my parents' house, I had felt like a child without responsibility, able to believe that I could be everything that I had longed to be. I had notebooks overflowing with family stories and my head full of ideas for a book. In that comforting haven, I felt I had found my place in this world at last - but perhaps I had just imagined it. Here in the reality of my urban life in London, the harsh vibe of this big city overwhelmed my spirit. The fragile hopes in my heart felt small and helpless in the tumult of its drive and ambition and commerce. The power of the *bomoh* in me seemed to diminish amid the hard asphalt and stone of this sprawling metropolis.

I looked out at the treeless avenue, the Regency terraces gouging a white stucco canyon through the late October grey. It felt like desolation. I sat down in an arm chair, unable to move. I could not cry. I felt no anger.

I had stepped off into the abyss. I had crossed into the wilderness. These women I had loved had brought me here. My longing to express the unseen, the unspoken, like a shaman mediating between two worlds, had brought me here. My mother and my family had given me a safe haven with their love for a while. I had allowed myself to dream and wish and hope for a while in the oasis of creativity and possibility that Shane had offered me.

But this was the reality. I was here in my life, in London, alone.

I wanted to stay sitting here as the afternoon light deepened. I had sat in this chair alone so often before, as if waiting in the wings. Maybe I could sit here a bit longer, until it got dark. And just carry on sitting here through the night. Only this time, there would be no performance to come of the beautiful girl in her beautiful clothes and beautiful little shoes. She was gone. Her audience, too, was gone.

This was me now; me, without disguise, without guile. Just me.

I had performed Her for so long, it suddenly felt terrifying to be alone. To give Her up was to give up all those years that I had worked so hard in creating Her, to admit that I had been living a lie all that time. I had suffered so much to become this construct, this idea of who I should be and here I was giving Her up. And in giving Her up, I would have to reveal the tiny, tender self that She had protected for so many years.

Undressing out of Her charm and polish and sophistication,

tentatively, hesitantly, I began to see who might be there beneath these loosening layers. In the stillness of the fading light, I sat and waited and I discovered myself still a child - the child who had put on a brave face back and forth over the vast curve of the earth, the child who had learnt to speak with the polish of public school, the child who had been so good at hiding her childishness.

I wanted to stay here in this chair. Just as long ago, I had sat on that tiled floor in the bathroom as a child, just me by myself - here, I could be small and sad and afraid. There was no-one to see me but me, no-one to be with but me. And it was nice.

But I knew I could not stay here. This was all of my own choosing. I had to step into this future I had set in motion. I had to finally grow up, become my own person. Come of age. And I would have to do it alone.

Would I have the courage after all?

Coming out is a rite of passage.

We are not chosen, like the beautiful debutantes in their white ball dresses. We choose. We do not come out into society. We leave it. We do not become part of the continuum by coming out, we step outside of it. We are not clothed in virginal white, we come naked into our new selves.

* * *

Once upon a time in China, a thousand years ago, there lived a young girl. Her name was Yexian. She lived with her step-mother and two step-sisters, who were ugly in spirit and ugly in demeanour. Her mother had died and her father had remarried but now, he too was dead and she was left alone in their care. They kept her out of sight because they were afraid that she was more beautiful than they. She was their servant, working all day and all night cooking and cleaning and doing the laundry.

She did her duty but she was sad and lonely. One day, when she was washing clothes by the river, she met a talking fish who became her friend. She liked having a new friend and it made her happy. The stepmother discovered the fish and killed it. She and her daughters ate the fish and they hid the bones away.

When Yexian discovered that her friend had been killed, she sat down by the river and wept. An old man saw her and taking pity on her, told her where the bones were buried. She retrieved the bones and kept them hidden and safe in her room.

There was a big festival and the whole village went to celebrate. But Yexian's step-mother and step-sisters forbade her to go for they feared that her beauty would outshine them. After the women left for the festival, Yexian sat alone in her room. She brought out the bones of her friend and talked to them, wishing she could go to the festival. But how could she in her clothes of rags?

Suddenly, a jade green gown appeared and a pair of golden slippers. Grateful to the bones of her magical friend, Yexian excitedly put on the gown and shoes and went to the festival. In her heart, she knew she was disobeying her step-mother but the urge was too great to join in the festivities and be happy like a girl again for just one evening.

At the festival, there were bright lanterns and dancing and music. Yexian took it all in with wonder and delight. Everyone noticed this beautiful young woman in the jade green gown and golden slippers. They have never seen her before they said to each other, who was she? And then, Yexian saw one of the step-sisters looking at her. Fearing that the step-sister would recognise her, Yexian ran away. And as she hurried away, she dropped one of the slippers.

A merchant picked up the slipper and sold it to the king of the neighbouring kingdom. The king was enchanted by this delicate, tiny slipper and reasoned that the woman to whom it belonged must be beautiful beyond compare for her feet to be so tiny and delicate. He searched far and wide for her but each time any woman tried the slipper on, no matter what the size of her foot, the slipper was always one inch too small.

The king's search brought him to the house where Yexian

lived. Her step-mother pushed her two daughters forward. They each tried the slipper on. Each time, it was too small. Determined to win the hand of the king, one sister chopped off her toes but still the slipper was too small. The other sister sliced off her heel and still the slipper was too small.

As the king was about to leave, he noticed a bedraggled serving maid in the shadows. He invited her to try the slipper despite the protestations of the other women. Yexian stepped forward and tried on the slipper. It fit perfectly and she was suddenly transformed into a queenly beauty in her jade green gown and pair of golden slippers.

The king chose her to be his wife and they lived happily ever after.

* * *

I first came across a version of this Chinese Cinderella story in the book *Foot-binding: A Jungian Engagement with Chinese Culture and Psychology* by Shirley See Yan Ma, who deconstructs the folk tale to explore the Female Archetype. There are a number of other versions of the Yexian story that can be found from different sources. There are also many versions of the Cinderella story across different cultures, from Korea and Vietnam across to Persia (now Iran) and Africa as well as Mexico and the Native Americans. However, most commentators seem to agree that the Yexian - or sometimes Yen Shen - story may be one of the earliest forms of the story that evolved across time and cultures to become the Cinderella fairy tale that Western audiences know. The first written account of it has been traced back to 850 AD, which was during the time of the Tang Dynasty, when the practice of foot-binding began.

For me, the most chilling element of the Yexian story is the detail of the slipper that is always one inch smaller than any foot that tries it on - until its rightful owner is found. It expresses in that throwaway line the desperate, determined, obsessive chase for impossible perfection that would come to dominate the Chinese psyche for a thousand years.

I never could relate to the Cinderella story as a child - nor the other major fairy tales: Snow White, Sleeping Beauty and Beauty and the Beast. They all seemed to feature heroines whose prized qualities were their beauty and the feminine virtues of patience and obedience. The plots of Snow White and Cinderella turn on their looks and the envy of other women - as does Beauty and the Beast to some extent, though Belle's sisters also envy her apparent riches and good life at the Beast's castle. The heroines are passive, patient, obedient, trusting - Cinderella waiting for the prince to find her with the slipper, Snow White with the apple in her throat and Sleeping Beauty with her pricked finger both waiting for the prince to kiss them awake, Belle given to the Beast by her father to pay a debt.

As a tomboy, I never felt that anyone would ever think of me as beautiful let alone envy me with such energy and vitriol that they would go to such lengths to make my life miserable. And should I in a million years find myself in the same quandary as these fairy tale maidens, I would never ever be able to sustain the level of patience and obedience that would be needed to win the day. More inexpressibly, there was something else. I did not really want a Prince Charming. I could not in my heart see myself living out a life as the pretty princess, making a lovely castle for him while he gadded about on his white horse doing whatever princes do when they were not at home. It was more interesting to me to be the prince.

And then I read the story of a girl just like me.

Once upon a time, there lived a little mermaid....

She was different from those other wimpy heroines to my childish mind. She is the youngest daughter of the Sea King, whose kingdom lies beneath the waves. Yes, she is beautiful but (according to the translation on the Hans Christian Anderson hca.gilead.org.li website): "She was a strange child, quiet and thoughtful; and while her sisters would be delighted with the wonderful things which they obtained from the wrecks of vessels, she cared for nothing but her pretty red flowers, like the sun, excepting a beautiful marble statue."

The statue is of a handsome human boy and she spends hours dreamily gazing at him and decking him in sea flowers. For me, the statue represented the inner landscape of the little mermaid's imagination - it is the first indication of a world beyond the waves and sets her as yet unacknowledged dream in motion. She loves to hear stories from her grandmother of the world above the sea where flowers have fragrance and birds sing sweetly and she can hardly wait to come of age when she will be allowed to go up to the surface.

The little mermaid is active and impatient and disobedient. She is a daydreamer, a brave heart and a being who lives between two worlds. When she is fifteen, she can at last go to the surface. There, bobbing amongst the waves, she sees a ship sailing by. She swims up to it and looks through a porthole. There she sees a handsome prince. It is she who sees him and not the other way round as in the other fairy tales. It is she who desires him, she who loves first.

It is also she who is the rescuer, not the prince - in a storm, the ship is wrecked and she saves him from drowning. He is in a swoon as she swims with him to land and there she leaves him.

The silly dolt never looks out of the porthole to see her looking in. Never wakes from his swoon in time to see her so never knows who rescued him.

Back under the waves, she withdraws into herself, becoming even quieter, holding her secret love and longing deep in her heart.

As one of the Sea King's daughters, she is cherished and loved by all, her beautiful voice is applauded and appreciated by everyone in the court - she has everything that a fairy princess could ever possibly want. Except the one thing that seems impossible, a life with a human boy in a strange and foreign world.

And so, she chooses adventure over safety, the impossible over the known. She crosses the dark, slithering dominion of the sea witch through dangerous whirlpools. She is terrified but persists, thinking of the prince. There, she asks the sea witch to transform her into a human. Whatever the cost.

She gives up her mermaid's tail for human legs but every step on those human feet feels as if she is stepping on knives.

Every step is an agony.

The sea witch demands payment in the form of the little mermaid's beautiful voice. In the fairy tale, we read:

> "But if you take away my voice," said the little mermaid, "what is left for me?"

> "Your beautiful form, your graceful walk, and your expressive eyes; surely with these you can enchain a man's heart."

And there is one last terrible condition that she accepts without flinching. The sea witch tells her:

> "The first morning after he marries another your heart will break, and you will become foam on the crest of the waves"

And the brave little mermaid agrees.

When I first worked on the script of *Bound Feet Blues*, I planned to structure it round a re-telling of *The Little Mermaid*. But the conceit became too cumbersome and it unnecessarily complicated the flow of the piece. So I cut out the fairy tale reference although a trace of the little mermaid remains in the structure and themes of the show.

Let me show you.

Act One: Under the Sea

Here beneath the waves, I am the mermaid in her father's kingdom, daydreaming over Suzi Quatro and ONJ, living in my imagination in the world of my little stories. Others around me, like the five older sisters of the little mermaid, fit in and accept their place in the kingdom in the sea, but I am restless. I listen to stories told by my mother and I dream of a strange and foreign land where it is cold and foggy and the people are pale and creamy. I listen to stories told by my grandmother and learn about the struggle and hardships of past generations, like the weight of the water over the fathomless sea. As the mermaid with her natural tail dances and twirls in the water so I, too, can dance and twirl, free and laughing at home in my bare feet. But I hold a secret in my heart that I do not know how to express even as my voice pours its beautiful words onto pages and pages of stories.

For generations of bound foot girls, this is where they have always lived, here under the ocean in the Sea King's world, the burden of the mothers passing down to their daughters like layers of sediment, the pressure of the dense water lying heavy upon their bodies. For a few short years, they are free to swim and play as they please and give full voice to their souls. But when they come of age, they rise to the surface and gaze upon the world of men, busy and noisy and important. If they are to enter adulthood, they must leave their father's world, lose their childish freedom and step ashore into the kingdom of the prince, their husband.

For young girls today, they can swirl and swim in the power of their humanity before they learn that they are different from boys, before they are taught they must become women. Before they silence themselves for fear of being bossy, before they stay quiet lest they outsmart and outshine the boys. Before they learn to define themselves by the prettiness and sexuality. Before they step into the land of adulthood.

Act Two: On the Land

The little mermaid emerges from the water and walks on land, every step an agony. She arrives at the prince's palace and he asks her who she is but she can only look at him with her large eyes without reply. He and all those who see her are enchanted by her delicate, swaying walk.

There is singing and dancing at the palace. The prince loves the songs sung by the slaves and little mermaid wishes that she could sing for him, thinking sadly that she has given away her voice to be with him. She dances for him a dance that no-one has ever seen before, so beautiful that everyone is smitten, not knowing that each step she takes is as of knives slicing through her feet.

She stays with the prince and they walk in the woods and hike in the hills. Her feet bleed and she leaves behind her a trail of blood but she never reveals her pain, laughing lightly as she walks with him to the highest mountain.

But at night, in secret, she goes to the edge of sea to bathe her feet.

The prince has a distant memory of a beautiful maiden who saved him from the shipwreck. He longs to find her and confesses his love for his mysterious rescuer to the little mermaid. She can only sit and listen and cannot tell him it was she who had loved him and rescued him all this time.

He is betrothed to another. This other maiden is beautiful and virtuous. The prince thinks it is she who rescued him and loves her at once - and virtuous as she is, his fiancée does not disabuse him of his mistake.

As the first rays of dawn streaks across the sky on the first morning after his marriage, the little mermaid dives into the sea, dissolving into sea spray.

Here on the land, in my twenties, I am the little mermaid, walking in beautiful little shoes, swaying in delicate rhythms before so many unseeing princes. I dance for them all, unable to see my fathomless sadness even for myself, let alone voice it to anyone. Every step is an agony. My disguise is a muteness that does not allow them to see me. These men, like the prince, long to love me, long to be rescued by me and yet, I cannot give them what they want and can only give them back my silence, my heartlessness.

Here on the land, I am the little mermaid, walking in the woods with Lizzie to a meadow full of buttercups, hiking through hills and canyons with Susan, my feet bleeding and without words for this thing that I feel. I laugh and play the friend, washing away my shame by the moonlit sea. And even when I find the words, so many words across the world with Shane, she looks away from me towards another.

Sitting in my flat that late October afternoon, it felt like dissolving of myself into spray.

For the bound feet women of China, they are mute for a thousand years of history, letting their stories be recorded by men whose inky calligraphy leaves a trail of lotus loving literature. Those beautiful tortured feet are sniffed and licked and sucked and categorized and immortalized by the words of men. The swaying delicate manner of the women crosses into legend. The women themselves do not speak to us. We see them, these delicate decorative objects in ivory carvings and antique paintings and later, staring out at us from sepia photographs in their beautiful embroidered robes. What hopes and dreams they might have had, what ambitions, what longings, we can never know. Were they ever known and seen and truly loved for who they were beneath their disguises, beneath their beauty, beyond their feet?

For women today, are we silenced by men who take their right to speak without asking while we fear to be bossy bitches? Does our smaller size and more child-like, higher voices mean we may as well be mute? Are we not seen and heard just because we are women? Do we dance for others - both men and women - smile and be nice, needing to be loved, no matter how we feel inside? Do we walk in pain through our lives because despite our courage and energy and drive, despite being the rescuer, we are mistakenly waiting to be rescued?

For every woman through the generations wherever we may have been born in the world, despite taking our destinies into our own hands, despite our volition and ambition and will, are our chances thwarted from the start by unforgiving pre-conditions from time immemorial? Have we always been set up to fail by cultural traditions woven out of fear and envy and covetousness? I think it is of potent significance that it is the sea witch, a female creature, who is the one who makes the deal with the little mermaid for her transformation and who has the right in return to levy the tragic price. For such traditions cannot surely endure without the collusion and internalisation of them by women as much as men.

Act Three: Into the Air

Even as the little mermaid's body dissolves into sea spray, another transformation begins, from ocean to land, from land to sea spray, from spray to air. The sea spray disperses in the bright sunlight and the little mermaid becomes a spirit of the air, an invisible being joining the myriad of invisible, beautiful daughters of the air floating and swooping and singing above the sea and land.

From mermaid to woman to sprite, she loses her burdensome body but regains her voice. No - not regains. Her voice of the air is a new voice, one of maturity and fullness, emerging from pain and self-knowledge. Immaterial as sunlight, she sings with her sister sprites, their voices dancing and playing free high up in the air as once she danced and played deep beneath the sea.

We can hear them in the wind and in the sound of the waves, in the call of the gulls and songs of the land birds. They speak to us in voices of the leaves and hum of the frogs and cicadas. Their breath touches us in a warm breeze, their lips kiss our brows while we sleep. They sing to us in music, curl themselves around the words that flow from our mouths. They are all the stories that we tell.

In this moment in history, for some of us, women like you and me - we have a voice more far-reaching than we have ever had in any other period. We can speak for ourselves. We can speak out in public. We can write, we can tell stories, make films, perform, and create music. We can own our own property. We own our own selves. We are the spirits of the air.

But for how long?

We can be clever and rational and brilliant, talented and inspired, articulate and intellectual. We can be pure mind and yet, the cultures we live in spread their nets to catch us like birds and drag us down from the air into our bodies. Always our bodies.

We are told how our bodies must look (not ugly). Our faces must be pleasing to the eye ('give us a smile, love'). Our bodies must be fecund (not old). Our bodies must be available (not a lezzie). Our voices must be mute ('shut up, dear'). A woman's body in an ordinary life can be beaten into submission by her husband, raped if she takes a wrong turn walking home. A woman engaging in public disagreement, debate and discourse enters as a body to be threatened with rape and made malice with. A woman running for public office, for the Presidency of the most powerful nation in the world, is first and foremost a body to be derided by sneering men.

This moment in history - how long will it last before the dark net closes in and tightens its noose? The darkness roars its pain across the earth. A school girl is shot in the head for striving to be educated. School girls are taken at will to become wives and slaves of religious warriors. Husbands are told they can rape their wives as of right. Rape victims are stoned to death for adultery. Two sisters are gang raped and hung from a tree by men that include a police officer. An all-female punk band are put on trial and sent to a corrective labour camp for singing offensive songs. Lesbians are raped to cure them of their misguided ways.

And so we must sing for as long and as loud as we can, fly

and swoop in defiance. Open up the sky with our voices, cascade through the darkness with our light.

How can it be that ordinary men whose hearts are warm and soft can close them up with such fury and hatred? How is it that they can look upon a woman and be filled with such rage and violence? What has their culture done to them, these who were once young boys and babes in a woman's arms, that their lips can curl with contempt and their fists ball around a rock or knife or gun in the face of a woman? What cloaks their eyes to a woman's humanity and values her only by the evenness of her face or largesse of her breasts or tiny delicacy of her feet?

By the measure of the energy and resources poured into keeping us bound and in our place for so many generations across so many cultures, how fearsome we in our natural, untamed, unruled, unowned selves must seem to those who are so desperate to control us.

So let us scare the hell out of them all. Let us be fearsome, unbound, uncontrollable, wild and free. Let us be Woman - at once frail and strong, tender and harsh, beautiful and ugly, afraid and courageous, wise and foolish, sexual and clever, in our bodies and of our minds, masculine and feminine, childish and adult, old and ageless, sacred and profane.

Let us be undefinable.

So in the penultimate scene of *Bound Feet Blues*, Ah Mooi flies across the ocean on a ship in a journey of transformation. She has given up everything, hoped for love and lost, given up herself to others - and now chooses defiance and her own happiness. We see her in the act of becoming - from earth-bound wife to a free spirit of the air, she is at once my great-grandmother and the little mermaid and me. She is a woman in a moment of personal history and all women across time, she is embodied in me and intangible as our psyche. The rhythm of the sea, the beating of her heart lives in the very sounds of the words, the energy of transmutation driving the narrative like a rising wind. She transcends her obedience and endurance and timidity and becomes one with the sea and sky, as wild as nature, as powerful as woman.

Even as our cultures try to bind us to our bodies like the mothers who bound and broke their daughters, for the appreciation of men, for our happiness and future, for our own good, we dare to be free. What power we have when we are unbound, what joy, what exhilaration! When we can choose for ourselves, express who we are, go where we please, create, make, take, give, live - it is not just we who are free, we offer back to those fearful and angry souls the freedom and power of their own despised hearts.

* * *

I had always thought that I was a freak when my yearnings to be a tomboy did not go away long after I had grown up. I had been afraid of my queer heart and I had hidden it all in a feminine disguise with that magical thinking that told me that if I looked like a normal woman and acted like a normal woman, I would be a normal woman - not just on the outside but also be one through and through on the inside, too. Now, when living outside in didn't work, I was going to live inside out at last. I started to dismantle the disguise. It didn't happen all at once. But, slowly, over time, I cut my hair and lived more and more in jeans and flat shoes.

I found Bally had made lace-ups for women. I tried on a black pair, two toned in matt and shiny patent leather. And a brown pair in suede and faux crocodile texture. I bought both. I thought they looked cool with jeans and the soft silk shirts I had brought back from Malaysia, worn open over a camisole. I began to take a few of my floaty skirts to the charity shop. Then some of my high-heeled shoes. But for work, I kept back smart skirt suits and black loafers with the lowest heels in my wardrobe.

It was all very well to have this grand idea that I would come back to London and be a writer. But I had already used up much of my savings taking these few months off in Malaysia. My parents had given me so much already to make a good start in life and

Silk shirt and jeans

had given me this safe haven now. I could not and would not ask them for money to give me more time so I could play at being a writer. I was twenty-seven, a grown woman, and I needed to do this myself.

At some level, despite their love and acceptance, I nonetheless felt I had let my parents down. The ideal of the eldest daughter was embedded in my DNA, I realised, even though I had railed and fought against it as a child. I wanted to make my parents happy even as they wanted me to be happy. Now, I would never have a husband or children or grandchildren. There would be no big wedding for my mother to look forward to and plan. No role for her as grandmother to my children. No future girl child who would be the eldest daughter of eldest daughters going back six generations. Even while I felt my family's love, I felt as if I had cut myself adrift from the flow of the generations. The internalisation of my heritage was so deep that, despite the evidence of my family's acceptance, I felt had failed them as a daughter.

At least I could prove myself still a success in the world of work. I wouldn't be their unemployed daughter playing at being a writer but their lawyer daughter who might make partner one day in a respected law firm in London. Hard work and success have their own prestige in Chinese culture and especially, if overlaid with Presbyterian ethics and the driven mind-set of my extended family. I would save face by getting a proper job and that sense of duty and obligation I had grown up with would be fulfilled.

At any rate, I knew in my heart that I didn't want to sit at home alone by myself with nothing but words and thoughts to fill the time. Without the women who had meant the most to me here in London, with the hurt of losing some of my friends, I had to keep busy, keep out there in the world. Writing would have to wait.

I found a job teaching English as a foreign language to business people and then locum stints as a lawyer in local authorities and finally a permanent job at a law firm in Lincoln's Inn, specialising in the not-for-profit sector.

I had a few gay male friends, charming and warm men who took me under their wing. But I knew no lesbians. Neither did they. They took me to First Out, a gay cafe by Centrepoint with a studenty feel. I felt self-conscious as we walked in as if that very act put a flashing light on my head and activated a booming announcement to the cars and people passing by: Here's a dyke!

Kyle got us coffee and cake while Charlie sat with me. They were like mother hens, excited to show their new chick the chicken coop. They wanted to hear all about how I realised I was gay. In turn, they shared their own coming out stories.

Looking around me, I noticed a lot of men and only a few women. They all looked like regular folk. The kind of people you would see anywhere in London. No-one stared at me.

It felt disappointingly…well…normal.

We picked up The Pink Paper and I pored through it in wonder. There's a newspaper for gay people! My friends pointed out the noticeboard where I learnt about lesbian and gay tea-dancing socials, a reading group at Gay's the Word bookshop, a lesbian feminist discussion group in Stoke Newington.

Kyle said, "There are not so many women out on the scene, generally. I don't know why."

"Maybe you need to look for women only groups," Charlie sipped his coffee.

"Oh, look, here - here's group for women who are just coming out," Kyle leaned across to a shelf full of leaflets.

When I walked into that women's group, I realised for the first time I was not a freak. Most of the women there had short hair and had a tomboy energy about them. Some had longer hair and their look was softened with a more feminine blouse or jewellery. But all of them wore sensible shoes. With my new short hair and tentatively boyish outfit, I fit right in. There were two of us first-timers, the others having been before. The facilitator had a warmth that put us at ease. Watching her easy confidence and self-assured kindness, I wondered if one day I would be able to be so comfortable in myself?

We sat round in a circle, sipping drinks from paper cups. And we took turns talking. About all the things we were not able to express for so many years of our lives. Our sense of difference and alienation. Of feeling like freaks. Of shame and fear. We talked about when we knew we were gay. Whether we had come out to our friends and family - how we had each done it (or not), what we had said (or not), what had been the fallout (or not). Some had known since childhood, others during college or later. Some had been married - were married still. Everyone had a unique experience, a singular story. But as the women spoke, there was one strong common catalyst for many of them.

"I fell in love with my best friend…"

"She was so kind and beautiful…"

"… my best friend…"

"I didn't know how to tell her…"

"… my best friend…"

"But she didn't feel the same way…"

I had this image suddenly of all these gorgeous, amazing, kind, warm hearted women out there, all these best friends who had changed the lives of these women here in this room. Did they know the impact that they had had? Did they fully appreciate the gift they had given to us?

Because even as I had felt the hurt of rejection in my own experience of coming out, I knew that I would always cherish those women who had touched my heart, for their warmth and generosity and kindness, and the love that they had for me. For sharing themselves with me for a short time - time enough and space enough for me to reveal myself to both them and me.

Looking around the circle of women, I felt as if I had been set free. There was nothing wrong with me - there never had been. I was normal just like all these women here in this room - and just like all those women out there in the world, whichever gender they loved. Because ultimately, what we all shared was our openness to the beautiful heart of another, our vulnerability to our emotions and our willingness to love.

I went to other groups - a book group, a discussion group, social groups and most notably the empoweringly named Lesbians in Management. I went tea dancing on Sunday afternoons at The Bell pub near King's Cross. Having always danced with men, I was a 'follower' rather than a 'leader', twirling easily in the arms of handsome women. This was my new frontier, most of these activities taking place in grungy venues on the edges of a London that I thought I had known. I felt as if I was entering a secret world just below the surface of the mainstream. I had found the groups in the listings section of The Pink Paper or from the flyers at First Out. They invariably took place in tired looking rooms of down at heel pubs on slow mid-week evenings or weekend afternoons. There were no signs or outward markings. You would have to turn up and look around, maybe scuttle upstairs or through a door to a back room. Or maybe follow another woman with short hair and sensible shoes and hope for the best. Each time I went along to a new group or activity, I would hover on the street corner outside, anxious and uncertain. Each time, it felt as if I was stepping through a doorway that had neon lights above it proclaiming, "Welcome, Rosa Klebb, you man-hating dyke, you!" And each time, once inside, I felt the relief being surrounded by ordinary women like me - there was a warm camaraderie there, a relaxation into our lesbian selves.

I began to make new friends. Tanya, a blonde with a page boy cut and the cheekbones of Tilda Swinton, educated me on lesbian feminist politics and told me about camping out at Greenham Common. Wanda, an Australian with curly dark hair, told me about lesbian SM practices and was rather snooty about my vanilla preferences. Olu, who came from Saint Kitts and who had a distant connection with Joan Armatrading, was still living with her husband but in a relationship with another woman. My new gang and I hung out at the Lesbian and Gay Centre in Farringdon, had drinks at the Wow Bar and coffee at First Out, danced at the Ace of Clubs.

The claw-like grip of my old stammer loosened, its talons unhooking from my chest and tongue. My lungs took in vast gulps of fresh, invigorating air. My voice flew and sang with every word. I savoured this fluency that had eluded me for so long, revelled in its musicality, danced to its buoyancy. I talked and talked with my new friends, laughed and teased and flirted. The trapped energy of years poured out. I took up more space where I sat, I moved with a new vigour, vitality coursed through my gestures.

My acne disappeared. I had no more use for the creams and gels

I had once smeared over my face with such desperation. I packed away my make-up. There was something invigorating about being gazed upon with acceptance for my unadorned face - I liked those looks of respect, acknowledgement, and appreciation. They made me bold.

The Wow Bar and Ace of Clubs were the two glamourous nights on every London lesbians calendar and they would emerge out of the mists once in a while, like *Brigadoon*, magical kingdoms swirling with more women than I could ever imagine. There were women of all races, of all shapes and styles - lipstick lesbians, tomboyz, diesel dykes, Tank Girlz, dungaree dykes. There were tattoes, buzzcuts, long hair, piercings, dreadlocks, Brylcreamed Elvis hair, glamour, lounge suits, cocktail dresses, brogues, high heels, Doc Martens, slingbacks. Women were flirting, kissing, lounging with limbs intertwined, sipping beers, wine, and cocktails. An exuberant energy crackled through these women-only nights as if all the pent up secret lives of everyone here had been let loose. Women eyed me and I eyed them. Someone brushed past, stroking my bum. In our daily lives, we were lawyers, accountants, social workers, teachers, technicians, police women. We fit in, kept quiet about our lovers and partners,

No more girly shoes

played along with the cultural norm of our straight colleagues and friends. But here, we could shed our buttoned down disguises and strut our queer energy, we could desire and be desired, be masculine and feminine, bold and tender. We were outsiders and there was a power in it.

Afterwards, at the stroke of midnight, these women-only nights would melt away again. We would put on our coats over the dazzling range of who we each had been that evening and head for the tubes and buses, indistinguishable from any of the other women out on the town that night. The mist would come down and when dawn burnt it away, the Wow Bar and the Ace of Clubs would be gone and their venues in Neal's Yard and Piccadilly would return to the heterosexual day to day.

One evening, I met up with Dana for drinks at First Out after work. She was a small firecracker of a woman with an air of the young Michael J. Fox about her. She was from South Africa and would often regale our gang with tales of ANC marches, surfing before breakfast and seducing women on her Eurorail travels - including a dazzling tour de force of a story about her affair with a married Turkish woman. I marvelled at the confidence she had in her sexuality - it seemed so far away from my own hesitance. We were sitting in the basement, chatting and laughing, when she looked across to some people coming down the stairs and grinned.

I followed her gaze and saw two women heading over to join us. I recognised the shorter one as Vicki, Dana's flatmate.

"Hey, what are you doing here?" They all greeted each other. "Good to see you!"

The taller of them had the bluest eyes I had ever seen. Her black curly hair, cut short, and her dark rimmed glasses gave her an earnest, writerly look. She was wearing a white man's shirt and brightly coloured tie, with a black waistcoat and black jeans. Her black boots looked like those that Mary Poppins had, high-ankled lace ups with a slight heel. On her slim frame, the effect was more

Annie Hall than butch dyke. Her pink lipstick shone lightly on her lips. My heart skipped a beat.

"Yang-May," Dana said, "This is Angie."

* * *

The evening that I met Angie, I had worn a sober cardigan to work over a white blouse and smart black tailored slacks. It had a hounds tooth pattern and a Chanel style rounded neckline. I thought it gave me a smart-casual but serious lawyerly air. I needed a haircut but had not had the time to make an appointment so my short hair was scraggly over my ears.

As Angie tells the story, what she saw was a woman with a bad haircut and a frumpy cardy.

And that is the irony of love. You can spend all your energy trying to look beautiful for most of your adult life, ready for The One to see you on some enchanted evening and on the one night that you are looking like a slob it's the night The One comes along.

Angie wanted to be a writer, too, and was going to a weekly creative writing class. As she spoke, she had a slight stammer which I found charming. Her voice was gentle and soft, like feathers stroking my skin. She was from Durban and had an accent like Virginia Wade's. She had been a teacher there and every day, her route to and from school took her past the airport. Every day, she would dream of escaping to London. At last, she saved up enough to leave and had come over on a one way ticket.

"So even if I got scared, I couldn't turn around and go back home," she said quietly.

She had come over with only a rucksack and £200.

"How did you survive?" I could not imagine the courage it took to start a new life in a new country with so little.

"I never wanted to be a teacher again. I would do anything but that - or prostitution," she laughed. She had worked in a warehouse with other South Africans and Ozzies and Kiwis, stacking pallets of CDs. A friend had got her a job as a staff writer at a small magazine which had since folded. She was now temping as a receptionist and writing theatre reviews for a magazine for Antipodean travellers in London.

She invited me to see fringe theatre shows in upstairs pubs around London. Afterwards at dinner, we would talk theatre and literature and move on to each other's lives and relationships. She had known she was gay when she was sixteen and throughout university had been involved in women's groups. She had only ever had relationships with women. I loved her quiet confidence in who she was. Despite the uncertainties in her work life here in London, she knew herself and had an assured certainty in her sexuality. It stilled me to be with her, like sitting by a moonlit lake. We went for walks in St James's Park on Saturday afternoons. We were going to be writers together - like Gertrude Stein and Alice B. Toklias, Vita and Virginia, F. Scott and Zelda. We talked on the phone till the early hours - with her voice breathy in my ear as I burrowed into my duvet, I would switch off the light and it would seem as if she were right there beside me in the dark.

We laughed that if we had met back in our student days, Angie would have hated me on sight with my uber-femme arrogance and overly decorative facade. And I would have hated her punk/ Goth/ lesbian activist scruffiness. I was nowhere near being The One for her back then or her for me. We had each needed to travel our own journeys of selfhood before we could embody all those qualities that would enchant the other.

Is it with hindsight that we create the myth of The One? We tell our 'how we first met' stories and everything in each of our lives seems like *kismet* - destiny leading us to that one moment across a crowded room. Is there really such a person as The One? Or is it that we fall in love with the person who embodies most the qualities that we long for? In Angie, the person she was when we met, there was the child-like tenderness of Lizzie, that blue-eyed desire that was at once electrifying and innocent. There was the androgynous gentleness of Susan, that skill for making a cosy nest of a life together and for making me laugh. And the confident sexuality and literary mind of Shane, an intensity of words and emotions that was captivating. Perhaps I had needed to be enthralled by them first before I knew what it was that I yearned for in another. And perhaps without them, there never could have been a me who embodied all that Angie longed for.

We met up late one Monday night after Angie's creative writing class. We sat upstairs at First Out with our drinks. The evening was busy but not crowded, with a mellow buzz in the air. I could not take my eyes off her. As we talked, I found myself trembling beneath her blue gaze. It was warm in the bar and yet, I could not stop this electrifying tremor.

I laughed. "I'm all a-tremble. I've never felt like this before..."

"Me, too..."

"I feel like a Jane Austen heroine..."

We were laughing as I took her hand. We sat like this for a moment, holding hands like teenagers, staring stupidly at each other, unable to stop laughing or trembling.

We leaned in and kissed. Her lips were soft and warm, her kiss gentle but with a confident urgency. I had never kissed a woman so publicly before.

It was breath-taking.

* * *

The drums clattered with rhythmic vitality. Whistles shrilled all around. There were women in jeans and T-shirts strutting arm in arm, men in dresses and enormous wigs dancing along in high heels. Rainbow colours were everywhere - on scarves and sun hats, in body paint, on fluttering flags. I walked with Angie in the thick of it all, our sea of queer bodies taking over the Strand. The noise of a thousand voices chanting, laughing, yelling, whooping swept us along. Banners proclaimed Lesbian and Gay Pride, Stonewall, Black Pride, Queer Muslims, Proudly Catholic, Out and Proud! Muscular men in tiny thongs camped it up for the crowd. Women in dashing suits and slicked back hair swished along - drag kings

At Pride, with Angie

channelling their glorious masculine energy.

I could not take my eyes off these women. I had never seen drag kings before. Drag queens, yes, handsome men as beautiful strong boned women, playing it for laughs or for sizzling sensuality. But women preening and striding in male drag. Oh my god! Here they were before my very eyes, a tumult of breathless memories of Katherine Hepburn as Sylvia Scarlett, Marlene in white tie and tails, Julie Andrews as Victor/ Victoria - and now, these drag kings here in the flesh. Their confidence and swagger were bewitching - and they knew it. Their feminine features framed in masculine clothing subverted expectations. Their movements were at once angular and yet retained an underlying curvaceousness. They had the old-school manliness of Clark Gable and Elvis and Errol Flynn and the modern femininity of Sigourney Weaver and Jane Fonda and Julie Christie.

Angie nudged me, laughing. "Close your mouth, sweetie…"

I had at first been uncertain about joining our friends for the Pride parade. "What if someone from work saw me?"

Kyle laughed, "Well, if they are at the parade, they'd be gay, too!"

Angie said, "Come on, we have to go. It's the one time in the year when we can be out there, taking over the streets."

Surrounded by our gang of friends, Angie and I walked in the midst of it all, taking in the kaleidoscope of homo bodies and queer styles. I could feel the cacophony reverberate through my whole being. I grinned at Angie beside me. She was wearing a black T-shirt shirt and jeans with Chelsea boots. I had on a slim fitting T-shirt over black jeans, a baseball cap completing the tomboy look. I strode along in a new pair of black brogues. It felt daring and strange to dress in this boyish way. That cheeky energy I had forgotten from my childhood crackled through me. The day felt fun, new, exciting.

Here on this one day, our transgression could be celebrated. Men dressed as women, women dressed as men. Women loving women, men loving men. In another time and another country, several hundred years ago, Chen Duansheng could only fantasise about a woman who dresses as a man and who loves both men and women. Her transgressive heroine Meng Lijun could have no happy ending. Once she is revealed to be a woman by her tiny bound feet, she can have no life out in the world where she might choose her work or whom she loves. And so she lives on suspended in the midst of her adventures - until one day, magically, she is re-animated several centuries later. Here, right now as you read this page, can you see her, dashing in her men's boots, tantalizing in her delicate make-up, stepping out into the presence of our imaginations and swaggering down the Strand at Pride next to me, as handsome and as beautiful as those drag kings that day?

Angie took my hand. It startled me and I began instinctively to pull away, but stopped myself. I relaxed into her easy affection and we walked hand in hand. We had never walked like this in the street before in the six months we had been together. We had never put our arms around each other's waists as we strolled in public, never touched each other in any gesture that would give away our relationship - not a tender drawing away of a stray hair from the other's forehead, not a gentle stroke of the cheek. Never a kiss on the lips. All those little moments in public that I had shared with the men I had dated, Angie and I held back from. But that day at Pride, it was a freedom to slip my arm around her waist, feel her hips sway against mine, lean in without thinking to kiss each other.

I was getting used to the L word. The old associations began to fade. Poor old maligned Rosa Klebb - if only she had got out of that sexist James Bond universe into an art house movie, she might have been portrayed so much more sympathetically. And the Shirley Maclaine character in *Children's Hour* - if only she had gone along to a lesbian encounter group, she might have seen that there was nothing disgusting about her falling in love with her best friend. Lesbian - that marginal, pathetic, ugly creature in my mind began to reshape herself into a strong, beautiful, confident woman who had nothing to be ashamed of and so much to offer the world.

It was not me who was ugly, or Angie, or any of our lesbian friends. We were not the pathetic, fearful ones. It had taken courage for each one of us to come out, some at the risk of alienation from our families and friends. Some in the face of abuse and violence. It had taken self-knowledge and acceptance to choose our own lives and to love whom our hearts love. It was the world out there that was ugly and fearful.

Pride

I remembered one evening when we had drinks with Dana and some other friends at First Out. Tanya had been late and in those days before everyone had mobile phones, I had seen a pay phone across the street. "I'll go and give her a call and see if she's left yet."

Dana had said, "I'll come with you."

"No, don't worry, it's fine. It's just across the road."

But she had insisted.

Outside it was already dark but still early in the evening. We crossed the narrow street. It was a side street with hardly any traffic and few pedestrians. I slipped into the red telephone box, digging in my pocket for change. Dana stood behind me, the heavy red door open. I picked up the phone and dialled. The answering machine picked up and I left a message for Tanya,"... anyway, so if you get this message, we're downstairs."

As I hung up, the heavy door clanged shut behind me. There were loud voices outside, muffled by the thick booth. I looked around. There were a gang of young men outside, mean-looking and shouting.

"Fucking chinky dyke!"
"Get out of there, you lezzie cunt..."
"Get off the fucking phone, chink bitch.."

Instinctively, I backed away. But there was nowhere to go in that tiny booth. I jostled against the phone and the receiver clattered off its hook. Through the panelled glass of the door, I saw Dana standing with her back to me. She was guarding the door, her stance strong and firm, ready for anything. She said nothing to the men, just stared them down. If they wanted me, they would have to go through her. She was stocky but small, not much taller than me. The men hovered, circled, shouting. There was no-one else in the street. She stood firm, shifting slightly as they circled, always covering the door.

I don't know what diffused their aggression. Perhaps Dana's resolute stance was more than they had reckoned for. Perhaps her still silence gave them nothing to hook on to. Perhaps some people appeared at the top of the street. The pack cackled, spat on the ground. And backed into a strutting walk down the street.

Dana eased open the door. "Come on," she said, not taking her eyes off the men as they rolled away.

We crossed back to First Out, Dana between me and the men like a shield, never taking her eyes off their receding backs.

I could hardly speak when we got back to our table. Our friends could see something had happened from our faces. Angie took my hand. Dana told the story. She was seething with quiet anger. She was more used to incidents like these and had developed a streetwise instinct for how to deal with them. Her boyish demeanour gave her a more obvious dyke energy that some people bristled at and she had had to put up with abuse throughout her life. I looked at her and took in her matter of fact statement. I could not imagine going through life like that - and still remaining warm, open and generous. I could not imagine having her courage. If she hadn't been with me just now... I went cold. If it hadn't been for her being there, for how she handled the men, I might have been beaten up by them - or worse.

I started to thank her.

She shrugged it off. "You're OK, that's the main thing."

I looked down at my soft silk shirt, jeans and lace up shoes. Had simply dressing this way with my short hair - and racial features - made me a target? I had done nothing to these men and yet they hated me with such ugliness. Or rather, they hated what I represented. An outsider. A sub-human. A Chink. A woman who did not make herself beautiful for men. A woman who by her very identity rejected men as a gender. A lesbian.

This was what I had feared for all those years. This hatred and loathing had kept me in my disguise, denying my feelings, strangling my ability to love, killing me slowly inside.

And here it was, grotesque and ugly and mean.

I reflected on that evening again as I marched through London at the Pride parade. I had looked at Dana, picking up her drink and chatting to Vicki. At Angie and our friends around the table. I remembered Dana's quiet courage. I remembered the men and women at the other tables around us. All of them had had experiences like the one I had had to face that night - many of them undoubtedly worse. I thought of the mean faces of the men at the phone booth, all that anger spoiling for a fight. The faces here in the bar in contrast were open, laughing, warm. The energy in here was mellow and easy going. I thought of the hidden courage of all these homos, fags, queers, lezzies and dykes in the way they nodded and smiled, teased and flirted, leaned in close in serious conversation, threw their heads back in laughter.

Striding along at the Pride parade, I was surrounded by a thousand more men and women like those in the bar that night. For all that each one of us had gone through, you might have expected the parade to have been one of anger and bitterness. We might have taken this one day of the year that was ours to march down the streets, like those men outside the phone booth that night, shouting "Fucking straight people, you're dead! We're fucking going to bash your ugly straight face in!" But there was no vitriol or hatred in the air. The energy was high with exuberance and celebration, an outrageous seizing of life and love. We blew kisses to bemused tourists along the route, gave out rainbow flags to straight folks who grinned and waved them in the air. Families marched together under a banner for parents of gays and lesbians, the emotion in their group written on their faces. This one day of the year, when we could proclaim our queerness to the open sky, was a defiance of shame, a reclaiming of our pride in ourselves. This one day was also a mirror to those who found energy only in anger and hate: these prancing, dancing people here, this could be you, too - you could celebrate life, too. It was an outstretched hand to anyone who cared to take it: come and join us and take pride in your humanity.

I had been so afraid of the L word. I had found solace in telling myself that it was the person I loved, not the gender so I could avoid thinking of myself as "that" word. But now…I cuddled against Angie beneath the city sky. It felt pretty cool to be a lesbian.

* * *

I couldn't quite bear to throw out all my girly shoes in one go but let each pair go over time. In their place, I hunted out solid, low-heeled shoes that made me feel strong and whole as I strode in them through the city streets. I had a funky pair of loafers with a top lip that covered the length of my foot with a lattice of brown and dark green leather. There was a pair of black brogues from Church's that made a muffled *kok-kok* sound as I walked and a brown men's style side-buckled pair. Looking for shoes became like a quest for rare artefacts - with my tiny, delicate size 3 1/2 feet, I couldn't buy men's, or even boys', shoes and it was rare to find women's shoes in a masculine style. So, whenever I saw anything that excited me, I would go in and try them on - mostly to be disappointed but on the few occasions when the shoes fit perfectly, I would buy up at least two pairs. I found that the trick was to wear two pairs of socks - one thin and one thick hiking pair - so that my feet became the more standard size 4.

As a gawky teenager, my sexless blouses had made me invisible. At Oxford and in my early twenties, my super feminine clothes had expressed my feline, female sexuality, balancing uncertainly on shoes that alienated me from myself. Now, I gave space to that other vitality I had been afraid of for so long. In this new frontier beyond the big hair and conventional girly look I once had, I found a lightness in experimenting with who I might be. I played with it as a child might play with a chest full of dressing up clothes - trying on the T-shirted and baseball capped look of an overgrown tomboy, the all black leathered up butch, the denimed androgyny of k.d. lang. Over time, a core comfortable self settled in. I lived in jeans and soft silk shirts that opened up to reveal a camisole beneath. The shirts were from Malaysia, brightly printed and fun. I jazzed up the look with blazers and a growing collection of leather jackets. If I needed to be smart, I had a range of neatly cut slacks or dark-coloured khaki style trousers. I wasn't trying to look like a man nor was I pretending to be a boy. It was about letting through that more masculine energy that I had kept tightly bound down for so long. I was still clearly a woman - slim, petite and feminine - yet infused with a more forthright, androgynous quality.

In my sensible shoes, London opened up before me. Angie and I would walk everywhere. The West End was only half an hour's stride away, through pretty side streets and across St James's Park in daylight. At night, we would walk home past Parliament Square, the bright eye of Big Ben's clock face watching us pass by.

Brogues, jeans and Angie

New to London, Angie had a curiosity about the city that I had lost and we began to explore it on foot at weekends, taking long walks through different areas, discovering hidden parks, Saturday markets, quiet residential streets just off busy thoroughfares.

In my girly shoes and skirts, my ability to walk long distances had been limited. My walk home from Victoria station late at night after seeing friends used to make me anxious as I tripped along with tiny little steps. It used to worry me to visit friends in the leafy suburbs, feeling like a target with my wobbly gait along dark, uneven streets. I had seen London for the most part from buses and tube tunnels and taxis. Now loping along beside Angie, it was a joy to awaken to the living city. We walked from through St James's Park and Green Park across Hyde Park to Kensington Gardens and had lunch in Queensway before strolling back through the white stucco streets of Lancaster Gate, past the Serpentine down through Knightsbridge and Chelsea. We explored the Thames path eastwards to Tower Bridge and westwards from Hammersmith to Gunnersbury and Kew. Night time walking lost its psychic menace.

A long time ago, I had been afraid of being a woman, of giving myself over to the power of men. And then I had found a potency in my desirability, that swaying, feline delicacy that had given me a sense of control. In my beautiful tiny shoes, I had carved out a dominion for my power - as all women have learnt to do over millennia and across cultures. But it was small domain, centred on my body and looks and the reflection of themselves that I gave back to the men who gazed upon me. And now, disregarding their gaze gave me the power to disregard their judgment. Not caring for their approval gave me dominion not just over my body but over the choices I made for my own life. My sturdy shoes gave me a strong stance and a swift gait. My feet could feel a connection with the earth, not just in my tippy toes but along their full length. I was no longer unbalanced but dancing with my shoes through the vigour of my whole body.

Research shows that taking up space when you stand, sitting astride and generally adopting the body language of an alpha male alters your brain chemistry to give you more confidence, a stronger sense of self and a more positive view of life and your abilities - take a look at Amy Cuddy's TED talk on "power poses". So why is it that women are culturally shamed when we live our lives with this style of powerful body language? Why is it only men are allowed to be mannish? Why are these shoes and boots that I love, that are sturdy and strong and can travel with you for hundreds of miles allowed in our culture only to men? Why are only men allowed to take long strides and stand firm on the ground? Why do we, as strong, capable, powerful women, still need to float half off our feet in a precarious balancing act of femininity? I don't want to be a man. I don't want to be mannish. I love being a woman. But I also love to take up space and stand astride or move in whichever way my energy flows, unrestricted by codes of feminine conduct. I revel in a body that can nurture itself into confidence just through the simple act of standing or sitting in a particular way. I celebrate a physicality that can give me a strong sense of self and a positive view of life and my abilities simply by moving myself in a powerful way. I love connecting to my physical self with vigour and solidity, to that energy that can propel me forward for miles in a stride or a swagger or a run without having to worry about my shoes or my feet hurting.

In my solid shoes in those early years of my new life, I discovered the adventure of walking. In the mornings, I would get out of bed with a fresh vigour, even earlier than I used to. Instead of taking the tube, I would walk to work, slowly giving up my skirt suits for smart trouser suits. I loved those early mornings, striding through a new London day. It took me 45 minutes through Strutton Ground, a cobbled market street, as the stall holders set up for the day; St James's Park, empty of tourists at that hour in the morning and the Strand, its centuries old buildings lit by the morning sun. I would turn left by the Royal Courts of Justice, sometimes walking through the ancient stone hall, and head into Lincoln's Inn. The journey was fifteen minutes longer than taking the tube but so much more beautiful. And I arrived bright cheeked and invigorated for an otherwise sedentary day of reading legal documents.

But there was still one more unbinding left.

I turned thirty-one that summer after I met Angie. For all my talk about becoming a writer and all my scribbling away in my spare time, what I had after so many years of fits and starts was absolutely nothing. There were half-finished manuscripts in beige document wallets and a mass of notes for story ideas as well as a growing number of floppy disks with snatches of scenes and chapters. And, of course, my bundle of notebooks full of family stories from my few months in Malaysia. I had always thought that I would have had a book published by the time I was thirty. It hadn't been an articulated thought or focused objective. It was just something in the back of my mind that I had sub-consciously expected to have happened by then.

Turning thirty feels like a milestone for twentysomethings. Many seem to have a quarter-life crisis at that point. In your twenties, you can still play with who you are, still have dreams of what you might become. It's a time for exploring, experimenting. But thirty. Thirty feels grown up. Old. Your friends are partnering up, starting to settle down, some are already even parents. Your career is becoming serious and you have responsibilities, leadership roles, expertise. Your life, that had been free-floating and malleable, is beginning to crystallise. Maybe even ossify.

And here I was, thirty-one, a respected lawyer in field I believed in, on track for partnership, building a breath-taking relationship, confident in the love of my family and friends - and yet, there was still something missing. In the next few years, as I drove headlong towards partnership, I would have to dedicate my life and focus to the law. There would be no more time for messing around with literary words, there would only be time - and energy - enough for legal words. While I had still been able to tinker with stories and ideas for books in my spare time, there had still been the chance that I might one day write a book, become a writer. I saw my childhood dream evaporating before my eyes.

Angie, St James's Park

I looked at Angie as we sat in the June sunshine in St James's Park. She had come over from South Africa with £200 and all her worldly goods stuffed into a rucksack. She had taken a menial job to survive and now worked as a temp and freelance writer. She had lived in a bedsit with no heating and shared a flat with strangers before moving in with me. There had deliberately been no safety net with her one-way ticket, because above all else, she had wanted to be in London and to try and make a new life here.

With her shy smile and quiet manner, Angie would not strike you as an adventurer. But in the soft expanse of the park, she seemed to me intrepid and brave.

"Weren't you scared giving up your job and just arriving in England with nothing?" I asked.

"Yeah, I was scared. Of course. But I hated teaching more. There was nothing for me in Durban. I never fit in there. I had to get away. And I had always dreamed of coming here. I had some friends here so that helped and they showed me the ropes." She smiled. "I don't regret all the hard times - it was worth it in the end."

I talked about my dream of becoming a writer. "I wish writing was like a backpacking adventure. I could just give it all up and go off somewhere and write…"

I paused. I looked at the people lounging in deck chairs and sprawled round picnic cloths. The grass was warm beneath us. Angie and her life in Durban spread out like a vapour trail behind her, emblematic of the journey she had taken. Both of us here, together.

"I don't even have to leave home to have my adventure," I said.

There was nothing to stop me giving it all up and stay home to write.

If Angie could grab her dream with no more than £200 and make good, I could surely grab mine with a whole lot more in savings and a roof already over my head. My mind opened like a flower to the bright sunlit sky. Somehow, being with Angie, I felt bold and alive. I laughed out loud with exhilaration at what was possible.

Over the next few weeks, we talked about our hopes and dreams of becoming writers and shaped them into a solid plan. I started a file which I titled "Escape Plan". Together, we worked out what needed to be in place for me to leave my job and I wrote everything down in that ring binder. I checked what savings I had. We made a list of our base expenses and calculated the minimum that we could live on, including utilities and food bills. I taught myself to touch type so that I could temp if we needed to top up our income.

I could have asked my law firm to work part-time. I could have asked for a sabbatical. But I had made up my mind in the park that summer's day and anything else would have been a cop out.

I had copped out for long enough already. I had tried to write in my spare time. I had tried to write in my few months in Malaysia. I had been talking about writing ever since childhood. I imagined myself in tired old age, sitting in a nursing home, quaveringly saying, "I'm going to write that book, you just wait and see…"

There were nights when I woke up at 3am in a cold sweat. It might all come to nothing, this wild idea to give up a high paying job to devote to a little childhood hobby. I might write and write and produce utter bollocks. Or I might end up with a book that only I felt was brilliant but no-one else did. And even if I were published, I might never earn enough to live on. I might be throwing away my career for nothing.

These fears had plagued me all my adult life. I had had the chance to re-invent myself as a writer when I had lost my job and gone back to Malaysia to collect my family's stories - but I had had a failure of nerve and returned instead to the familiar, a tried and tested career as a lawyer. I had given myself lots of good reasons why I had to get a proper job again - I couldn't sit at home alone, I needed to pay the bills, I needed to honour my family and all that they had done for me. But ultimately it had come down to this: I had seen myself as a writer all my life and if I tried to actually become one and failed, who would I be then? It had been safer to nurture a hope and a potential than to risk the reality and failure.

The only person stopping me becoming a writer was me. And time would run out one day.

I needed to take myself seriously as a writer.

I didn't need a safety net.

In October that year, I walked into my supervising partner's office and handed in my notice. I was wearing a black trouser suit and my black brogues.

* * *

The first few chapters of *Ancestral Voices* were a disaster. The writing was turgid, pretentious, overly detailed. The story was convoluted and incoherent. There was no narrative progression. I had spent the last six months on the book and was everything I had feared. It was utter bollocks.

I stood at the windows of my parents' house in Malaysia. I had come back home for a few months with Angie to re-immerse myself in Malaysia as I worked on my magnum opus. Beyond the streaks for rain outside, I could see the flame tree. Its canopy had the shape of a huge umbrella and was laden with scarlet flowers, brought into bright relief by a sprinkling of feathery emerald leaves. I had never seen it so beautiful.

"Mum, is it my imagination or has the flame tree become redder?"

My mother was sitting at the marble breakfast table in the cool, tiled hall behind me. She looked up from her crossword. "It's gorgeous, isn't it?"

Angie got up from the rattan rocking chair where she had been reading a book and came over to look out of the window with me.

My mother went on, "The flame tree takes about twenty years to reach its full maturity. I planted that tree when we first came to this house - so that would have been when you were six years old. So it's about now that we can see it in full bloom."

I remembered the scrawny little tree of my childhood, all feathery leaves and no blossom. I thought of my mother planting the sapling. She would have been my age, around thirty-one, with her three little children. It would have taken faith and trust to nurture the tree week after week, month after month, year after year for twenty years. It would have taken patience and a confidence that she would see the tree would grow into its full magnificence over the course of two decades. It took the faith and the love of a mother - that same patience and trust in the future that it took to nurture her children into adulthood.

There was something in that unremarkable act of planting a tree that was both simple and epic. It gave me goosebumps.

It didn't help my funk about my book though. I had thrown away my career as a lawyer to write and my worst nightmare was coming true. I couldn't write for toffee. This grand dream of writing the Malaysian *Roots* or *Wild Swans* was no more than pie in the sky. I should never have given up the day job.

Later that afternoon, I threw myself onto my bed in my old bedroom with a copy of a John Grisham novel I had found in my mother's bookshelf. Angie lounged on my sister's bed trying to write a letter. The rain was still coming down. We were both beginning to get cabin fever and I needed to be distracted from the crisis of my book.

The front cover of the novel had a marbled green-grey background. Carved boldly across the top was *The Firm*. I leafed to the first page and started to read. I was not expecting much from this blockbuster populist book. It was going to be badly written, I thought, but it would pass the time.

And suddenly, I was sucked in. The writing was transparent, hardly noticeable. It was the characters who mattered. And the story. In its first pages were ambition, intrigue and a cocky energy. I kept reading. And reading.

When it was time for dinner, I broke off but had to go back to it as soon as I could. I had not been so addicted to a book since my childhood.

As I reached the denouement, breathlessly along with Mitch

in the chase and the discovery of the Firm's secret, I kept saying out loud, like a sports commentator noticing each technique and strategic play, "Oh my god, this is so good. Wow, that's clever. Nice pick up. Great twist…"

I was in my pyjamas in bed by now. When I got to the end, I looked up at Angie as she came out of the bathroom. I closed the book and held it with a proprietorial air. "I can do this!"

I stopped thinking about *Ancestral Voices*. I was going to cut my losses. Forget the last six months. Here in my old bedroom, where I had spent my childhood writing adventure stories and experimenting with cliffhangers and prose that kept you on the edge of your seat, I realised what I was really good at. I had been trying to write what I thought a 'proper' novel should be, one that ought to be taken seriously, one that should be profound and that should discuss grand themes. But to be deep and meaningful and taken seriously did not mean that the story had to be thrown out in favour of turgid prose or that it should not be a rip-roaring read. After all, look at Dickens and Hardy, the two great Victorian novelists whose works explored serious social issues and universal themes while telling moving stories that grabbed your imagination.

So, starting from now, here in this room, what did I have in front of me that could give me a new novel? What did I know from my life? The law. What skills did I have as a writer? I thought of Lizzie reading my unfinished manuscript, the sound of her turning the pages faster and faster. I could do simple, page-turning prose, that was for sure. A legal thriller, that was going to be my new book.

It struck me that all legal thrillers at that time had white protagonists, usually male. They took place in modern cities, usually American but London, too. Meanwhile, Chinese women only ever appeared in books about three generations of women - and invariably, bound feet would be involved. Or a Chinese woman in a modern setting would be some sort of prostitute or sing-song girl like Suzy Wong. And here I was a modern Chinese woman, a lawyer jetting between two modern cities, as ambitious in whatever I did as Mitch, with not a bound foot in sight. Where were the legal thrillers featuring someone like me?

Later that week, the Peter Sarstedt song came on over the radio, *Where Do You Go to My Lovely?* It tells the story of a beautiful, highly educated woman who moves in the best circles, speaking and dressing like a star but who grew up in 'the back streets of Naples' and whose first love was the narrator whom she has forced herself to forget in her 'burning ambition' to make a good life for herself.

In the news, there were stories upon stories of landslides due to the heavy rains. A number of high-rise residential blocks had collapsed due to subsidence. There was speculation in the press about shoddy workmanship by greedy developers and accusations of buildings being put up cheap and fast in landslip areas.

And every day, I could not take my eyes off the joyous red of the flame tree outside the windows.

I grabbed an old legal pad of my father's and sketched the outline of my new novel. The working title was *The Flame Tree.*

To everyone who knows her in London, Jasmine Lian is a high flying lawyer from a good background. She is the youngest partner in her law firm, working on a construction project to build a university in the rainforests of Malaysia. She is about to marry Harry Taunton, a rich man from a landed family in Sussex. But she has a secret past and everything she seems to be is a lie.

Her work and a promise she made to her mother take her back to her roots in Malaysia. There she meets again her childhood love, Luke McAllister, a passionate environmentalist. They find themselves on opposite sides of the battle over the construction project as monsoon rains soak the hillside where the university is being built.

Unknown to Jasmine, dark forces are at play behind the scenes of the project involving gangsters, blackmail, violence and murder. Will she discover the truth about her top client?

Her mother, too, keeps a secret that many years ago set in motion the terrible events that will come as Jasmine's past collides with her present.

And over it all, the flame tree presides, its growth and coming to maturity a symbol that matches Jasmine's growth through the course of the book. In the finished novel, what Jasmine's mother tells her about the flame tree in her garden is almost verbatim my mother's words to me that rainy afternoon.

I finished *The Flame Tree* in eighteen months back in London. With the guidance of friends Tim and Alice Renton, I pitched the manuscript as 'Amy Tan meets John Grisham' to three literary agents. To my astonishment, all three wanted it and I was in the unique position of being able to choose the best one for me, Rogers Coleridge & White. Gill Coleridge got me a two book deal with Hodder & Stoughton and out of that came my second novel, *Mindgame*.

In many ways, *The Flame Tree* was a success beyond what I had ever dared to hope. I was on the BBC and LBC. The book was reviewed in *The Tatler, the South China Morning Post* and newspapers in Australia and Canada. Hodder flew me out to KL and Singapore for a two week book tour. I sat in a suite in the Regent Hotel in downtown KL as a stream of journalists took their twenty minute turns interviewing me. I gave book readings and signed books till my wrist hurt. I was interviewed on Malaysian radio, the book launch was reported on the prime time TV news and I was flown to Singapore to appear on breakfast TV. Malaysians saw themselves, their dynamism, the ambition of their new nation, the drive of the present generation and also the sacrifices and history of those who had come before. *The Flame Tree* spoke as much to a local audience as to a Western one and reflected back to East Asians who they were and who they could be. The book was a sensation in Malaysia and became a bestseller there, outranking Ken Follett.

All those years of fear. Fear of giving my whole self over to my dream only to find that my writing was utter bollocks. It had happened. My worst fear had come true. Six months of earnest, intense blood, sweat and tears working on *Ancestral Voices* only to find that my writing was a failure.

I had stood in that place of failure and I had not fallen apart. My world had not fallen apart. Out of that failure, I had found a new perspective and a fresh energy that I would never have come to if I had not failed. In the funk of that rainy day, looking out at the flame tree from my old bedroom window where I had scribbled my adventure stories as a child, it was as if my mind had been reset by the failure of *Ancestral Voices*. I had wanted to write a novel about the Chinese migrant experience and about three generations of mothers and daughters, just like Amy Tan and Jung Chang's books - that was a topic for a Chinese woman to write about. But what I was good at was action and adventure and what thrilled my heart was as much as masculine energy as a female one. So I had rebooted out of that failure to write a book that crossed genres to embrace both my Eastern and Western selves, my *yin* and *yang*, my rational lawyer mind and animistic heart, my ambition and my authentic tiger soul.

But *The Flame Tree* slid into obscurity in the UK. Its crossover uniqueness was what had made it exciting for my literary agent and publisher but that was also its flaw. It did not sit in any category. It was set in a previous British colony but it was not 'colonial lit', that genre favoured by book awards that is firmly set in the colonial past with its exoticization of the 'natives' and the colourful locale - the book is set in the cut and thrust of board rooms and high-rise modern cities. It was not a 'proper' legal thriller with the expected settings of the urban West and featuring heroic white protagonists and evil East Asian ones - in fact, in a subversion of that genre, the book casts white characters as the villains. Nor was the novel another Chinese woman's book which has an expectation of stories telling of the sufferings and hardships of Oriental women from generations past - the heroine is a 'take no prisoners' high achieving lawyer.

The best of what I had hoped for had come true. I had become a writer and a bestselling one at that. But the worst of my fears had also happened. I was not a bestselling author in the country where it mattered most to me, here in the UK. My savings were running out and I was tired of working part-time at a low level secretarial job to top up the kitty so we could pay the bills. I had had a respectable advance for the two books but it was not going to be enough to live on while I worked on my third book. It was clear that if I wanted to make it as a writer, I would have to refocus my creative energies on books that would be more commercially recognisable within the expectations of the various genres I could fit into. Professionally, it would have made sense to stick to thrillers and to pick up on the new trends emerging in that genre at that time: big pharma conspiracies, forensic psychology and cyber-security. But after two books back to back, I was tired and I felt exhausted even thinking about spending at least the next year and a half writing a new thriller on topics that did not excite me. Or more riskily, I could switch to colonial lit or three generations of Chinese women lit.

I could make that switch, I thought. After all, *Ancestral Voices* fell into those latter two categories. And my family story was the real book I had always wanted to write. With my new found professional status as an author, I could re-work it into something more readable. I could novelize it or develop it as a simplified, less over-written memoir.

But, as I've already said elsewhere in this book, that task turned out to be easier said than done, and led me into fifteen years of creative stillbirths and miscarriages.

Often during that decade and a half I felt like a failure as a writer. I saw other writers who had launched their debut novels around the same time as I had produce a volume of work and establish their careers. I saw others, new and younger than me, catch me up from behind and overtake what I had achieved. Seeing them work hard, create fresh new stories, develop their skills - it all fired me up to keep struggling with this next 'proper' book that I was determined to launch to the world. And yet, nothing was working. Nothing gained traction in my imagination or on the page.

I had failed as a lawyer when I lost my high flying job once through redundancy. Then when I had gained back my legal career path, I had thrown it away and lost the opportunity to rise to the top of a respectable profession. I had thrown away prestige and my expensive education to temp and work at low-level typists jobs while I wrote and my savings had run out. I was back in the corporate world - doing well and making a difference in my own way but my very success in that arena made me feel more starkly my failure as a writer.

I was living my worst fear. I had been a 'wannabe' writer once. I was now a has-been. It was embarrassing to tell people that I was a writer when the last book I wrote was over a decade ago. I did not know if I could ever produce another book again. That old fear I had had in my mind of me in a nursing home in my old age talking about becoming a writer now changed to a scene where I was still scribbling notes for my next book, muttering to myself, "Yes, yes, this is the one, the next big one, just you wait and see."

A has-been. There is so much failure crammed into that cringe-making portmanteau word. But failure is not the end. Failure is a beginning. Failure as a writer led me to a rebirth. A re-invention. I never thought I would be a performer. Never saw myself as a creative artist.

In the same way as I had never seen myself as a lesbian.

I had been so terrified of failing as a woman. Of being rejected by my family and friends for being gay. I had been paralysed by my love for women I should not love, so afraid that I would destroy those friendships. I had lived in fear of abuse and threats from those who thrived on their energy of hatred. And what I had feared had happened. Friends had rejected me. Those friendships with Lizzie and Susan and Shane had been destroyed. I had been a target of abuse and threats.

And yet, here I am. All those terrible things that I had been so afraid of - when they actually happened, I had handled each one. I had felt hurt and sadness and anger and fear. I went through moments where I felt lost and alone and devastated - at times lasting a short period, at others for much longer. But ultimately, those emotions had not annihilated me. I had the help of friends and my family and I went to talk therapy and talked and talked. I would rather not have had those feelings of pain and distress, of course. But I realised as I lived through all those things I had feared, the fear had been more crippling and more destructive than the reality of those things themselves.

At each step along the way, I had had a choice. Whether to express my tomboy nature or to bind it up in favour of becoming like every other girl. Whether to take my writing seriously or not. Whether to give up my legal career or not. Whether to return to it or not. Whether to allow myself to love whom I love or to force myself to be 'normal'. Some choices had consequences that were more difficult or fearsome. The well-trodden, obvious choices were easy. Do what everyone else is doing, fulfil your own and your family's expectations of what a good life should look like and all should be well. But choosing the conventional path, the one that everyone else took, had led me deeper and deeper into a maze of falsehoods and inauthenticity where ultimately I lost myself. It had been those choices that scared me the most that had been the ones that had set me free.

My friends - the ones who mattered - are still here. I have made new friends, like beautiful new flowers planted in a devastated space. I got through the threat of violence because of one of these brave pals. My family and I are closer now because I can be my whole self when I am with them. And Angie walked into my life.

Through failure, I at last became a writer.

And I have at last become myself.

* * *

I had an idea long ago of who I should be. That idea of the beautiful, desirable young woman had shaped the decisions I had made about how I would dress and behave and who I was going to love. That idea of the high-flying lawyer gave me a high-pressure lifestyle to match that I never wanted. That idea of being straight and normal just like everyone else broke me.

Ideas shape our lives and shape our cultures.

Foot-binding was an idea that that endured for a thousand years. It became so embedded in the Chinese soul that over forty generations, women's identities became bound up in their feet. Those tiny delicate feet were as potent and as private as the most intimate parts of our women's bodies today, defining them as not just women but desirable women. My shoes over the decades have unconsciously defined for me my life as a woman. As a child, I had felt genderless and free, in the bare feet that nature had given me and in my unisex Bata trainers that spoke of movement and play. As a hunched up teenager, I tried to fit myself into the idea of femininity as I forced my feet to fit into girly shoes with wedges and heels, my gawky stride sending me tumbling as my ankles twisted against the imbalance even as my body battled the ripping pains of the Curse and hormonal hell. At Oxford and as a Bright Young Thing in London, I slinked and swayed and seduced with my body and my shoes, luxuriating in that idea of female desirability and loathing myself for it all along, the pain and uncertainty in my feet a manifestation of my psychic desperation.

Today, I have a couple of pairs of biker boots in both black and brown, ankle boots patterned with metal studs, sleek Chelsea boots. They are piled up in boxes in the wardrobe and in neat rows under the bed. I have running shoes, gym shoes, trail shoes and gardening shoes. I love my comfy grey hiking boots which make me feel like a robust outdoorsy type when I wear them with rolled up skinny jeans. There's a black pair of smart desert-style boots which make a satisfying *kok-kok* sound when I walk on a wooden floor - and which I've been a little shy to wear since I declared to

Barefoot after a sprint on the beach

the world in *Bound Feet Blues* the thrill I get from that sound. I also still have my black Church's brogues and a range of flat lace-ups and loafers. And I am on the lookout for the ultimate pair of cowboy boots.

From the tomboy look and blazers and leathers that I experimented with when I first came out, I have evolved a personal style that I feel most comfortable in. I am not particularly butch or especially femme. I have only two rules: no skirts, no high heels. Sometimes, there's jewellery, sometimes not. I wear make-up when I feel like it and go *au naturel* at other times. The effortlessness of being a grown-up woman that I had imagined as a child, that ease with myself and my own body, I now have.

When I snap shut the powder compact even now, that click always makes me think of my mother in front of her triptych of mirrors, finishing up and rising as a perfect, beautiful woman. As I turn my head this way and that in front of the mirror in my bedroom now, the one I share with Angie, I see my mother's features in my face and shape of her lips in the glistening pink of mine. I see her in the way I wipe away a lipstick smudge to the side of my lips, touch up my eyebrows with the dark pencil, check the evenness of the rouge on my cheeks. Only, instead of her *cheongsams* or fashionable tailor made dresses, I am wearing jeans and a leather jacket over a camisole and instead of *tik-tok* shoes, I stand feet firmly planted in a pair of biker boots.

I love looking at shoe shop displays, especially those which cater for a more androgynous taste like mine. These days, there seems to be a move towards more styles for women that involve low or flat heels and options in styling that are playfully masculine. Ugly shoes that are bulky and make a statement against the classic feminine stiletto are also staking their claim. Kurt Geiger make black boots for women now with a flat wide fitting and high lacing that would look good on a street hooligan. More and more women are dressing as they please, regardless of the dominant culture of high-heels and typically feminine fashion. And there is something sexy about these women with their hint of tomboy or gypsy or subversion - I see the men in their orbit gaze upon them with appreciation and desire because these women's sex appeal lies in their confidence and vitality that is fully expressed in how they dress.

I never thought that it would be possible to be a woman and at the same time, be me. I never thought that I could meet the world on my own terms.

Now, I have a new idea of what it means to be me.

I feel at my most powerful and confident in boots and brogues.

Story Performer – credit: Paul Cox

I love being able to stride out and walk for miles and miles across London. I love walking into a meeting and taking charge of it. I love flirting and teasing and laughing at parties, standing firmly on both feet.

That dread and anxiety that I woke up to day after day for almost thirty years is gone. That low level unhappiness that permeated everything in my life, miring me down in distrust

372

and isolation and bitterness has slithered away. There is such an exuberance and delight now in that simplicity of living through my days as me. It is as if I have connected with a primal power that is creative and at ease and brimming with joy.

But I'm not a shoe fascist. I'm not saying that you have to wear boots and brogues to be free and happy. For anyone who loves to wear stilettos and high heels, I can only admire his prowess and skill. If you've ever seen any of Yanis Marshall's choreography featuring hunky guys dancing in outrageously high heels, you will see what I mean. Go on - google 'yanis marshall men dancing in high heels' and delight in their cheekiness.

I'm also not advocating that you turn lesbian to clear your stammer, acne or back pain. It worked for me though I recognise that it's not everyone's cup of tea. But there's something to be said for unbinding ourselves from inner conflict and finding an at-oneness within ourselves that is a pretty good antidote against these symptoms of stress.

I'm not saying that women are better than men or that we should hate or blame men for everything. It's clear that for some men, the fact that we menstruate and give birth seems to make it difficult for them to see us as fully human like they see themselves to be. And men can be bound, too, by their dominant culture, limited, frozen, trapped in expected roles. For me, the freedom to be who you choose to be is genderless. It is about empathy and compassion for those who are not like us - and ultimately, freedom for each one of us.

What makes you feel most confident and strong and free? What gives you the greatest joy and delight in your life and who you are? What connects you most at the deepest, most fragile level with those you love? Whether it is high heels or Chelsea boots, loving a man or a woman, being male or female, and all shades between, that is not for me to say but for each one of us to choose and luxuriate in - and to allow others that same the freedom to do so.

Growing old together

Angie and I have grown old together. From the first breathless few months, through many years together, we have created a life to call our own. She has given me a haven where I have felt able to reveal my naked soul to her - and I, too, for her. We are intimate lovers together, and also playful and enterprising and creative and serious. As civil partners, we feel like equal partners in a joint adventure through life, neither husband nor wife to each other but creating the traditions of our partnership as we go along. We have seen what it means to be there for each other in sickness and in health, and also for richer and for poorer. I offer her the mirror in which to see the most beautiful of who she is and I see myself too in her reflection, both of us cracked glass made whole.

We live in a little suburban house with a messy garden that we don't have enough time for. We natter with our neighbours over the garden fence. We spend hours at our computers writing and blogging - and, okay, I admit it - faffing on Facebook. We see friends for *al fresco* lunches, walks in the countryside, picnics in the park. We see our international families whenever we can. I commute to work four days a week and spend the rest of the time on my creative projects. I have no particular ambition to be a corporate or even a creative star - but I do care deeply about

With Angie, New Years Eve 2013/14

giving it my all whether it is in my professional life or my creative work. It's not really the 'proper' high-flying life I thought I would have but it is also not outrageously 'improper'.

But it's a life that has allowed me to be myself. To express who I am, to engage and be active in the world through my work and my creativity. To be happy.

This book is not about shoes - as you've probably worked out by now. It's not about bound feet or fashion or beauty. It's not about being gay or straight or male or female. It's not really even about me.

It's about the people around me. It's about you. And all of us.

I have been able to have the life that I have now because of Angie - and because of the love of my family and friends. And because of the people I work with in my professional life and my creative endeavours. I have the freedom to be all of who I am because of the people I come into contact with every day - neighbours, acquaintances, and strangers - who don't care about my race or sexuality or gender. And because of those who uphold a society that protects my right to own property, my opportunity to vote and to work and also whatever I wish to say, who I choose to sleep with, what god I believe in or not and who I am beyond gender - a society that protects me simply as a human being.

We have seen for a thousand years in China what can be done and consented by women to be done to women because their society did not uphold that a woman, that ethereal other creature, could or should have the same freedoms as a man, the one human norm. These women's internalisation of that practice made brutality honourable and created a tradition that millions took pride in. The bound feet women of China are, for me, an emblem for all those today who are required to be broken and bound by reason of their otherness from the norm. We see that brutalising of 'the other' in the present day in many cultures around the world. We see it in our own Western democracies even now and even in spite of the strides that we have made.

If you have ever felt that exuberance of being alive, that joy at fully being and expressing your whole self, that sense of aliveness that comes from the vulnerability of opening your heart, and that intensity in knowing the fragility of our human spark - if you have ever felt how good life can be, even for one brief moment, then you know what it means to be given the space to be free.

This book is not about shoes or beauty or me. This book is about allowing ourselves whatever our gender, whoever we are - and all those others, even those whom we may not understand, who may not be like us, who we may profoundly disagree with and even dislike - allowing all of us that space for such exuberance and joy and aliveness.

BOUND FEET BLUES - THE STORY

The Crossing

The crossing to Malaya will take three weeks with a fair wind. Ah Mooi - the woman who would become my great-grandmother - huddles with the other 3rd class passengers on board the junk. They terrify her, these crowds of stinking bodies – the leering men, the jostling for food and water at meal times. The big sky terrifies her, the heaving of the boat terrifies her. And she is so unsteady, so unable to fight for her rations.

But one day, something draws her up onto the deck. She stands up, clinging to a rope, holding her weight up with her arms.

She feels the power of the swells beneath the ship. She feels the sun on her face. The sea spray showers her in bursts as the boat skids onward. It is as if she is reborn. She sees infinity in the vast endless horizon.

Everything in her old life was so certain, so uncompromising – going back for a thousand years. Everything ahead of her is an unknown. Out there beyond the horizon, is a new country where they don't care about bound feet – can that be real?

Is it possible to throw away tradition, just like that? To make your own life, your own choices, your own traditions?

She has never seen the world move past her so fast. The wind buffets her body. The sea swooshes by.

Her world is no longer shrunken, no longer defined by her tiny painful steps.

It is as if she has taken flight.

She looks up and gives herself over to the arching sky, laughing like she has never laughed before, a woman in ecstatic joy.

Acceptance

In Chinese tradition, when you get married, you must bring your spouse to the family to be formally accepted. This is done through the tea carrying ceremony. The newly- weds carry tea to the elders. If the elders do not drink the tea, that means they reject you and your beloved. But if they drink the tea, it means they accept you and your spouse into the family and the bonds between all of you become even stronger.

It's 2008. Angie and I have been together for fourteen years and it is the day after our civil partnership. Angie has eyes as blue as the arching sky and a shy, gentle manner that makes my heart takes flight.

We're at my sister's house in London and the whole family is there - my parents, my sister, my brother and his family. We are all dressed casually and I'm wearing my biker boots. When my parents got married, they performed this same tea ceremony to their parents - as did my grandparents to theirs, going back innumerable generations.

Angie and I carry tea to my father. He sips the tea and says, "We all in the family cherish you both."

Then Angie and I carry tea to my mother. She too sips the tea. She says to me, "I am so proud of you, my *noi*". She says to

Angie, "Ever since you came into Yang-May's life, we have seen how happy she has become. The whole family is grateful to you. Thank you, Angie, my *Sum Po* – my daughter-in-law."

Today, Angie and I have been together for twenty-one years. I see all of her. And she sees all of me.

She sees Bruce Lee and John Steed. She sees the sulky four year old in the fluffy white dress. She sees in me the mother who would do anything for her daughter's happiness. She sees the daughter who dares to live unbound. She sees the slinky young woman in the red *cheong sahm* and she sees the *pondan*. She sees in me my mother and my great grandmother. She sees the feminine and the masculine, the shameful and the desirable, she sees my endurance and my defiance. She sees the lover and partner always by her side, she sees me bound and she sees me free.

* * *

It's a beautiful September day in 2012. I'm almost fifty and I'm walking side by side with Angie. We are hiking the South Downs Way, 100 miles along the Southern Coast of England from Winchester to Eastbourne – and there's a gang of us, all of us in our hiking gear. We have walked 95 miles and we turn the corner. There stretching out ahead of us are the Seven Sister, seven hills rolling out over the white chalk cliffs like the hem of an embroidered gown. On our right, the infinite sea glitters in the bright sun.

Looking up at the delicate beauty of the landscape I have a sense that I own the world and I break into a wild, unfurling race; up the first hill, then the next, and the next. My feet leap up the steep slopes, instinctively finding the best path. I am wearing old battered hiking boots, sturdy on the outside and soft as bedding on the inside. It is like dancing on air.

On this bright day, here with my friends, here with Angie, I love the gift of this fragile body. I love feeling my heart pumping so hard. I love the stickiness of my sweat. I love the fire in my chest as my lungs gasp for breath. I love my small feet that have carried me this long, long way. I love my short chunky legs that have pistoned me up the hill, my muffin top that will always be there no matter how far I run. I love my smaller than average breasts, my crooked teeth, my squashed nose, my short sighted eyes, my grey hair.

I love the beauty of my imperfection.

And this is my power.

A New Journey

29 March 2014, Red Lion Square, London.

We said our goodbyes, the workshop participants and I, and straggled down the stairs from the tiny classroom tucked into the eaves of Conway Hall. It was the Saturday after the scratch night in the main hall and the final class in the series of performance workshops. The afternoon before, I had met with Annie Kwan and accepted her invitation to take *Bound Feet Blues* to the South East Asian Arts Festival in six months.

I had hoped that this final class would help me set a clear path for gathering everything I needed to create a showable theatre production of the work. I knew I could finish the script - I was a writer so that part was easy and within my comfort zone. But to pull together a production almost out of thin air, beyond the classroom in the real world ...

The series of workshops had focused on creating the artistic piece in terms of the content, structure, dramatic voices and loose ideas around how it might be staged and performed. It was beyond the remit of the course to teach the business of theatre production. But in that last class, I had scribbled madly as Sean the course tutor and the other participants had shared their knowledge and experience of bringing solo work to the stage at the Edinburgh Festival and elsewhere. So I had a list of what I needed to put in place but the path was far from clear.

Outside, in Red Lion Square, my head was spinning. It was a bright spring morning. The trees in the square were just beginning to leaf. The dappled sunlight was warm on my face. I started to walk towards Holborn to take the bus home.

The list tumbled around in my mind. I needed a venue. What theatre would take any notice of a book writer asking them to programme her first solo performance into their autumn season?

"That's what a producer would normally do," I remembered Sean saying. How on earth would I find a producer?

"A producer wouldn't take you on without a viable production and for that you need a director at the very least," someone else had said.

"And you'd need to think about set and lighting…"

"… costume…"

"… a stage manager…"

"… music…"

"… publicity, posters…"

"You'd need to get funding, of course."

People threw more ideas at me. The Arts Council gave grants. I would have to make an application, produce a budget. But all those other things needed to be in place first, especially a venue.

"What about crowd-funding?" There were loads of websites for that. I would have to entice people to give me money but they would expect something in return.

The clamour of voices rang in my head. My fellow workshoppers had been trying to be helpful. But now, as I walked along the square, it was all too overwhelming.

I stopped. I couldn't walk and think at the same time.

"Or," someone had said, "You could just do it upstairs in a pub somewhere. Just hire the room and do what you did on Wednesday night."

I could do that, couldn't I? I looked up at the wispy clouds in the bright sky. That would be the easiest. And most do-able with little to no budget.

But something stirred in me. It was physical reaction that was so strong I felt sick. No. Upstairs in a pub was the wrong thing for this piece.

It needed to be in a theatre.

The strength of that instinctive response surprised me. Who was I to think that I could really pull of a full theatrical production with no professional drama training and no knowledge of the theatre business?

Was this just hubris?

There was nothing wrong as such in doing it upstairs in a pub. That could be my fall back. But I realised that I needed to go as big and as far as I could with this piece. Maybe it was hubris - but so what if it was. Fear of the judgment of others had held me back so many times before in my life. Fear of failure, too, had been the other binding. If others thought me arrogant and over-confident in thinking that I could really put on a theatre piece from a standing start - well, so what. If I failed, at least I would have failed knowing I had thrown myself at it with everything I had. The alternative would be giving up before I had even started just because of what other people might think. If I pulled it off, such others might still have their sneery opinion but I would have a production of *Bound Feet Blues* on the London stage - and an experience that no-one could take away from me.

I let the sun play on my face. Of course, these other people whom I imagined judging me were really just my own internalised fears. Culturally, we are not meant to have a vaulting ambition - or at least, to let that ambition show. We should not let others see our self-belief or confidence, especially as women. We must not grab the limelight, be too pushy, ask for what we want. Instead, we should be modest, demure, humble, wait to be asked. We must let others shine, be self-effacing, wait for others to praise us, wait for opportunities to be offered to us. We are kept in place by the fear of being named and shamed as pushy, bossy, demanding, boastful, big-headed, bragger, and of course, that ultimate B-word that has all those other words rolled up into it: bitch.

I laughed to myself. The message of *Bound Feet Blues* is all about defying convention and literally, stepping into your own power. And here I was skirting around my power. It doesn't happen just once and then you're done, these transformations. The metaphor of the caterpillar turning into a butterfly works only so far - it assumes that once you are out of your cocoon as a beautiful winged creature, that's it, your work is done. In reality, throughout the course of our lives, we are offered time and again moments of transformation and we have to keep choosing yes or no each time. The work of metamorphosis is our life's work. So not just one unbinding, but many.

As a young woman, I had played the China Doll with such desperate conviction and it had pleased Her to see so many taken in by the illusion. I had performed my life with such drive and skill but the false self that I had created had made me ill. Later, I had briefly played butch to Her femme, trying on the tomboy and enjoying the vigour of that more masculine energy. And finally, I had simply let myself be me. It struck me that through *Bound Feet Blues*, here I was performing my life again - but this time within the artifice of a theatrical setting. And curiously, the act of creating on stage the illusion of Her and me and all the people who lived in my memory and imagination had a depth of authenticity that my performance of me in my real life had never had. In giving myself over to the theatre performance, I had re-enacted the pain and sadness and loss in my life, but also the joys and love and connectedness. I had expressed in public through body and voice private experiences I had not spoken of for decades. I had invited in the spirit of the women who had shaped me and rediscovered a wholeness in the past and present, self and family, personal and universal, inner truth and outward action.

The journey that had begun in the grey rain in my garden three years before had led me to this bright morning in this London square. I remembered the terror as I had stood in the shadows a few nights ago in an endless moment of not-beginning. That night in the cavernous auditorium of Conway Hall just behind me, that too had been an unbinding - yet another layer of fear and uncertainty unfurling to reveal a new talent, a new courage.

I simply let myself be me

It struck me that the story performance that I had created that was neither a storytelling nor a play, neither book nor dramatization, had the essence of a shamanistic ritual performance. The ghosts of the living and dead in my family expressed themselves in me, the stories of silent women and an unspeakable practice played out in my voice and gestures. I felt at once a kinship to Ah Mooi, my great-grandmother who was not my great-grandmother and also to the Malay mistress, the *bomoh* who had given my family the power to conjure spirits and to make visible the invisible. In the performance, too, was Chen Duansheng's solo voice recounting the adventures of her tomboy heroine Meng Lijun whose fictional life defied a culture that bound her to gender and immobility and whose spirit lives on now in drag kings and women who love regardless of gender. And, at last, after a lifetime of impasses, this creative work that had no 'proper' category gave voice again to the stories that had been passed down to me by the women in my family. More so than my novels, it was also the culmination of that gift of storytelling that my mother had unconsciously bequeathed to me in her recounting of books and movies and musicals.

Bound Feet Blues was my inheritance, and also my legacy.

So here was another moment on the brink of a precipice, here in the dappled light of Red Lion Square. I had to take *Bound Feet Blues* as far as it could go. Did I dare to take that next step? To keep on becoming and unbinding? To live in my power?

Start with what's in front of you, I thought. I breathed in the fresh spring air. I took a few turns up and down the pavement. My mind felt calmer. Who did I know who knew about theatre?

Jessica.

She was a director as well as a voice coach and had worked on mainstream shows as well as in alternative theatre.

I dug out my mobile phone and dialled her number. She had come to see the scratch night performance and had been positive and encouraging in her feedback. But there was a difference between working with me for a few hours as my voice coach and taking on the role of a director for a theatre piece by a novice performer.

The call was ringing. It was a huge ask. She probably wouldn't want to work with me. In which case, I would ask her if she knew anyone else whom I could approach.

She picked up.

We had a chat about the scratch night. We talked about where I had been strong and where my voice could have done more. I told her about my meeting with Annie Kwan and the invitation to be part of the festival.

"I have six months," I said, "I don't really know where to start with putting together a theatre piece. But whatever happens, I need a director." I took a breath. "Will you be my director?"

Without hesitation, she said, "Of course, I would love to be your director."

"Really?"

"Yes, it's a strong piece. It's unusual - the themes, what you're trying to do. It has something important to say. But you need technical skills in your performance and I can help you with that. And we can work on shaping the staging of the piece and the visual flow..."

We began to talk about the creative aspects and how we could work together as writer/ performer and director. We talked about the production logistics, what needed to be in place, funding and the business side. This was her world and she outlined a clear path for what we would need to do.

"Look, we need to have a proper meeting about all this," she said.

We arranged a date and a time and I hung up.

I walked along the square and headed towards the busy roads intersecting at Holborn Circus. The dappled pavement gave way to glaring white slabs, traffic lights, street furniture and busy traffic.

I laughed. It was spring. New leaves, new light and all that.

A new journey had begun.

Showcase performance, Tristan Bates Theatre,
Oct 2014 – The Crossing

Addendum

London, May 2015

Bound Feet Blues - A Life Told in Shoes showcased at the Tristan Bates Theatre in Central London on 13 October 2014, as part of the South East Asian (SEA) Arts Festival 2014. It was written and performed by Yang-May Ooi, and directed by Jessica Higgs. The show was produced by Eldarin Yeong Studio. The production was supported by funding from Arts Council England.

The showcase garnered 4+ Star reviews.

A full production has been scheduled for a three week return run at Tristan Bates Theatre in November/ December 2015 as part of the SEA Arts Festival 2015. The original creative team has been joined by Hua Tan (set and lighting design), Carol Alayne (costume), Crin Claxton (stage manager) and Helen Lewis (publicity).

The full production is being supported by funding from the Arts Council England and sponsorship by The Housing Finance Corporation and Maclay Murray Spens.

Sources

The following are a list of sources which I have referred to in researching this book, and also notes which may be of interest.

Stilettos

A root of modernism in China: Ibsen by Sheila Melvin, International Herald Tribune, date unavailable - http://www.nytimes.com/2006/09/15/world/asia/15iht-ibsen.2822242.html?_r=0

Cheongsam, Wikipedia entry - http://en.wikipedia.org/wiki/Cheongsam

Cheongsam: an everlasting elegance - https://cheongsamfashion.wordpress.com/

Hanfu, Wikipedia entry - http://en.wikipedia.org/wiki/Hanfu

List of Hanfu, Wikipedia entry - http://en.wikipedia.org/wiki/List_of_Hanfu

The Cheongsam – The Treasure of National Chinese Apparel by Hongxia Liu, Asian Culture History Journal, Vol 1 No 1, Jan 2009

Traditional Han Chinese Clothing, Travel China Guide - http://www.travelchinaguide.com/intro/clothing/hanfu/

Tik-tok shoes

In the Lim family, Great-Grandmother No.1 was called *Koo Ma* and the other wives were known as *Ah Ma* (Mother), *Yee Ma* and *Sum Ma*. Apart from Ah Ma, the other three nomenclatures are variations on Aunt Mother. For the purposes of this book, I am changing their titles to refer to their number/ ranking – hence *Tai Ma* for Eldest Mother – to make it easier for the reader to identify the different characters.

Lotus feet

Aching for Beauty by Wang Ping (University of Minnesota Press, 2000 – Kindle edition)

Chinese Footbinding, BBC - http://www.bbc.co.uk/dna/place-london/plain/A1155872

Chinese Footbinding: The Wuzhen Footbinding Musuem - http://reneeriley.wordpress.com/2011/06/27/chinese-foot-binding-the-wuzhen-foot-binding-museum/

Consequences of Foot Binding among Older Women in Beijing, China by Steven R. Cummings, MD, Xu Ling, MD, MPH, and Katie Stone, MA – American Journal of Public Health Oct 1997, Vol 87 No 10

Footbinding: A Jungian Engagement with Chinese Culture and Psychology by Shirley See Yan Ma (Routledge, 2009 – Kindle edition)

Footbinding: A Painful Tradition In China By Liliana Melo –
Research Paper, Nov 2006

In China, Footbinding Slowly Slips into History by Kit Gillet,
Los Angeles Times, April 16, 2012 - http://articles.latimes.
com/2012/apr/16/world/la-fg-china-bound-feet-20120416

*The Emperor And His Women: Three Views Of Footbinding,
Ethnicity, And Empire* By Dorothy Ko – Denver Museum of
Natural History, Nov 1998, Series 5 No 15

*The Tian Zu Hui (Natural Foot Society): Christian Women in
China and the Fight against Footbinding* by Brent Whitefield -
Southeast Review of Asian Studies Volume 30 (2008)

Kok-kok shoes

Aching for Beauty by Wang Ping (University of Minnesota Press,
2000 – Kindle edition)

*Chen Duansheng and Meng Lijun: The Woman Author and
Heroine Ahead of the Time* by Gao Huan - academic paper

Chen Duansheng, Oxford Reference - http://
www.oxfordreference.com/view/10.1093/
acref/9780195148909.001.0001/acref-9780195148909-e-167

Classic Chinese Cinema:The Love Eterne, Taste of Cinema -
http://www.tasteofcinema.com/2012/classic-chinese-cinemathe-
love-eterne/

Hangzhou website - http://eng.hangzhou.gov.cn/

Huangmei Opera, China Vista - http://www.chinavista.com/
experience/huangmei/opera.html

Huangmei Opera, Wikipedia - http://en.wikipedia.org/wiki/

393

Huangmei_opera

Lover-Sister: Female Same-sex Desire and Women's Agency in Feng Shuangfei by Wenjia Liu - Intersections: Gender and Sexuality in Asia and the Pacific Issue 35, July 2014

The Love Eterne on Youtube - https://www.youtube.com/watch?v=OCA5ukcIrSc

The Love Eterne, Wikipedia - http://en.wikipedia.org/wiki/The_Love_Eterne

You can listen to my recording of Grandpa Lim telling the story of our family at bit.ly/limstory

Bound feet

I relied on notes of interviews with various family members and in particular, Great-grandmother No. 4, Wong Hee, made in 1990 and at other times. I am also indebted to my Great-Uncle Willie's privately published book about our family.

Biker boots

Footbinding: A Jungian Engagement with Chinese Culture and Psychology by Shirley See Yan Ma (Routledge, 2009 – Kindle edition)

Multicultural Cinderella Stories by Mary Northrup, American Library Association website, May 2000 http://www.ala.org/offices/resources/multicultural

The Little Mermaid by Hans Christian Anderson as published online by Zvi Har'El - http://hca.gilead.org.il/li_merma.html

The Story of Ye Xian, author unknown, http://iss.schoolwires.com

Ye Xian, Wikipedia, http://en.wikipedia.org/wiki/Ye_Xian

About the author

Yang-May Ooi – credit: Paul Cox

Yang-May Ooi is a bestselling author, award-winning TEDx speaker and acclaimed story performer of Chinese-Malaysian heritage, now living in London.

Her first novel *The Flame Tree* topped the Malaysian bestseller charts and was closely followed by *Mindgame*, possibly the first - and only - Malaysian lesbian thriller (both published by Hodder & Stoughton, now re-issued by Monsoon). She is the co-author of *International Communications Strategy*, which was nominated for the FT Goldman Sachs Book Award. Her TEDx talk *Rebel Heart: How Small Acts of Rebellion Can Create Powerful Change* was described as "electrifying" and "one of the best and most moving talks at a TEDx event".

Bound Feet Blues - A Life Told in Shoes is Yang-May's unconventional memoir and tells the stories behind the story of her solo theatre piece of the same name. *Bound Feet Blues*, the story performance, garnered 4+ star reviews at its showcase debut and has been described by reviewers as "powerful", "engaging, eye-opening, funny and moving" and "beautifully performed and directed". The book's publication co-incides with the return *Bound Feet Blues*, the solo show, to London's West End for the three week run in Nov/ Dec 2015. Find out more at www.BoundFeetBlues.co.uk

Index

Urbane Publications is dedicated to
developing new author voices, and publishing
fiction and non-fiction that challenges, thrills and
fascinates. From page-turning novels to innovative
reference books, our goal is to publish what
YOU want to read.

Find out more at

urbanepublications.com